shared faith.
bold vision.
ENDURING PROMISE.

THE MATURING YEARS OF MESSIAH COLLEGE

THE MATURING YEARS OF MESSIAH COLLEGE

Paul W. Nisly

To order this book, contact Messiah College Bookstore, P.O. Box 4509, Grantham, PA 17027. Telephone (717) 766-2511, ext. 3050. Email: <bookstore@messiah.edu>

Cover image: Shirley Groff
Cover design: Messiah College Office of Marketing and Public Relations

Photograph credits: Aerial map (p. xix) courtesy of Bub Manning, Principal, The Quandel Group, Inc.; all other photographs courtesy of the Historical Library and Archives of the Brethren in Christ Church/Archives of Messiah College.

ISBN: 978-0-692-00794-5

LCCN: 2010924427

The paper used in this publication is recycled and meets the minimum requirements of America National Standard for Information Sciences — Permanence of Paper for Publication and Documents in Libraries and Archives, ANSI Z39.48-1992.

Printed in the United States of America

0 1 2 3 4 5 EP 5 4 3 2 1

To my family, with love,
Laura and Nancy,
Janelle, Lamar, and Randal,
who were unstinting in their support.

The tragedy of life is not death; it is destined for us all.
The tragedy of life is to die with convictions undeclared
and service unfulfilled.

Ernest L. Boyer, Sr.

The past is never dead.
It's not even past.

William Faulkner in *Requiem for a Nun*

Have no fear for what tomorrow may bring.
The same loving God who cares for you today
will take care of you tomorrow and every day.

Francis de Sales

Contents

Introduction

"As human beings we have a real hunger for stories," muses American author Paul Auster in an interview for London's Sunday Times. "Similarly we compose and create a sense of ourselves in the world. We construct a narrative for ourselves and that's the thread that we follow from one day to the next." During Messiah College's Centennial year we have celebrated the diverse stories that come together to form a communal narrative thread that is woven throughout our history — stories that reveal our triumphs and challenges, and remind us of subtle shifts in perspective as well as watershed developments. Through our shared collective memory, we come to understand who we have been in the past, who we are in the present, and who we shall become in the future.

Professor Paul Nisly has given us a treasured gift by writing a reflective history of the College from the 1970s through the present. With his accumulated experience of teaching full-time at Messiah College for 35 years, he brings a unique perspective and depth of knowledge to this topic. With truthfulness, candor and insight, Professor Nisly has chronicled the story of the College's growth and maturation during the past four decades. Professor Nisly's commitment to incorporating many different voices who share their individual perspectives creates a collective memory that will enrich our understanding of the unique mission and identity of Messiah College.

Throughout this Centennial year, stories of the last 100 years have recalled God's faithfulness to our beloved College. In addition to this published history, another significant Centennial initiative has been the research and presentation of the College's Multicultural Century Research Project by colleagues Hierald Kane-Osorto '07, former associate director of multicultural programs, and Bernardo Michael, associate professor and director of the Center for Public Humanities. Their research reminds our community that reconciliation has always been an important part of Messiah College's heritage and history. Understanding our past is essential to our current self-understanding as we labor together to become a hospitable campus community that reflects the beautiful diversity of God's kingdom.

During Centennial Homecoming 2009, Messiah College also hosted StoryCorps, an independent nonprofit project whose mission is to honor and celebrate one another's lives through listening and whose stories are regularly featured on National Public Radio. The Centennial Committee facilitated interviews between Messiah College faculty, administrators, trustees, and students from past and present eras. Recalling and sharing stories, StoryCorps suggests, reminds us of the importance of listening to and learning from those around us. These stories enable us to celebrate our shared humanity and they "tell people that their lives matter and they won't be forgotten."

Even as we honor the stories of our past and pursue our mission in the present hour, we are keenly aware of challenges confronting our nation and all of private higher education including Messiah College. Historian David McCullough, who presented a lecture on campus as part of the Center for Public Humanities Symposium, emphasizes that history is "an aid to navigation in perilous times. We are living now in an era of momentous change, of huge transitions in all aspects of life — here, nationwide, worldwide — and this creates great pressures and tensions. But history shows that times of change are the times when we are most likely to learn.... We should embrace the possibilities in these exciting times and hold to a steady course, because we have a sense of navigation, a sense of what we've been through in times past and who we are."

I am grateful to Professor Nisly for capturing important questions and insights into the history of "what we've been through and who we are," for the countless hours that he dedicated to this project, and for his remarkable ability to write in a style that engages and embraces the reader. Professor Nisly reminds us that Messiah College's history is dynamic, not static; the starting point of meaningful dialogue, not its conclusion; and that each one of us plays a vital role in developing and nurturing our identity and mission. It is my fervent hope that this volume will guide us in the future as we face opportunities, challenges, or even the uncertainty of "perilous times." May we follow the example of our predecessors and remain steadfast and hopeful because we are convinced that now more than ever, the Church and society need Messiah graduates to lead and serve a complex 21st century world.

Kim S. Phipps
President, Messiah College

Foreword

Some Reflections

When Messiah College president, Dr. Kim S. Phipps, first asked me to consider writing an updated history of the college, I thought the project would be an interesting challenge. After all, I had been a faculty member at the college for some 35 years; and in addition to teaching a broad range of courses in literature and the humanities, I had been the chair of a large and diverse department for 24 years, as well as serving on many college committees. But I soon realized that the proposed project was more than a challenge: it was a daunting task.

Among other questions were these: who was the perceived audience? To what extent was the book to be celebratory of college achievements; to what extent could it be evaluative? Should the authorial voice be personal, or should one attempt to convey an objective stance? To what extent is objectivity even possible when one is so close to the subject? How would the present work relate to Dr. E. Morris Sider's major study, *Messiah College: A History*, which ends in the early 1980s?

In the end I believe this present study is not strictly a history, but a reflective essay, an historical essay which attempts to incorporate many voices and varied perspectives. Over the course of more than 80 interviews I have spoken with past and present administrators and trustees, retired and active faculty members, and alumni from both on and off campus. All have aided in enlarging my understandings of the college, and a number are quoted here. At the same time I acknowledge that these voices are filtered through my own interpretive screen. I have also been assisted by the helpful insights of a reading committee, comprised of Randall Basinger, Susanna Caroselli, Gerald Hess, Joseph Huffman, and John Yeatts, whose insights and suggestions have strengthened this work.

A major question, one which defies easy resolution but is a major focus of this study, concerns the *identity* of the college. Who are we—religiously, academically, corporately? To what extent do we have a unified vision, a shared mission? How does the religious heritage of the college continue to inform our mission? How can we have deep commitments without being doctrinaire? How can academic freedom and strongly held religious commitments coexist?

The task is, of course, formidable: how can one hope to give a fair and coherent picture of an institution which has grown immensely and changed significantly in the past 35 to 40 years? How does one describe adequately the multiplicity of programs and services, on and off campus, which the college offers? On a more interpretive level, what are the major issues, questions, and challenges which the college faces? Are there major "watershed" moments in the history of the college, moments which decisively influence the future direction of the institution? How does one adequately incorporate the viewpoints and voices of those who may be — or perceive themselves to be — on the margins of the institution?

For these questions — and many others — there are no easy answers. My attempt in this reflective historical essay is to offer some possible windows through the views of others as refracted through a personal lens. In the final chapter, in addition to reflecting on the past, I offer some more personal views about the present, specifically about causes for celebration, some matters of concern, and evidences of commitment. This work is an invitation to further conversation.

Acknowledgements

To write some words of acknowledgement and thanks is both a pleasant privilege and a significant challenge — pleasant because I have been blessed by the gracious help of many people, a challenge because I fear that I will miss recognizing some deserving persons. No one writes in isolation, but in this project — perhaps more than in most — I am deeply indebted to many.

First, I wish to thank Messiah College president, Dr. Kim S. Phipps, for taking the risk of asking me to write this updated history as part of the centennial celebration and for twice reading the manuscript. I appreciate the freedom she has given me to shape the narrative, to ask hard questions, and to confront some of the perplexities and ambiguities which are part of our story. I thank her as well for providing dedicated office space to allow me the privacy which I requested and needed, and for providing a secretary to transcribe the many interview tapes.

I am deeply grateful to Gina Hale who transcribed most of the tapes, as well as typing the first draft of the manuscript. Not only did she work tirelessly and cheerfully despite sometimes straining to understand the taped dialogue, but she was also a great listener, supporter, and encourager. My thank you seems most inadequate for those many hours, but it is sincerely offered.

To the committee of five "Readers," Randall Basinger, Susanna Caroselli, Gerald Hess, Joseph Huffman, and John Yeatts — all of them colleagues at Messiah College — who read the manuscript, chapter-by-chapter, as it was gradually emerging from the cocoon of my office, I give deep thanks. Some read the manuscript with an eye for minute details; others were looking for larger patterns and themes. All were helpful as they encouraged, challenged, and — at times — corrected. Their readings have certainly clarified and strengthened the text. A number of other persons have read portions of the manuscript. With apologies to any whom I am missing, I wish to thank H. David Brandt, Chad Frey, Richard Hughes, Joseph Longenecker, Beth Hostetler Mark, Douglas Miller, and David Vader for their insightful readings and good suggestions.

Thank you to Glen Pierce, archivist at Messiah College, and to your student assistants, including Melissa Lewis, for your willingness to locate resources — whether photos or printed text — for this study. And a great word of thanks, Glen, for your work in the formatting of the manuscript. My hearty thanks to Rebecca Ebersole Kasparek for her practiced editor's eye and helpful suggestions regarding the format. A sincere thank you also to Shirley Groff for her many photographs of Hostetter Chapel and to Stephanie Perry in the Office of Marketing and Public Relations at Messiah College for designing the book cover.

Finally, a heart-felt thanks to Erin Jones, a Messiah graduate and former advisee, who read the final — or almost-final — copy with an extremely careful copy-editor's eye. What a gift she brought! And to my son Lamar, professor of English at Bluffton University (OH), the one who was always my first reader and usually my last, thank you for your many insights, your wisdom, your patience, and your candor. I have been blessed.

To the more than 80 persons who agreed to be interviewed and have their conversations taped, my thanks. Without your help the present work would literally not have been possible. Some type of historical essay might have been written, but it would have been composed from a very limited and narrow perspective. So thank you.

I am grateful for my many wonderful colleagues, with some of whom I have shared well-nigh 40 years, and all of whom have — by their lives — been writing the history of Messiah College. And thank you, thank you, to the generations of students who have blessed my life far beyond my desserts.

Now a personal word from an earlier past. All of us no doubt have had significant mentors whose lives have influenced and shaped us. I honor Dr. Hubert R. Pellman, a person who modeled for me the life of an excellent teacher, a dedicated Mennonite pastor, and a caring friend. And although I never expected to follow his example in this area, he also wrote the history of his college!

Finally, I am forever grateful for the unwavering love and support of my late wife Laura, who lived with courage, loyalty, and deep joy despite her significant health problems. And to my wife Nancy, my sincere thanks for your kindness, encouragement, and love while I have been preoccupied with this project during the early years of our marriage.

The Messiah College campus in winter in the late 1940s.

The Messiah College campus in the summer of 2009 with many developments and additions.

Chapter 1

A Brief Retrospective

*A Few Signal Developments
in the 1960s and Early 1970s*

On April 13, 2008, two persons of national prominence, U. S. Senators Barack Obama and Hillary Clinton, who were then the democratic presidential candidates, spoke at a Compassion Forum hosted by Messiah College. The campus was abuzz with scurrying news reporters, detail-oriented secret service agents, and feverishly working campus personnel. The resulting live broadcast by CNN and wide coverage by other national news media brought unprecedented national recognition to this college, which was begun a century ago by a small denomination with visible separatistic leanings. In significant ways this broadcast reminds us of the multiple ways that Messiah College has gained national prominence. The event marked another point in the maturation of Messiah College as she prepared to honor one hundred years of service as a Christian educational institution.

Approaching her centennial observance, Messiah College celebrates moving from extremely modest beginnings to a strong, vibrant institution with more than 2,700 students, over 170 faculty members, more than 55 academic majors, and many opportunities for studies in urban and international venues beside the main campus in a small suburban village in south-central Pennsylvania. Operating from a position of growing academic strength, the college has introduced several graduate programs. From twelve students enrolled initially to almost three thousand currently, from living in quiet obscurity in a rural village to experiencing national attention, Messiah College has changed dramatically. What are some of the significant developments which have shaped the institution? Are there "watershed" moments or decisions which have—at least in retrospect—been formative in the direction of the college?

In his significant study, *Messiah College: A History*, Dr. E. Morris Sider traces in considerable detail the early years of the college's development. Perhaps it might be helpful to outline a few of those earlier events, especially in the last half century and then comment more fully on several:

1946: Junior college accreditation from the Pennsylvania Council of Education

1950: Authorization to grant Th.B. and B.R.E. (baccalaureate) degrees

1951: Official name change from Messiah Bible College to Messiah College (and Messiah Bible College had evolved from the earlier Messiah Bible School and Missionary Training Home)

1960: Retirement of President C.N. Hostetter, Jr.
Inauguration of Arthur Climenhaga as president
Submission of application for Middle States Association academic accreditation
Graduation of last academy class

1963: Academic accreditation (provisional) by the Middle States Association of Colleges and Secondary Schools

1964: Initial Program Approval for teacher education certification in Biology, Chemistry, English, Mathematics, and Social Studies by the Commonwealth of Pennsylvania
Resignation of President Arthur Climenhaga
Inauguration of D. Ray Hostetter as president

1965: Merger between Upland College—formerly Beulah College (CA)—and Messiah College

1966: Full academic accreditation with Middle States Association of Colleges and Secondary Schools

1968: Establishment of Philadelphia campus

1970: Revision of academic calendar to include a January term

1971: Initiation of a major general education review

1972: Approval of covenant relationship between Messiah College and the Brethren in Christ Denomination

Clearly, some of these events were more important than others in the development of this growing institution. The change of name from Messiah Bible College to Messiah College marked a developing consciousness of the institution as moving beyond its earlier, more narrowly defined educational goals. It also became clear to the president, C.N. Hostetter, Jr., that the college needed to achieve regional academic accreditation if it were to mature and reach a wider audience. Hostetter was a church man par excellence, but he was also an educator with an eye to the future, and no doubt he was disappointed that he was not able to achieve accreditation during his tenure as president, though he had made good progress.

Instead, it was during the relatively short tenure of Dr. Arthur Climenhaga that Messiah achieved the regional accreditation which the college sought. Among other benefits was the possibility of offering a number of teacher education certification areas, a beginning which has grown and developed enormously in the years following the initial program approval by the Pennsylvania Department of Education. Of the initial college accreditation, Dr. Harold Engle, who was for many years the chair of the Board of Trustees, says, "Arthur probably deserves [credit for] what he felt was his greatest contribution to Messiah, the accreditation." In some ways, of course, his was the climax of a process which had begun a number of years earlier.

Mark G. Garis, who is an alumnus of both the academy and the college, offers an interesting view of those formative years of moving toward accreditation: "I didn't expect to go to college; I didn't expect to stay for four years, but God led me step by step." When he and his classmates graduated from the academy (in 1956), Garis says, "We were about the first ones and a group of us, 29 of us, stayed on [to continue studies at the college] . . . President C.N. Hostetter was saying . . . we can't get certified because we can't get students to stay and they have to look at our graduates and so on. And I remember we as a class were close . . . and we said 'let's stay on and let's be pioneers.' That's what he called us, 'Pioneers' . . . and we stayed on, and they began the first Middle States evaluation because we loved the college. It was small, of course, about 200 students, but we understood that somebody had to step out and take the risk." Clearly, the risk was worth taking, because years later Dr. Mark Garis, who

S. R. Smith (1910-1916)

C. N. Hostetter, Sr. (1917-1923)

Enos H. Hess (1923-1934)

C. N. Hostetter, Jr. (1934-1960)

Arthur M. Climenhaga (1960-1964)

D. Ray Hostetter (1964-1994)

graduated from the college in 1960, would serve for many years on the Board of Trustees, including a number of years as chair of the Faculty and Academic Affairs Committee, as well as assistant chair of the Board. How little could he have dreamed in those early years that the college would grow and expand beyond any expectations which those "pioneers," those "risk takers," might have imagined. Their hopes were more modest: that their degrees might eventually be recognized as coming from an accredited institution. With initial accreditation now achieved, the college could move forward and seek state certification for a number of elementary and secondary teaching areas.

Soon after achieving provisional accreditation for the college, President Climenhaga was asked to serve as executive director of the National Association of Evangelicals. Climenhaga apparently found the fund-raising necessary to his position as college president not particularly to his liking, nor did he enjoy the detailed aspects of administration. Besides that, he had already achieved a major goal for the college, and more than he could have realized, the college was poised to move into a new era.

So it was perhaps fitting that a young man, one who was in the line of two previous presidents of the college, D. Ray Hostetter, was invited to the presidency. His father, C.N. Hostetter, Jr., who was president from 1934–60, had had the longest tenure of any of Messiah's presidents at that time, and he had shepherded the institution through the extremely difficult years of the Great Depression. Having come to the campus as a six-year-old lad and being himself a graduate of both academy and junior college, Ray would have had few illusions about the challenges that faced this young institution. His grandfather C.N. Hostetter was the second president of the young college (from 1917–22); and as a youth while his father was doing graduate work and living in Winona Lake, Indiana, Ray and his brother Lane lived with his grandparents. Besides this extensive family involvement, Dr. Hostetter says, "I knew all the presidents [of the college] but one."

He returned to Messiah College as an adult, first to teach history and physical education. Later, after a five-year stint in the business world selling ice cream, he was invited by President Climenhaga to join the college as the first director of development and was later named a vice-president. In earlier years the president himself had basically been the development officer (in addition to all the other responsibilities of the presidency), but Climenhaga sensed the importance of having additional support in this significant area of financial growth. Nonetheless, after his relatively brief tenure as president, Climenhaga left the office to follow his sense of call to the leadership of the NAE, and Ray Hostetter was inaugurated as president in October 1964. A new era had begun.

In 1965, a year after Hostetter's accession to the presidency, Upland College in California merged with Messiah College, with the latter thus becoming the only college of the Brethren in Christ denomination. In 1964 there were 270 full-time-equivalent (FTE— a number based on student credit hours taken) students at Messiah with 44 percent identified as Brethren in Christ; by 1967 after full accreditation, there were already 427 (FTE) students with 47 percent Brethren in Christ. Clearly it was important that the college maintain her ties to the founding denomination, but at the same time the young president realized that if the college were to grow beyond a fairly limited size, the institution would need to reach a much wider constituency.

In some ways, though, the seeds of a more diverse audience had already been sown in the founding documents. The minutes from June 18–29, 1907, of the incorporating Board record this statement of admission policy:

> Applicants for admittance to the school may be admitted irrespective of race, color, sex, creed or faith, who believe in the deity of Jesus Christ under the following conditions:
>> (A) Who are not members of secret or oath-bound societies, excepting they promise to release or relinquish their affiliation with the same.
>> (B) Who do not make use of profane or vulgar language, and who are not addicted to the use of intoxicants in any form . . . (p.14).

Although the numbers of students from traditions other than the Brethren in Christ denomination varied from year to year, and although within the church there was a desire for purity of doctrine and practice, there was also a stated openness in the admissions policy to a larger, more diverse student body. But the college was owned by the denomination, and thus the governing Board of Trustees were all members of the denomination. And in the larger educational community there was the strong perception that the college was primarily a Brethren in Christ institution. From his vantage point as a former president, Ray Hostetter says, "I contend that the college never was narrowly sectarian and the [Brethren in Christ] church was never narrowly sectarian even before the 1950s, even though they stressed much more categorically separation from the world. But . . . they moved away from a categorical separation from the church in the 1950s and this [the change in the college] was part of that." The college, in fact, probably gave further impetus to the lowering of the barriers that separated the denomination from the larger culture, including the Christian church. In any event, as Dr. John Yeatts, professor of the psychology of religion and associate dean, argues, "While neither Arthur Climenhaga nor Ray Hostetter were attempting to move the college away from the Brethren in Christ Church, they were both in some ways more interested in strengthening the college's ties to the broader Evangelical church than to the college's Anabaptist roots."

And as the college was enlarging her boundaries, President Hostetter felt the college needed to move to a different governance structure. Along with other interviewees from this period in the college's history, Hostetter identifies this as a "watershed time." "The Board of Trustees," he says, "was always exclusively Brethren in Christ when we moved from an ownership and full controlling relationship of the denomination of Messiah to a covenant relationship with Messiah . . . [but] the intention was not to move away from the church but to move out from the church." The distinction between "moving away from" and "moving out from" the denomination was probably not always easy to maintain or communicate. What Hostetter sensed was that, among other things, the college needed a broader base of financial support, perhaps in part a result of his experience in his first major fund-raising campaign — a campaign to build a much needed science hall. Of that time, he says, "It was our first campaign to the community and we raised those funds without a [single] member of the Board of Trustees being outside the denomination." In recalling those years and that major decision to change the controlling governance structure of the college, Hostetter is passionate to communicate that his desire was to continue to be strongly related to the founding denomination. "We moved to the [decision] in order to . . . reach out further not only for sources of leadership but for sources of income. But I still contend it was not a movement away."

The covenant was approved by the Board of Trustees in April 1972 and was then brought for approval to the Annual General Conference (June 28–July 2, 1972). The minute record provides both the background rationale and the wording of the covenant itself. The availability of government funding was one of the key issues, according to the minutes. "Governments, state and federal, recognize the financial dilemma of the private college as well as they do the positive contribution which they make to the educational life of our society. As a result they are moving in the direction of making available public funds to assist the private college." The implicit assumption seems to be that if the college were to continue to be owned by the denomination, these new public funding sources might not be available to the college.

Messiah College, according to the minutes, was not currently (in 1972) in "a state of crisis . . . however, it is not reasonable to assume that the trend which has brought crisis to many colleges will not eventually affect Messiah College." Thus the administration, the Board of Trustees, and the denomination's Board for Schools and Colleges "have cooperatively sought to find a way whereby these new developments in financial support will be recognized and at the same time the historic, traditional, and theological ties between the church and the college can be maintained." Although the covenant between college and denomination moved the legal ownership from the church to a self-perpetuating Board of Trustees, there were still a significant number of church leaders on the board, including the presiding bishop and a representative from each of the five U.S. regions, as well as a representative from the denomination's Board for Schools and Colleges. In addition to these commitments for the governing board, the college covenanted to "teach the Christian faith and biblical studies within the Brethren in Christ understanding of Christian truth." Beyond issues specifically theological, the covenant also included behavioral expectations: "To pattern the life of the college community in a manner consistent with Brethren in Christ ethos patterns and the Church's understanding of Christian discipleship."

From the vantage point of some thirty years one can see that the college was already confronting the question of identity. The "historic, traditional, and theological ties" were being affirmed, but the denomination itself was — at least in some ways — moving from its own earlier more separatistic understandings to being more acculturated into the larger American and evangelical culture. The decision, for example, of Dr. Arthur Climenhaga, former president of the college and long-term missionary and churchman, to accept the leadership of the National Association of Evangelicals suggests something of his desire for close connections with Evangelicalism and may be seen as a harbinger of the change which was beginning to occur in both denomination and college.

In the printed rationale for the covenant, finances are noted as a significant — perhaps primary — reason for the needed change in governance structure. At the same time the door was being opened to a more diverse Board of Trustees, an increasingly wider range of theological views on the faculty, and a considerably more religiously heterogeneous student body, many of whom came from theological traditions quite dissimilar to the Anabaptist, Pietist, and Wesleyan backgrounds of the founding denomination. As both the number of students and faculty grew rapidly, and the percentage of Brethren in Christ members concurrently declined, the identity of the college became less coherent than it had been in earlier years. In the course of these reflections we will return to the question of identity, but at the moment we can assume that the decision to have a covenant relationship with the church was indeed a "watershed" moment in the college's history. No administrator or trustee or faculty member could have been prescient enough to envision fully the changing face of the college in the coming years of unprecedented growth.

More than the new college-church covenant was at play, of course, but the growth during the seventies and eighties was stunning. In 1969 the full-time-equivalent (FTE) student body was 565; by 1979 it had more than doubled to 1,185 (FTE). Then in the next decade the numbers almost doubled again for an FTE of 2,245 students in 1989. The changing goals for the desired maximum number of students became a source of some amusement on campus. In 1972, for example, with 801 (FTE) the goal was an ambitious — as it seemed then — 1,200 students. But by 1979 with 1,185 students the goal had essentially been reached. The next "limit" was 1,500; then 1,800; then 2,000; then 2,400; and finally 2,800. These were heady times: the hiring of faculty and staff could never seem to keep pace with the seemingly relentless growth in the student body; the campus was experiencing the addition of more buildings almost every year, especially residence halls; the budgets were healthy because usually there were more students on campus than had been budgeted for the previous spring. The growth continued through the 1990s and the first years of the twenty-first century, but the rate of growth had slowed dramatically. The 2,245 (FTE) of 1989 had become 2,702 (FTE) by 1999, a healthy growth rate, but far less than that experienced in the previous decades. In 2003 the college reached 2,914 (FTE), the highest point ever, and in the years since that the enrollment has ranged between 2,700 and 2,900 with some minor fluctuations from year to year.

For college personnel who had been accustomed to years and even decades of continuing growth, the leveling of the student body population brought some necessary adjustments in expectations for the funding of new initiatives. At the same time, this virtual steady-state enrollment has given the college time to catch its breath, as it were, and reflect more carefully on present identity and then to think more carefully about future hopes.

Chapter 2

Reaching Out
Developing an Urban Campus

The articulation and acceptance of a covenant between the college and the denomination in 1972 was clearly an important step in the development of a larger identity for Messiah College. But this development did not occur in a vacuum. Several years earlier President D. Ray Hostetter had already been considering a major new growth possibility. Messiah, located in the quiet little village of Grantham, was both geographically and culturally isolated from urban life. Hostetter began to dream about the possibilities of linking with an urban campus, a rather audacious dream for a tiny denominational college that in 1967 had 429 (FTE) students with almost half the students (47 percent) coming from the founding denomination. Additionally, this was during an era of great ferment — and sometimes turmoil — on many major university campuses.

The genesis of the idea of an urban campus apparently developed at a conference in Chicago which Hostetter attended along with Ernest Boyer, member of the Messiah College Board of Trustees and later chancellor of the State University of New York, and Albert Meyer, executive secretary of the Mennonite Board of Education. According to the memories of some, the initial ideas were sketched on a napkin over dinner! All three of the educators were enthusiastic about exploring the possibilities.

As he recalls those early days of exploration, Hostetter says, "I went to considerable detail in laying the groundwork for the Philadelphia Campus. I visited the University of Pennsylvania; I visited the University of Pittsburgh; I visited Penn State; I visited Temple to see what would be the most appropriate larger institution that we could connect with, and they were all ready to go and were all encouraging to us to connect with them." But of the several potential sites available, Temple University on North Broad Street in Philadelphia was chosen. "Temple had two things in their favor," according to Hostetter. "One was their tuition to us would not be as high [as some other universities]. . . . Temple University had another thing in its favor, we felt, and that was that it was in the inner city, and here we are a rural campus. We needed the insights of both worlds, and so those are some of the reasons we chose Temple." At the time when the Temple-Messiah connection was being established in 1968, it was the first such arrangement between a Christian liberal arts college and a major urban secular university in the United States. Further, as Dr. John Yeatts notes, "It is remarkable that Messiah chose the North Philadelphia ghetto, rather than the Oakland area, where the University of Pittsburgh is located, or the West Philadelphia area around the University of Pennsylvania. We decided to live with the poor and oppressed." Not only was North Philadelphia an economically depressed area: the Messiah campus was planted in an area which had been rocked by race riots only a few years earlier.

Hostetter's dreams were ambitious: "My initial vision was that college [in Philadelphia] might even become *larger* than the Grantham campus." The Board of Trustees, while not projecting that degree of growth, in 1971 approved long-range enrollment projections which from 1974 to1980 would be steady-state at Grantham but would increase steadily in Philadelphia from 140 in 1974 to 350 in 1979. That level of growth never happened, of course, with the enrollment usually ranging from 60 to 80 students even after the program was well established.

But Messiah College committed significant resources and personnel to develop this new venture in reaching out beyond the comforts of the main campus, though a major grant from the U.S. Office of Education provided assistance, both with start-up costs and for later program development, with a total of $300,000 being given by the federal government in the first several years. A Philadelphia Advisory Board was established to give overall direction to the new program and to provide a linkage to the larger Board of Trustees. In the 1967-68 year of planning Dr. Daniel R. Chamberlain, academic dean-elect at Messiah College, served as a consultant, working out a plan with the Temple University leadership whereby Messiah College would provide general education courses and Temple would offer courses in selected majors. The first year (1968) opened with nine students and five professional staff members, not all of whom were full time. Dr. Gerald Swaim was named as dean at Philadelphia, and Ronald J. Sider, who was completing his doctorate, was a teaching faculty member.

To prepare for new faculty, staff, and incoming students, the college bought three contiguous row houses on North Broad Street and began to renovate them for use that fall. In addition to dormitory rooms for students and apartments for faculty, plans included a dining hall, kitchen, lounge, two seminar rooms, and faculty offices. Because renovations were not completed by the beginning of the fall term, students were housed downtown in the "Y" for the first several months, though with its separation from the main center it clearly was not an ideal location.

The goals for the Messiah–Temple program were ambitious. As noted in the October 8, 1968, Philadelphia Advisory Board minutes, they included the following ideas as articulated by Dean Chamberlain:

- Preparing students to live in an urban culture.
- Providing a wider range of disciplines and courses than could be possible at Grantham.
- Offering cultural enrichment [in a large-city context].
- Providing opportunity for service and involvement in an urban society.
- Bringing increased effectiveness to the Grantham campus.
- Providing opportunity for "creative cooperation which would be of mutual benefit to both institutions."

Dr. Paul R. Anderson, president of Temple University, spoke on its behalf, affirming that "Temple is delighted with this opportunity for cooperative effort with other educational institutions and believes that the Messiah–Temple effort will be mutually beneficial." The groundwork had been laid, and the prospects seemed bright for this creative engagement between a small rural Christian liberal arts college and a large urban university.

Three row houses on North Broad street, adjacent
to the main campus of Temple University.

The basic design was that students at the Philadelphia campus
would take one course each semester with Messiah College faculty on
various ethical and philosophical topics. In that first year two
innovative interdisciplinary courses were developed and offered:
Christianity and Contemporary Problems in the fall, and Modern
Images of Man in the spring semester. (Interestingly, variations of
those courses were later offered at the Grantham campus.) Those
Messiah courses offered the students in this largely unfamiliar
urban culture an opportunity to discuss significant issues in a
structured classroom setting with their colleagues and one or more
faculty members.

Ronald J. Sider, who had the major responsibility for teaching at
the center in those early years, recalls that during his seminary
program he had written a paper, "Where Is the Most Strategic
Location for the Christian College Professor Today?" a paper in
which he argued for some type of creative intersection between the
Christian college and the secular university. As he described it later,
such a connection was the "ideal location where you had the best of
the secular world with all its complexity and excellence and at the
same time you had the strength of the Christian college." So Sider was

A mural of Grover Washington, Jr. (saxophonist, 1943-1999) painted by
Peter Pagast and sponsored through the Mural Arts Program.

dreaming about some future possibilities — but was considering job
offers at other institutions — when the dean at Messiah, Dr. Carlton
Wittlinger, contacted him by letter, describing this second campus
which Messiah was planning in Philadelphia. The possibility engaged
him immediately: "I thought . . . this is exactly what I said I was
interested in, and I called him, and the next day I was on a plane, and
I knew immediately this was what I wanted to do, [what] I sensed
God wanted me to do."

Sider's enthusiastic engagement led him, then, to help develop
courses which were not only of abstract interest but involved deep
personal engagement with the issues. This was 1968, a year of major
political-social events, a propitious time for both a new faculty member and a new program to engage in current issues. As Sider recalls
his course on Christianity and Contemporary Problems, "There was
a big section on racism and a big section on global poverty and a big
section on war and peace . . . and it was certainly the doing of that that
contributed to my being modestly ready to do the first version of *Rich
Christians in an Age of Hunger*." In his book — and one can assume
in his teaching — Sider challenged the Christian evangelical world to
a renewed sense of engagement with the pressing social issues of the

Don Wingert, the director of the Philadelphia campus,
in conversation with a student in the dining room.

time. Far from withdrawing into the relative quiet and security of
suburban life, Sider confronted Christians with the challenges and
opportunities of urban life. Perhaps this particular emphasis went
beyond what the president had envisioned for the campus when he
and other early planners were developing the initial outlines of the
new campus, but the choice of location and the ferment of the times
provided fertile soil for new intellectual and spiritual seeds to be
planted.

Students coming to the Philadelphia campus would, of course,
take most of their courses at Temple University. For some, this was a
time when they could choose selected courses, not available at
Grantham, to enrich their major. For others, majors became available
that were not previously possible. The 1974–76 Messiah College
catalog, for example, lists the following majors as now available, with
the usual pattern being students taking the first two years at
Grantham, the last years at Philadelphia: psychology, sociology,
social welfare, urban studies, journalism, art, modern languages,
speech, RTF (radio-television-film), theater, physics, philosophy.
Later other majors such as political science, computer science, and

engineering became available, all requiring extended time of study at the Philadelphia campus.

But as the student body at the home campus became larger, more faculty were hired and many more majors were offered at Grantham, thus no longer requiring the extended time at the urban campus. While some faculty were enthusiastic about the Messiah-Temple connection, others strongly desired to bring their majors "home," in part because, understandably, they wanted to teach more upper-level courses to students in their majors. As he reflects on the early vision for the urban campus, President Hostetter laments the lack of sustained growth at Philadelphia. "It was stunted because as soon as we would develop a new program here [at Grantham] it was easier to keep the kids here." In a recent interview, he says that at the beginning (in 1968) "we had three or four hundred students here [in Grantham]. I would [like to] have seen three or four hundred students in Philadelphia. . . . I would have been happy to buy out a city block in Philadelphia." For various reasons that dream was trun-cated, no doubt primarily because majors begun at the Messiah– Temple campus were — time after time — brought to the Grantham campus, much to the disappointment of Donald Wingert, who served loyally and well as director of the Philadelphia campus for 23 years. Thus the current Messiah campus on North Broad Street consists of five buildings, not a city block as Hostetter had dreamed.

In response to a question about the type of students who were attracted to Philadelphia and the educational opportunities available on the urban campus, Sider argues that there were several factors: "There were clearly people who were coming for the major. . . . [But] I think there were some that were kind of fed up with a small, rural campus and wanted a broader context. I imagine as we developed the image a few came because of it [the urban setting] and probably others didn't come because of it. I think probably the image of the big bad city was a much bigger problem [for recruitment]."

And it was not only the challenge of the urban environment which troubled some, but the confrontation with other philosophies and ideologies, both secular and Christian. Temple University, after all, was — like many major universities — a seedbed of "radical" ideas during these turbulent years. In October 1970, two years after the

opening of the urban campus, the Student Affairs Committee of the
Board presented a paper to the Board of Trustees. Ultimately the
writers favored continuing with the current arrangement, but there
was a strong note of caution in their tone. "In our Student Affairs
Committee," they write, "it was apparent that Messiah College is now
experiencing its first major interaction with Temple University.
Fortunately, at this moment it does not involve the fundamental
belief in Christ; eventually this could become the issue. Our primary
concern is that we be prepared to meet such a challenge. . . . Messiah
College must be capable of defending its view or it could be
overwhelmed by the ideologies brought to the campus by those
returning from Temple University." From these comments, at least,
one could assume that some students were bringing challenging ideas
from their interactions at Temple, ideas that brought concern to
some. "We favor maintaining our Temple campus," the paper
concludes. "However, we need to constantly evaluate Temple campus
leadership and strengthen the area of Christian apologetics." The
proposals for a response to the perceived challenges include the
following possibilities: "a series of six lectures at the Temple campus";
"a convocation at the Temple campus"; or the "establishment of a
chair for Christian apologetics." The reference to the "Temple
campus" is not altogether clear from this distance, though one can
assume that the Messiah campus at Philadelphia was meant, not
the large university. The Student Affairs Committee of the Board of
Trustees approved the report, but there is no reference to other
specific actions that were taken.

The minutes of the Philadelphia Advisory Board meeting in the
same year (October 1970) record the following: "Dr. Hostetter reports
a tendency of polarization between the two campuses. . . . The
Philadelphia students are regarded by the Grantham Campus as
more liberal and condescending. There are some faculty members
who are less than enthusiastic regarding the Philadelphia program."
By the following year, however, Dean Chamberlain reports "that there
is a better understanding and a more sympathetic attitude on the part
of the Grantham faculty towards the Philadelphia program." For
whatever clustering of reasons — student reluctance, parental fears,
limited faculty support — the growth was slower than desired: in the

fall of 1968 there were nine students; in 1969, 19; and in 1970, 25. The growth to 350 by 1979 as projected by the Board was highly ambitious, and, as we have seen, never fulfilled.

Despite the slower-than-desired increase in numbers and the various intellectual and cultural challenges, the urban campus provided a significant opportunity for growth. In an interview, Merle Brubaker, who served as chaplain at Philadelphia from 1971 to1973, articulates the vision succinctly: "The vision was to be a presence on a state university campus and to have the advantage of that resource for Messiah College students at every level possible and every major possible." The opportunities were rich and varied: obviously being in classes at a major university brought Messiah students experientially in contact with persons whose beliefs and practices were often quite unlike their own; taking the required Messiah class with their own colleagues provided opportunity to think together about these challenges; the small-campus intimacy in dining hall, chapel, and residential living all helped provide an "at home" feeling in a larger environment that was for many unfamiliar and could sometimes feel threatening. Students and faculty lived in close proximity at the Philadelphia campus and often developed an esprit de corps hard to imagine on a larger campus. The Middle States Association team in their 1972 report wrote with commendation about the program: "Care should be taken to insure the continuation of the 'informal-living-learning center' atmosphere, and the present closeness of faculty and students — all of which seems to be contributing to a very high and distinctive educational experience. This type of operation is expensive, but the cost appears to be fully justified by the results." Those students, faculty, and staff who lived and worked there generally seem to agree with this early assessment. Recalling those years, Ron Sider says, "[We were living in the center from] the end of 1968 until the summer of 1975. So we had all kinds of interaction with students. I've never had that kind of interaction again. I think that we made a pretty strong impression [on students] in terms of my concerns of being a Christian and being concerned with the poor and needy."

But recruitment for the urban campus continued to be something of a struggle, even though students after living and studying there — almost without exception — became loyal supporters of the program. The college did work hard to introduce new students to the Philadelphia campus. Merle Brubaker recalls that in "those early years [1971 to1973] when we were there, the freshmen [from the Grantham campus] all came down on a weekend; we took about six or eight groups; [in] six or eight weekends every freshman came, and we introduced them to the city. We took them to the churches where black people used to be kept in balconies and were not allowed to be in the main part of the sanctuary, and gave them a real introduction to the racial implications of the city."

In addition to these weekend introductions, the Philadelphia campus offered four-credit Cross-Cultural Studies courses in the January and May terms. The January course offered three "satellite courses," as Yeatts has described them, one in the African American community, a second in the Hispanic communities, and a third in the Asian communities. In May the course was focused on the African American community. Not only were students involved in the usual academic study, but they also lived with families in the community for a week to ten days in order to have a more experiential immersion in another culture. But coming for a three-week short course did not require the same level of involvement in the urban scene as being a longer-term student. In an intriguing observation, Merle Brubaker muses about his perception of the difficulty of recruitment: "Students come to Messiah College in order to avoid a city university, and when we try to persuade them to go [to an urban campus], you have a self-selected group that is going to be very hard to convince to reverse an earlier decision that they made . . ."

One of the early possibilities which was dreamed about by some was establishing a four-year program in Philadelphia, thus recruiting students from the very beginning for the urban campus. Speaking of that dream, Ron Sider recalls, "I was trying to persuade D. Ray [Hostetter] at the time to develop . . . on the Philadelphia model the first black evangelical college, using the Philadelphia campus and expanding it into a four-year program to really attract a lot of African Americans. And he was intrigued and basically said, 'I'll do it if you stay [at Messiah]. I thought it was a good idea, but I didn't feel called to . . . make that the reason I stayed." The idea of an evangelical urban college with a major goal the recruiting of larger numbers of African Americans offers fascinating possibilities — though the barriers to development would no doubt have been formidable. Perhaps a major urban branch of Messiah College could have helped to foster dialogue between white and African American evangelical theologies in a way that could have contributed to the growth and understanding of God's kingdom. But Ron Sider left Messiah in 1978 to teach at a seminary; the fervor of the Civil Rights era was becoming a memory; and Messiah College was still primarily attracting young white college students, though efforts were made to recruit a more ethnically diverse student body. How would a more inclusive campus climate become a reality on both the Grantham and Philadelphia campuses? To those challenges we turn in the next chapter.

Chapter 3

Growing Pains
Encountering Protest and Diversity

The late 1960s and early 1970s were turbulent years on many college and university campuses. Peaceful protests sometimes became violent; orderly marches occasionally turned into riots; anti-war sentiment sometimes morphed into the burning of ROTC buildings. Most stunning were the shootings at Kent State University in the spring of 1970. On May 4 at Kent State some members of the Ohio State National Guard fired into a crowd of dispersing demonstrators, killing four and injuring nine. At hundreds of campuses throughout the nation students went on strike, faculty refused to teach, and many universities were shut down, some for days, others for weeks.

At Messiah, as well, the college was closed and the campus evacuated during a few days early in 1969 — but not because of student riots. The cause of the excitement generated during those days was not student activism, but a train derailment, which actually did have some connection to the war in Southeast Asia. On Thursday, January 23, 1969, a freight train jumped the tracks, with cars reportedly carrying Class A explosives totaling 150 tons, including grenades, mortar shells, and machine gun shells. According to an army munitions expert at the scene, had the explosives detonated as expected, Old Main would have been blown off the map. The army ordered the evacuation of nearby campus buildings, and the college was closed for several days, with students returning the following Wednesday.

Any actual protests at Messiah College, by contrast, seemed fairly muted and quite orderly. In fact, student Glen Heise, writing for *Ivy Rustles*, the student newspaper, passionately laments the apathy on

A few of the freight cars derailed in January 1969. Munitions destined
for the war in Southeast Asia were strewn across the campus
near the entrance to the college, resulting in the evacuation
of nearby campus buildings.

campus, suggesting with apparent frustration that an appropriate
college motto "would be that well-known phrase, 'I couldn't care
less'"(May 26, 1969). The college did, however, experience some
increased student activism during those years. *Ivy Rustles* records a
number of events, some involving only a few students, others having
a wider impact. The February 20, 1969, issue carries a report of a
mobilization of a "Clergyman and Layman Concerned" meeting in
Washington, which seven students, members of the Messiah Peace
Society, attended. Among other activities, the seven were able to
meet with several Pennsylvania legislators, namely, with Senator
Richard S. Schweiker and an aide of Senator Hugh D. Scott, as well as
with two congressmen. Later that spring, in April, five students,
along with their faculty sponsor, Dr. Howard Landis, represented the
college at the National Convention of the American Association of
Evangelical Students (AAES) held at Asbury College in Kentucky. At
the conference Messiah student leaders Glen Pierce and Don Eshle-
man presented a resolution which had been prepared by Messiah

students and had earlier been adopted by the Northeast Region of the AAES. According to the report, "The resolution called for positive action, such as prayer, relief, or service to the Vietnamese people in response to Christ's commands" (*Ivy Rustles*, May 26, 1969). Reportedly, at the national convention the resolution "brought hot debate" and was narrowly defeated by a 23-22 vote.

Throughout the United States protests against the war were increasing by the fall of 1969, and a national Moratorium Day was declared for October 15. The Moratorium was marked by nationwide assemblies, peace marches, and speeches, all having the purpose of bringing pressure to bear on the United States political leadership to bring an end to the war in Southeast Asia. The editor of the *Ivy Rustles*, Mark Charlton, wrote, "The participation of Messiah College in the Moratorium marks the first time that students at this college have mobilized for such an effort" (Oct. 13, 1969). And he encouraged students to voice their concern in a "legitimate, nonviolent, and effective way" through active involvement in the effort. At Messiah the Moratorium was announced very early that morning by the ringing of a large bell near the library by students Esther (Dourte) Spurrier and Beth (Hostetler) Mark. Volunteers continued to ring the bell throughout the day. Classes were cancelled from 9:30 to 11:00, and a service was held which included a peaceful march to major campus buildings, addresses by several people, a homily by Father Thomas Knadig from Mechanicsburg, and a lengthy litany. The opening prayer issued a call for greater personal accountability for the nation: "Help us to establish a consciousness of our responsibility for policies carried out in our name and lead us to the formulation of concrete actions to change war to peace, hate to love." Later that day the Messiah Peace Society organized students to distribute literature in the Harrisburg community about the war in Southeast Asia.

At the Philadelphia campus a number of Messiah students were involved in activities at Temple University and in the city. According to a student's report, "The highlight of the day was the rally at John F. Kennedy Plaza. Nearly half the Messiah group joined the Temple students in a twenty-block march to the gathering of nearly 20,000 protestors. The beauty of the rally setting seemed itself to be a protest to the ugliness of war; the courage of 100 draft card burners seemed to speak of man's nobility rather than his hostility." Clearly the Temple University connection was stretching the college well beyond her early rather separatistic stance as a "Bible School and Missionary Training Home." A month later in November, seven Messiah students at the Philadelphia campus participated in a march on Washington. Reportedly, the "representatives from Messiah in Philadelphia enjoyed the feeling of euphoria which many experienced during the day's activities, but they left with the knowledge that euphoria alone does not bring peace" (*Ivy Rustles*, Dec. 16, 1969). The number of students involved in these major demonstrations appears not to have been large, but the influence on campus conversation must have been significant.

At Messiah there were some protests both on and off campus in response to the May killings at Kent State and Jackson State. Alumna Karen (Hostetler) Deyhle recalls the activities of the Peace Society: "Right after Kent State, some of us made four fires on the pavement … [across from the church]. We had shifts [of students] to keep the fire attended to at all times." The fires — one for each of the Kent State dead — were reportedly kept burning for a day or two, and prayer vigils were held during that time. According to another alumna, Nancy Heisey, "We also took four wooden crosses and marched down the median of Route 15 for a mile or so, and drivers shouted stuff at us." According to Karen Deyhle, a "busload and many cars" went several miles to Carlisle to join a march on the road in front of the Army War College. Later a number of students with a faculty sponsor also went to march with protesters in Washington, D.C. Regarding those days, Beth Mark reflects, "I always thought it was a good thing that college leaders didn't try to stop the fires/protests at that time."

By the following fall, essays in the student newspaper called for involvement on the local or grassroots level. One student observes, "The days of the huge demonstration are probably gone, but the huge demonstration was not defeated. . . . The peace movement has now moved into an arena of trying to change society on a local level while calling attention to the fact that the war machine still exists" (*Ivy Rustles*, Nov. 11, 1970). In one sense, of course, Kent State showed dramatically the limited power of demonstrations and the seemingly overwhelming authority of guns and bullets. Although there was a large public outcry and many campus protests, there was also a new realism which recognized lethal power and the limitations of protest.

A year later, in April 1971, the national coordinator of the Student Mobilization Committee to End the War in Southeast Asia issued a call for new strikes, rallies, and memorials. His call was printed in *Ivy Rustles*, but the response seems to have been limited. The same issue (April 30) printed a "Young Voters for Peace" pledge which students were invited to sign and return to the office in Portland, Oregon. The (potential) signer pledged to vote only for those candidates who committed to "withdrawal of all U.S. military personnel from Indo-China by a specified date in the immediate future" and who insisted "upon the exercise of Congressional authority over decisions affecting matters of war and peace." One wonders how many Messiah students signed and submitted the voting pledge, though there seems to be no written record of responses.

Not much evidence exists about Messiah faculty and administrative involvement in the anti-war movement, though some faculty were involved in the October 15, 1969, Moratorium activities, and Academic Dean Dr. Daniel R. Chamberlain spoke at the on-campus rally. One strong spokesperson for pacifism was professor of the history of Christianity and chair of the Division of Religion and Philosophy, Dr. Martin H. Schrag, who taught some of the required Bible courses. In those courses, according to Beth Mark, Schrag "included teachings on the biblical underpinnings for our peace stance. His passion for the topic was contagious and convicting, leading a core group of students to become activists." Schrag also wrote several essays for the student newspaper. In the May 14, 1971, issue he wrote, "For some time I have been wanting to make a statement regarding the war in Indo-China. This article is my channel for stating that I disassociate myself from American participation in the war. I am not at war with the people or government of North Vietnam. They are not my enemies. I divorce myself from the conflict. . . . To have the peace of Christ in the heart means the motivation for participation in and support of war is gone."

Meshach Paul Krikorian   Rachel Flowers

Again, in a later issue of the campus paper, Schrag wrote, "Behind the ease with which some American Christians go to war lies the assumption that God in actuality has a special relationship with the United States. . . . In this scheme of things America entered wars only under the directive of God and to further His purpose." A deeply committed Anabaptist, Schrag rejected this view of the United States as a specially called and chosen nation. At the time of his writing few on campus might have made the case as pointedly as he did, but there were still significant numbers of faculty and students who would have accepted the broad outlines of Schrag's position. Furthermore, the strong anti-war sentiment in the U.S. against the increasingly unpopular war in Southeast Asia probably made his strongly worded arguments more acceptable than they might otherwise have been. Many opposed the war even though the basis of opposition was not the same as Schrag's theological position. The student bulletin board, fittingly called the Wittenburg Door, had frequent postings by students debating the involvement of the United States in the war in Southeast Asia.

The war did eventually end, of course, and campuses everywhere returned to a greater focus on more local concerns. One of the on-campus issues at Messiah College was the involvement of persons

Vincent Flowers   Martha Bosley

from a variety of ethnic and social backgrounds on a campus which was traditionally overwhelmingly white. Perhaps a few words of earlier background would be helpful.

The early roots of the Brethren in Christ denomination reach deep into Swiss German (largely Mennonite) soil. The college was founded within that tradition, and then from that tradition recruited most of her students in the first half-century. At the same time, for most of a century the church has been heavily involved in missionary work in Africa, particularly in (present-day) Zimbabwe and Zambia. Thus over the years a number of African students have matriculated in their denominational school in the States. Perhaps the first international student at Messiah, however, was not from Africa, but from Turkey. Meshach Paul (M. P.) Krikorian, who fled his homeland following the intense persecution of Armenian Christians, including the killing of his parents and a sister, came to Messiah at the invitation of the first president, S. R. Smith. After some time of study, he left in 1915 to continue his academic work and eventually became an ordained minister in the Brethren in Christ church. No doubt many of these international students confronted significant cultural adjustments, but they were also welcomed because of their connection to the church and to missionaries who were known in the church.

Although the number of American students from non-Caucasian backgrounds was small in the early years, Hierald Kane-Osorto, past associate director of multicultural programs, has discovered three African American students who studied at Messiah. Rachel Flowers attended Messiah Academy from 1917 to 1919, which as Kane-Osorto says "was an amazing discovery ... [because] it was 8 years after Messiah was founded in 1909." Her brother, Vincent Flowers, followed her lead, and in 1923 he enrolled in the academy, from which he graduated in 1927, with an ambition to become a pianist. Two years later, in 1929, another African American woman, Martha Bosley, graduated from the academy, and she then returned as a student at Messiah Bible College for a year in 1931–32. Apparently she later matriculated at another institution, where she completed a nursing program and became a registered nurse. Little has yet been discovered about the Messiah campus experiences of these early "pioneers," Rachel Flowers, Vincent Flowers, and Martha Bosley.

But many years later some non-Caucasians did not find the campus a hospitable, welcoming environment. Writing in the campus newspaper (*Ivy Rustles*) in October 1973, student Anne Gilliam cries in pain, "At present I find being on Messiah's campus very hard and very frustrating because white people *don't care*! They are tired of hearing about *racism* but they don't do anything about it. Meanwhile, because of their insensitivity, I am dying." Without necessarily assuming that she is speaking for all black students on campus, she is clearly crying out her own frustration at the lack of understanding which she perceives. Nor did she herself always voice the same degree of outrage. Writing a few months later in February 1974, Anne offers an invitation to the third Black Cultural Weekend: "We, the black students of Messiah College, feel that in order for a real community of Christian fellowship to exist at Messiah's campus, we have to be sensitive to one another's needs. So it is vital that you give us your support during the entire weekend." After describing some of the planned activities, she ends with this invitational tone: "We really want everyone to have a dynamite learning experience and a beautiful time in our Lord." The weekend activities, which opened with a dinner featuring ethnic foods, included the showing of black films, "visiting choirs and speakers," and concluded on Sunday with a

"Black worship service." Despite voicing her frustrations, Anne Gilliam and others had not given up in their efforts to bridge racial barriers and misunderstandings.

A few years earlier, in 1971, a Black Student Union had been formed on the Grantham campus. The primary objectives, as noted by student reporter Linda Carey, were "To promote black programs on campus and to attend any off-campus event that will relate to the black students . . . spiritually, socially, or academically" (*Ivy Rustles*, Feb. 8, 1971). In addition to these goals, students projected "encouraging the establishment of a Black Studies program here at Messiah." A year later, student Jacqueline Gibson reported on a meeting with participants from area colleges in which they proposed an "African American Semester" to be located at one of the participating colleges, the program to be run by a black coordinator and staffed — at least in part — by black faculty. In addition — and probably more realistically and helpfully — the group urged that "each individual school should seek to improve and/or develop its own black curriculum so that black courses will exist at every school on a permanent basis" (*Ivy Rustles*, Feb.16, 1972). Messiah had already taken a modest first step in that direction when Professor Clyde Ross offered Afro-American Literature for the first time in 1971, a course that later became part of the regular continuing American literature offerings and one which was popular with both English majors and others.

The conversation on campus continued, and in the April 4, 1972 *Ivy Rustles* a student editor raised questions about racism, "I must ask if racism really exists on our campus or if one faction among us is CAUSING it to happen," the clear implication in the essay being that some black students were stirring up unnecessary controversy. The editor argued further, "We must get back to the point where race is no issue and skin color is overlooked." Not surprisingly, his editorial provoked vigorous discussion and dissent. The following issue (April 20) carried several lengthy rejoinders. One person wrote bluntly, "When you refer to the Messiah College where the problem of racism did not exist, you are in reality referring to a time when Messiah was so completely immersed in white Anglo-Saxon Protestant culture that the extremely small number of people

Black Student Union members, with Dr. Martin Schrag, advisor.

from other cultures who were on campus did not dare to speak." In the same issue another writer said, "We should raise the roof, not because we want to destroy, as campus patriots often assume, but to make the college a better place."

Reflecting on issues of racial diversity in the early 1970s, Dr. Gerald Hess, current interim dean of the School of Health and Natural Sciences and professor of biology, writes, "My first faculty retreat was held at the Philly Campus in August 1971...with [African American preacher] Tom Skinner as speaker. My sense is that Messiah faculty in 1971 were concerned about racial issues, but [we] faced a steep learning curve on such issues." The administration and faculty did become actively engaged in responding, and that same April (1972) President D. Ray Hostetter created an ad-hoc faculty-student "Committee on Discrimination" as it related to Messiah College with Dr. Martin Schrag serving as chair and student Frank Demmy as secretary. Already by May 8 the committee issued their first report in which they both listed some of their goals and offered a strong critique of perceived problems on campus. The committee wrote, "We want to thoroughly define racial discrimination in a way relevant to Messiah College and to measure its extent at Messiah.

Second, we want to prepare a formal statement by which the college may be guided concerning racial discrimination . . . [including] a Biblically-based philosophy of race relations. Third, we want to formulate some specific recommendations to the college community for dealing with racial discrimination as it exists at Messiah."

Rather bluntly the committee articulated their perception of existing problems on campus: "It has been brought to our attention that there is a very ugly overt racism among us, and this has been demonstrated by a number of incidents involving obscenities directed at Black students. The greatest problem is, however, not open racism but hidden racism and ignorance. Minority students feel crushed and misunderstood by a white culture that is insensitive to their needs and to their heritage, and is often hostile to their attempts at self-expression." On a strong positive note the committee wrote, "The Committee emphatically believes that all of us need the presence of minority cultures at Messiah to enrich and deepen both our Christian faith and our human experience. It is our conviction that if Messiah College rejects the witness of minority cultures and withdraws into a cultural isolation forged by fear and ignorance, she will do so only by betraying her Lord Jesus Christ."

By November of that year, the committee had prepared a twelve-point theological statement which was clearly Anabaptist in its orientation. The focal point of the document was the transforming power of Jesus Christ: "Jesus Christ was the historical culmination of God's solution to the sin problem . . . Christ sets aside more barriers than those of race or nationality, for he also abolishes barriers of sex and class distinctions. . . . The days of discrimination are over. The new humanity created by God in the church tolerates no discrimination of race, class distinction, sex or nationality. . . . We are truly one in Christ." Although the initial statement was primarily theological in focus, it does include some specific suggestions for change. For example, the committee argues, "Because there is one people, created by God and uniquely made one in Christ, to prohibit intermarriage . . . is to oppose the New Testament concept of personhood." Finally, they conclude, "to continue to accept the racial categories of today's world after one has been converted to Christ is to deny Christ's lordship over one's life and is, therefore, not merely error but mortal sin." In January 1973 the preliminary study was distributed to faculty with the stark title, "Racism at Messiah College," and a faculty forum was scheduled to provide opportunity for full discussion by the faculty.

Then in May 1973 the writers brought their conclusions and recommendations to the faculty in the "Final Report of the Committee on Discrimination in the Area of Race." The committee notes that both overt and covert racism exists on the Messiah College campus and identifies a few instances of overt racism. But covertly, they write, "racism is manifested in the constant application of pressure on the oppressed group to denounce its own racial identity and conform to the roles and expectations assigned to it by the ruling group. Every manifestation of racism reduces the power of the oppressed group and this weakens its capacity to resist." In words of strong critique, the committee writes, "Black students feel mistrusted, misunderstood, and separated from the life of the community. . . . The final straw for many minority students is the apathy of many white students to even recognize the problem. . . ." The committee brought many recommendations for change, including more assertive recruitment of "minority" faculty and students, the addition of more cross-cultural experiences, as well as more black studies courses, and the integration of black studies in the curriculum more generally. The 23 page report concludes with this stirring call to repentance: "Let us come together on our knees, let us move our concern for justice from our heads to our hearts, and let us forge from the white heat of conviction and repentance a new commitment to Jesus Christ and to the new way of life which he ordains for all who would call themselves his disciples."

The previous fall Dr. Ronald J. Sider, from the Philadelphia campus, had written a series of three lengthy essays on racism which were published in the student newspaper. In tone and content the essays were more scholarly than the usual fare in college newspapers. Sider concludes his first essay in the series with this appeal: "Is it not time for the church of Jesus Christ to take some dramatic visible steps to end the scandal of racism in that body where there is to be neither Jew nor Greek, slave nor free because all are one in Christ?" (*Ivy Rustles*, Oct. 31, 1972)

That same fall a racist incident at the Philadelphia campus provoked the presentation of a series of demands by black students. When conversations with the students did not lead to resolution, the Philadelphia Advisory Board and the Executive Committee of the Messiah College Board of Trustees met in joint session in Philadelphia on February 1, 1973. Among the demands were the naming of a black director for the Philadelphia campus and the hiring of black faculty, with the students having "veto power" over these hiring decisions. In response the joint committees reaffirmed their "intentions of naming a black director and [agreed] that we press the search with more vigor." Not surprisingly, they declined giving the students veto power, though two black students were named to the search committee for the director's position, along with several administrators, three local African American leaders and a few others.

Then in a letter dated February 6, 1973, President Hostetter addressed a letter to two black student leaders, summarizing some of the conclusions of the joint committees, which had met a few days earlier. Among other matters he wrote, "A letter of apology for past neglect, for some overt acts of discrimination, and for covert discrimination is now being prepared." He indicated that students would not be given veto power in hiring decisions, but representatives would be included on the appropriate committees. Students were also encouraged to "propose [Black Studies] courses that are uniquely suited to Messiah College as a Christian College" and which would not duplicate courses available at the Philadelphia campus (through Temple). The demand for additional scholarship money for black students was acknowledged but no specific promises were given. And the demand that students from Philadelphia be permitted to commute from their home and be considered Messiah students was denied because of the important learnings of the community life experience at the "Living–Learning Center" of Messiah College.

Over the next months the search led eventually to the hiring of Dr. Abraham Davis, an African American professor who had been teaching at a sister college. He had come to read and lecture at Messiah College during a speaking tour while he was on sabbatical and was well received. Recruited by Messiah, Dr. Davis served first as acting dean of the Philadelphia campus from January to June in 1974; and then, returning in September 1975, he was named as dean and served for over two years before requesting release from his administrative post. He continued for several years as professor of speech communications, as well as being involved with community relationship building. One college release describes his role as having his "time divided between several humanities classes and a newly developed minority advocacy program."

In addition to the student demands there was also a community group from north Philadelphia, the "People's Community Developer's Corporation," which brought a series of twelve "expectations" to the college administration. The Philadelphia Advisory Board modified a few expectations, but with those few changes accepted the list. One of the precipitating concerns for the Corporation, apparently, was the fear that Messiah College would expand too aggressively and take over large amounts of local real estate. In retrospect, the concern seems a little surprising because the April 26, 1973, Advisory Board minutes record a current Philadelphia campus enrollment of 43 students, a gradual increase from the nine in the first year (1968), but the Corporation included the "expectation" that the student body not grow beyond 300 resident students. The Corporation also defined expected geographical boundaries for college expansion, "with any purchase negotiable with the Community." Partly in response to the concerns, the college actively cooperated in the revitalization of the housing of one city block in north Philadelphia near the campus.

Although this community group did not address faculty hiring, they included significant expectations for student numbers: "the College will use its best effort to secure a student body at Philadelphia and Grantham which will be 10 percent non-white by 1975," an ambitious goal when one considers the thirteen African American students enrolled (in 1973) at the time of the writing. With a current total student body of 808 (FTE), the needed recruitment of almost 70 additional students to meet this "10 percent non-white" goal would have been extraordinary. To be fair to the record, the Philadelphia Advisory Board recommended "the acceptance of these 12 expec-tations . . . as a basis of continued negotiations and relations with the People's Community Developer's Corporation." In addition to the growth of the number of "non-white" students, the Corporation also asked that the college "use its best effort to have a college Trustee Board and Advisory Board which will be 10 percent non-white by 1975." The possibilities for meeting those goals were much greater for the Philadelphia Advisory Board than for the larger Board of Trustees. Whatever the extent of realistic hope that these "expectations" could be met, the college administration was at least open to the conversation.

On the Grantham campus the ferment continued as well, and in that same spring semester (1973), the student senate responded to black students' demands for an apology with a statement which opened with these words: "We, the undersigned students, wish to signify by our signing that we apologize to the black students for any inhumane, unjust, or unkind actions toward our black brothers and sisters. We realize that we are sometimes blind to the things we do which hurt others. Forgive us for this, and help us to open our eyes." The apology further expressed the desire to change and "to strive together to create a Christian community on our campus." Whatever the ultimate impact of the black student demands and white student apologies, clearly the black students were becoming actively engaged in college life and insisting on further change.

Some years earlier, in 1967, John Howard Griffin, white author of *Black Like Me*, had lectured at Messiah College about his experiences traveling in the South as a "Black" man. Writing in the May 9, 1967, *Ivy Rustles*, student Glen Pierce (now the Brethren in Christ archivist at Messiah College), reported on Griffin's speech to an "overflow crowd" at the largest venue then available on campus, the Alumni Auditorium. After a lengthy reporting of Griffin's appeal to the audience's sense of justice, Pierce took a more editorial voice: "Some personal reflections seem inevitable following such a lecture." After listing two modest gestures which Griffin had offered to Messiah College students, Pierce then asked, "Is there not a challenge here for students at Messiah to become more involved than these rather passive gestures? . . . Could we find several Christian young people from the Negro community in the deep South who have the desire and the abilities to enter college, but who lack funds, and see that they are enrolled next fall at Messiah College?" He took his own challenge seriously and helped to establish a "Negro Scholarship Fund" to fund a student. Small cards with stark black/white contrasting blocks were printed with slogans such as "Join the NSF rebellion"; "Cast Your Vote Against Prejudice"; "Make an Investment in Freedom. NSF!" Pierce and his committee were successful in raising some $600 for a major scholarship. Through the contacts of Dr. Martin Schrag, Edna Curry from Mississippi was recruited as the recipient of the scholarship.

In her reflections on her coming, she writes for the student newspaper, "I have been asked many questions since being here such as: Where did you hear of Messiah? Are you Brethren in Christ? How do you like it at Messiah? . . . Before I came I did not know what to expect. By reading the catalogue, I surmised Messiah to be a Christian College, but then I asked myself many questions: are all the students Christians? Would there be students who would not accept me as an individual?" (*Ivy Rustles*, Oct. 12, 1967) She affirms that she has "been warmly accepted by students as well as faculty." Her courageous spirit in coming to an institution of which she knew very little is quite stunning. One wonders what she thought late at night in her dorm room as she reflected on being the only African American woman on campus. (There were at the time two male African students, one from Zambia, the other from Tanzania.) Did Edna Curry find a hospitable "home away from home" as she entered this unfamiliar environment, in addition to facing the significant adjustments common to many students in their first year on campus?

Two of a series of 14 small black/white cards printed with red lettering. The nomenclature reflects common 1960s usage.

Edna Curry.

In her word of reflection and appreciation (in the second month of her coming) she writes, "Being here at Messiah has been a wonderful opportunity for me, and I am enjoying my experiences very much." She did return the next year as a sophomore and is listed as a nursing major. However, she did not continue in the following year; presumably she transferred to a nursing school to complete her program of study. Given her affirming words, one could speculate that possibly Edna Curry, another pioneering student, might have been quite surprised at the strongly expressed frustrations of a later generation of students.

The late sixties and early seventies were years of flux and change on many campuses, both Christian and secular, and while Messiah College was by comparison much quieter, changes were coming. The peace movement on campus did create some levels of consciousness-raising, and the somewhat greater ethnic diversity brought a climate where students who had felt themselves on the margins began to express some of their feelings of frustration at the perceived lack of understanding by the larger community.

Through seeking to embrace greater diversity, the college was continuing to redefine herself. Messiah didn't move far toward the "expectation" of 10 percent non-white students by 1975, but the next two decades were a time of unprecedented growth.

Chapter 4

The Remarkable Years
The Growth Decades (1970s–1980s)

In the November 1972 report of the Middle States Association evaluation team, the reviewers address a short section to the issue of growth: "The Admissions Office is confident that an increase in student population can be realized but the projected 25 percent increase to 1,200 students by 1980 may be a larger expansion than is realistic in light of current factors in American higher education. . . . It will be necessary to provide an astute Admissions program to insure the desired degree of expansion without reducing academic standards or diluting the Christian commitment."

The questions raised by the Middle States Association team were no doubt reasonable given usual patterns of enrollment growth, but, in fact, by 1980 the college had enrolled — not 1,200 — but 1,267 (FTE) students. We have already noted that the student population more than doubled from 1969 to 1979, and then, remarkably, almost doubled again by 1989. Another way of describing this amazing growth is to observe that in the thirty-year tenure of President D. Ray Hostetter, the student body grew from 270 (FTE) students to 2,288 (FTE), more than an eight-fold increase. At the same time Christian commitment remained strong — though denominational diversity increased — and academic standards actually were strengthened during those years (as we will observe more fully in later chapters).

Not surprisingly, the rapid growth of the college in the 1970s and 1980s had its genesis in an earlier day. Elbert N. Smith, grandson of Samuel R. Smith, the first president of the college, served in multiple roles (as director of admissions, controller, and professor of courses in Christian education). He reports that in 1966 in his role as director of admissions, he was able to recruit at least 100 freshman students for the college, and in his words, "I told Dean Carlton Wittlinger, 'We have 100 new freshmen. If you treat them well, and we keep adding each year, in four years we will have 400 students.'" Not impressed, Dean Wittlinger reportedly retorted, "Smith, that will never happen!" But in fact the October 1966 Board of Trustees minutes report a "total enrollment" of 427 students (FTE figures not included).

That surprising growth may be attributable to the recruiting net being cast more widely. The April 29, 1966, Board of Trustee minutes — the last year of Smith's service at Messiah — include his admissions report: "Admissions personnel this year contacted 136 schools, blanketing the area surrounding the College for a radius of 75 miles. Contacts were also made with high schools beyond this radius, some by personal visitation, many by letter. . . . Catalogs were sent to all high schools in Pennsylvania, Maryland, Delaware and much of New Jersey." Nor was the church neglected: "All Brethren in Christ pastors and pastors of other interested congregations were requested to submit a listing of juniors and seniors attending their congregations."

Smith left Messiah in 1966 to become a pastor in California, and that summer Paul L. Snyder was named director of admissions, a post which he held for ten years. By 1976, Snyder's last year as director, there were 950 (FTE) students. Snyder continued to encourage enlarging the student pool beyond the denomination. Among other efforts he invited church youth groups to bring high school juniors and seniors to college basketball games on weekend evenings. Snyder also made contacts with Youth for Christ, a large parachurch Evangelical organization, and arranged to have Messiah College represented at a large summer convention in Ocean City [NJ], a meeting which became a major venue for recruitment.

The student body continued growing rapidly, and often at academic conferences colleagues from other institutions would ask, "What is the secret of the remarkable growth at Messiah College?" One usually fumbled for an adequate response probably because the answers are multiple, rather than singular. We believed that we had a solid academic program — but so did many other colleges who were not experiencing growth. We acknowledged that God was blessing us in many ways — but God blessed many other colleges as well. We were unashamedly Christian in our commitments, but so were scores — perhaps hundreds — of other colleges. We had good facilities — but they often seemed crowded because of the continuing rapid growth. In short, the unprecedented growth seemed not related to any single reason, and certainly no formula would be adequate to explain it.

Indeed, it would appear that President Hostetter, who had considerable business acumen, did not anticipate the growth to continue at the pace at which it occurred. In a paper sent to faculty on January 6, 1971, titled, "Consideration of National and Institutional Assumptions and Guidelines in Forming a Long-Range Plan for Messiah College," he identified the following educational assumptions, among others:

1. The private sector of education will attract a declining proportion of college students.
2. There will be drastic changes in education.
3. All colleges will be forced to look seriously at accountability.
4. Diverse forms of education beyond high school will be established and accepted because of society's feeling that colleges and universities are too inflexible to solve academic and productivity problems.

So, as Hostetter understood, the perceived challenges in the contemporary educational climate were significant, and to expect continuing growth in the student body and expansion in the academic program seemed unrealistic. Yet remarkable growth became the expected norm.

Many new majors were added during those decades of growth, particularly in professional study areas such as computer science and accounting, nursing and engineering. Additional faculty and staff were recruited every year. And it seemed that one or more buildings were always under construction during these years, as the following list will suggest:

1972
- Eisenhower Campus Center
- Lenhert Maintenance Building
- Covered Bridge (built in 1867; moved to campus 1972)

1973
- Bittner Residence

1977
- Murray Library (major addition to existing library)

1978
- Starry Athletic Field

1979
- Smith Apartments

1981
- Climenhaga Fine Arts Center (Music, Theatre, Visual Art)
- Fry Apartments

1983
- Naugle Residence

1985
- Sollenberger Sports Center
- Mellinger Apartments

1988
- Witmer Residence

1989
- Kelly Apartments

1991
- Frey Hall (Mathematics, Engineering, Business, Art)

So the growth in student body, number of faculty and staff, and additional programs and new buildings during those two decades was little short of amazing. And still the question remains, why? Many of those directly involved in leadership during those years affirm that the developing of a covenant relationship with the Brethren in Christ denomination opened the door to a much wider potential constituency. Dr. Harold Engle, who served as chairman of the Board for over twenty years, says of the decision to move to a covenant agreement rather than ownership by the church, "We basically had no choice [but] to move to a broader Board and to keep operating as a church related [institution]. I think this . . . was the

inevitable thing . . . we lost something philosophically as a denomination, but [we] gained in the broadened concept of Christianity: less
narrow-minded, more understanding from the world viewpoint."

The enlarged focus included major recruiting efforts beyond
the Brethren in Christ denomination. Perhaps no single person was
more important in this reaching out to an enlarged constituency than
Ron E. Long, who initially came to Messiah College as a student in
1962 and returned later to work on campus as part of his alternative
service as a conscientious objector. Soon he was assisting in the
Admissions Office part-time, where he continued even after joining
the music faculty. In 1976 he was named director of admissions and
financial aid, and, in 1981, director of admissions, financial aid, and
communications.

Ron Long devoted his considerable talents and strong work ethic
to enlarging the pool of applicants for admission to the college. He
recalls his basic approach: "I used the acronym SPAM: you have
Suspects, Prospects, Applicants, and Matriculants . . . [It is an]
enrollment funnel. You know you start at the top of the funnel with
these 'suspects,' and some weren't college material obviously. . . . We'd
collect hundreds of names which we could follow up with. . . . You
know you needed to have suspects to turn them into prospects,
[then] turn them into applicants."

In addition to sending music ministry teams on extended
summer trips to visit many churches, Long also recruited at parachurch organizations. He continued the contact with some Youth
for Christ leaders who had organized a "two-week conference down
in Ocean City [NJ]. Thousands of kids [were] there, some of them
not Christians, but most of them were . . . We'd kind of do the
warm-up [music]. Kids would come early to get a good seat; these
were big productions down in the convention hall . . . and that's
how they [our quartets] got in and then we'd have booths. The other
colleges hated me . . . because we had access to all these kids . . . so
we'd set up a display and . . . that's how I built a prospect base of
Christian kids."

Besides going to these large venues, Long significantly expanded
advertising in journals such as *Campus Life,* where he eventually
managed to place the Messiah College full-page ad inside the front

cover, a highly advantageous location. He also included "tip-in" cards for selected zip code areas where Messiah was attempting to recruit students. These self-addressed reply cards made it simple for "suspects" to get information and become "prospects." In addition, Long says, "We were the first [Christian] college, to my knowledge, that had an 800 [telephone] number . . . Some of the marketing things [which we used] would have gone against the grain because this is education; we don't market education like toothpaste."

But market we did, as academic dean and later academic vice-president (1977–1988) Dr. H. David Brandt notes, "I think Messiah was well ahead of its time with Ron Long in the marketing efforts of the college. Ron and his people were well ahead in understanding the need for positioning. . . . You probably also remember the giraffe which was used as a hook . . . [in] 1977–78 or thereabouts. . . . We had this giraffe [on our ads], and people would ask, 'Why the giraffe?' And . . . [Long would say] 'I don't know; did you read the ad?' And if the answer was yes, 'That's why the giraffe. It worked; it hooked you.'"

Little was left to chance under Long's leadership: he himself approved letters sent out to "prospects," and he personalized those letters which responded to specific student inquiries. Because both financial aid and the college communication office came under his leadership, recruitment efforts were clearly focused and the potential audience carefully cultivated. Unrelenting in his demands on himself, Long required excellence from his staff as well. And the pool of prospective students grew enormously, thus making greater selectivity possible, even while the student body was growing.

With the continuing growth in the student body, the increased numbers of academic majors, and the vastly enlarged facilities, the reputation of the college was being strengthened. But there was growth in other ways as well. Dr. James (Jay) H. Barnes, dean and then later vice-president for student development from 1980 to 1995, reflects on those years: "I'd say growth in quality was at least as remarkable as growth in size of the student body. I think the quality of the faculty [and] quality of the facilities certainly changed dramatically. . . . The professionalization of faculty, of student development, of campus ministries during that time was a significant factor in elevating Messiah's profile among its peers." Barnes notes also that being recognized in *U.S. News and World Report* at a significantly higher ranking "probably surprised us . . . [with] an affirmation from outside that we had become a different institution in size and scope and quality of programs."

The larger student body made possible — and necessary — significant strengthening in the student development area. In the year or two before Barnes came, small numbers of students had been creating mayhem with behavior which went beyond pranksterism to destructiveness. Fires were set in some dumpsters; several students broke into faculty offices; and at one point a few students even removed ceiling tiles and managed to break into the on-campus U.S. Post Office. As Dr. Dorothy Gish recalls that time, "It was almost anarchy." Because the situation had become so chaotic, the person in leadership in student development was released, and Dorothy Gish was asked to serve as acting dean of students. It was, as Gish describes it, a "difficult time, very difficult, but I learned early . . . [that] you don't go from anarchy to [working at] a desk spot. And so what I did was to move my office directly across from the dining hall so people would know there was a dean there. I ate all my meals in the dining hall." Change wasn't immediate — but change did come with a visible dean. But Gish had no desire to continue in that role.

After an extensive search, Jay Barnes was brought to the campus. With his quietly effective, though firm, leadership style, supported by an increasingly well-qualified staff, Barnes helped to provide stability in the student life area during this period of burgeoning growth. Not only was there stability, but there were greatly expanded student services during those years. From 1,267 (FTE) students when Barnes came in 1980 to almost double that (2,399 FTE) when he left fifteen years later, not only was there growth in numbers, but expectations for services grew dramatically. For example, the role of residence director changed considerably as Barnes describes it: "Many of the RDs were involved full-time in something else [when I came]; some [were] involved in coaching or off-campus work; then [they] did a little bit [of] part-time with residence hall supervision." Eventually many RDs had significant load time dedicated to their work in the residence halls.

Eldon Fry praying with the campus ministry team.

In addition to a much expanded residence life staff, other areas were either newly added or significantly expanded during these years as well. A full counseling program headed by Dr. Philip Lawlis, a psychologist, and a health center under nurse Ruth Brubaker provided a needed range of services for students. Also, increasingly students and parents expected more help in planning and preparing for careers following graduation. Dr. Donna Dentler, associate dean for community educational services and career development, with the able assistance of Dr. Dorothy Gish, developed effective models for student planning throughout the four years of college. Rather than simply learning how to prepare a resume in their senior year, students were assisted in taking a larger view of Vocation (calling), beginning early in their academic program. Faculty advising was also strengthened, and faculty were encouraged to be mentors and do far more than help students select and register for courses for the following semester.

Another related area which was developed and expanded was college ministries, with the calling in 1984 of Eldon Fry as director of campus ministries (which later became "College Ministries"). His newly created full-time position moved well beyond the earlier college chaplaincy position. In Fry's own words, "The role was really a new position; we'd not had this position before on campus. It was to work with student organizations, particularly around areas of student on-campus ministry, off-campus outreach, and . . . international ministries." Later, some of these areas would become more fully developed with other structures and leaders, but Fry's coming marked an important phase of increasing college focus on various outreach ministries. Initially, in 1984, the chaplain, David Parkyn, continued in his role with one-fourth time administrative load, having primary responsibility for chapel programming. In the following academic year Parkyn was on leave, and Fry was asked to serve as chaplain, a role he continued to fill until he left the college in 1997, before returning eight years later. With his warm spirit and heart for service, Fry was well received by the students whom he served and led.

The strengthening of the cocurricular area is well summarized by Barnes' reflections on those growth years: This period "was a chance for student development and campus ministries to mature into professional programs that were stronger contingents . . . [of] what was already a pretty good academic program. . . . The philosophical emphasis on educating the whole student became more of a reality during those years as campus ministries and student development came into their own."

Not all faculty and administrators were happy with the major focus on student development programming. There was some sense of competition for funding, particularly because of the major expansion in cocurricular personnel and programs. One person recalls that an administrator would sometimes say ironically in budget planning meetings that the student development office wouldn't "be happy until . . . [they] have a counselor for every student." Barnes acknowledges that "at times there was a tension between the academic side and the student development side that wasn't entirely helpful. We should have been talking more to each other."

But despite some stresses and growing pains, a positive sense of hopefulness pervaded the college. The student body was growing; new programs — both curricular and cocurricular — were being added; in short, change and growth seemed to be part of the institutional DNA. Although from time to time announced maximum numbers of students were projected, few seemed to take those limitations seriously. And a future "steady-state" environment was virtually impossible to imagine. For the entire decade from 1979 to 1989 the college had an average of 106 more students *each fall* than in the previous year. Not only were there more students each fall, but usually there were more students than had been calculated in the annual budget plan for the following fiscal year, thus providing additional revenue to support the college program. In some ways Messiah College was experiencing the American Dream as the institution grew from her modest beginnings as a Bible school through the trials of the Great Depression, to developing strength as a junior college and academy, to a four-year accredited liberal arts college in the 1960s, and finally to a rapidly growing institution increasingly recognized as an emerging leader in Christian higher education.

The two decades through the 1970s and 1980s became a period of enormous change for the college. A new academic calendar was designed and approved; an innovative, ambitious interdisciplinary studies program was planned and implemented; intercollegiate athletics moved to a new affiliation and greater national recognition; a major endowment gift brought the potential for increased long-term financial stability and strength; and faculty/staff salaries and other benefits became more competitive.

Chapter 5

A Time of Change
Calendar and Curriculum

The growth of the student body in the 1970s and 1980s was, as we have observed, nothing short of remarkable. Along with that growth were other significant changes in the college, though some were less physically obvious than the increased numbers of students on campus. Innovation and change have often been part of college life on many campuses; certainly at Messiah the theme of change has been one of the major subtexts as the college has moved from a fairly defined focus in the Brethren in Christ denomination as a "Bible school and missionary training home" to a "Bible college" and then to the much enlarged scope of a liberal arts college.

One specific focus for change was the academic year calendar, an aspect of college life which would seem fairly routine and mundane on one level, but one which could offer the possibility for significant innovation. The first change proposed was for a common theme of study in a January "Intersession," with the initial topic, "Man and His Environmental Problems," being considered by the entire faculty and student body during eight days in January 1971. The topic apparently led to lively discussions with one result being that the Messiah College Student Senate composed and approved a letter to be sent to all "friends" of Messiah College. According to the February 15, 1971 Faculty Meeting Minutes, the Student Senate proposed sending the letter "to all College personnel, all alumni, and all interested persons or groups on the College's mailing lists." The ambitious plans set forth in the letter, endorsed by the Student Senate, encouraged "population control, support of all legislation dealing with ecology and population limiting, and support of ecology candidates." Not surprisingly, though the faculty "recognized the need for action in this area," they turned down the request for endorsement of the rather sweeping proposals and suggested that MCSA prepare an essay or a series of essays for publication in one of the college's regular publications such as the *College Bulletin*. One could hope that the students kept their interest in environmental issues despite this limitation by the faculty, but there seems to be no written evidence of further public response.

After the initial experiment with an "intersession," a calendar subcommittee of the Long Range Planning Committee was formed in September 1971 for the purpose of studying the calendar in conjunction with the "strategies for change and knowledge utilization project." According to the report of the Calendar Study committee attached to the Faculty Meeting Agenda, the following concerns were to be addressed:

1. To develop a structure to evaluate curriculum period-ically and to provide for the building of new curri-culum.
2. To introduce more flexibility and voluntarism into the curriculum.
3. To increase inflexibility [sic] ["flexibility"] in the amount of time needed to complete the degree.
4. To use the campus facilities more efficiently.
5. To lengthen the school year and hence increase the faculty salaries.

The goals were wide-ranging, the plans ambitious. The plans included visiting several colleges, scheduling an all-college workshop, administering a questionnaire, holding an all-college forum, and eventually proposing a newly revised calendar. By March 19, 1972, the Calendar Committee reported on its findings, including responses to the questionnaire, which, among other things, offered several different calendar models. Overwhelmingly, the faculty favored a new model rather than the current fairly traditional two-semester calendar, though there was not unanimity of response on a desired calendar. As the academic dean, Dr. Daniel R. Chamberlain, recalls the process, "The initial proposal was that we would have a 1–3–1–3 calendar. In the fall there would be a September term, then October through December; . . . then a January . . . [and a spring term]; and then in the summer 1–1–1." The proposal was designed for significant flexibility, even allowing a faculty member not to teach in September, for example, thus creating more extended time for work on a research project. Additionally, the expectation was that a student might wish to extend a summer work schedule, and then catch up during the following year. In the March 21, 1972, Faculty Meeting, however, the faculty were less than enthusiastic about this fairly radical shift, and the motion was tabled for further study. One administrator thought the issue should have been brought to a vote, but Chamberlain, recalling the situation, says, "We could have passed it, but people would have chafed about it the whole time, and they would have soon destroyed its intentions and its purposes; and it would have been divisive. You can win battles and lose wars."

The committee brought a revised proposal for a 4–1–3 calendar (with the numbers referring to months) with a three-week January term and a twelve-week spring term for a total of a fifteen-week spring semester, a proposal which was accepted in December 1973. The January term was originally intended to be primarily for the offering of innovative, non-catalogued courses, including a number of off-campus cross-cultural courses to a variety of places including — in those early years — England, Greece, and Israel. There was also the hope that there would be faculty and student exchanges with other colleges that had adopted some variation of the January term. Colleges across the country, including Messiah, distributed their January term catalogs. A few students participated in the exchange programs, but almost no faculty became involved, though the idea had seemed attractive. The logistics of working out the details of faculty exchanges apparently seemed too complicated to many.

The attempt to offer mostly innovative, non-catalogued courses also had limited success because many students were concerned lest taking too many electives would jeopardize their timely meeting of graduation requirements. Thus, more and more, faculty reverted to teaching regularly catalogued courses. The Middle States Association already in November 1972 noted a potential concern: "The courses to be offered in the coming January [1973] are in the main a rather pedestrian, unimaginative group — too many of them in fact just being regular semester courses. If the college decides to stick with its

4–1–3 calendar, it will have to be much more creative if it is to realize the potential benefit of the January term."

Despite the limitations of the January term and the resulting shortened spring term, the basic format has been in place ever since its inception in 1972. Perhaps most successful have been the many off-campus courses, which have provided opportunities for students and faculty to study in many venues from Florida to Guadeloupe, from the Bahamas to Scotland, from Ghana to Hawaii—to name a few. Although most popular have been cross-cultural courses, which can meet one semester of a language requirement, many other disciplines have been involved, including anthropology and family studies, music and biblical studies, art and literature.

A more recent variation of the January term is that a faculty member can now choose to lead a cross-cultural course in May rather than during the winter, thus providing greater flexibility in scheduling and more pleasant weather for travelling in countries in the northern hemisphere. The short-term off-campus course is now so fully institutionalized that it's hard to imagine a return to the more traditional fifteen-week semesters, which would eliminate the possibility for January term off-campus courses.

At virtually the same time as the calendar review was underway, Messiah College was also considering some significant revisions of the general education requirements. Specifically, faculty, with the strong encouragement of Dean Chamberlain, were thinking of ways through which some of the academic disciplines could be brought together in one course or in a series of courses. As Chamberlain, recalling his argument, says, "I think the separation between the disciplines is done much more for the convenience of faculty and for pursuing specialization than it is for providing a good education to the students. . . . To see life steadily and to see it whole is much more what education ought to be at the undergraduate level." On the theoretical level, one may believe in and argue for the integration of several disciplines: for example, history, philosophy, religion, and literature. But deciding *how* these disciplines should be brought together when that means reducing or eliminating specific disciplinary courses becomes an interesting challenge for curriculum planning committees.

Committing to a wide-ranging discussion of general education philosophy and practices at the same time that the calendar study was in process brought some faculty objections. Minutes from the April 8, 1970 Faculty Forum note the following: "Concerns were expressed that too many new big innovations were to be introduced at once, particularly regarding the General Education program and the Intercession [sic], which might reduce the effectiveness of each. Each program should be meaningful, carefully planned and postulated on full faculty support and involvement or they will fall flat." Despite these hesitations by faculty, both the calendar study and the review of general education goals and practices went forward.

Earlier that academic year the faculty had already committed five full meetings to general education review, beginning with a consideration of goals and moving to an examination of specific course proposals for a sequence of team-taught interdisciplinary courses. The scope of disciplines to be included was ambitious, and involved practically all areas of college studies except mathematics, natural sciences, languages, and physical education.

Thus, in the planned sequence, writing, speech, art, music, history, the social sciences, literature, philosophy, and religion were all taught in these interdisciplinary courses. The courses included both large-group lecture sessions (with lectures given by professors from their own disciplinary background) and small-group discussions with a single instructor, who needed to lead discussion and conduct evaluation of material which may have been outside his or her area of expertise.

The challenge of developing such an ambitious course of study was formidable, but the faculty was relatively small, and Dr. Chamberlain, the academic dean, was strongly committed to the philosophy of an interdisciplinary approach. By the fall of 1972 a sequence of five courses was approved, with the first four being six-credit courses, and the fifth a three-credit course. The first-semester freshman course, Shapers of Man, introduced students "to the methodology of religion, philosophy, and certain social sciences" and stressed oral and written communication. The next three courses in subsequent semesters were "Ancient Ideas and Institutions," "Peoples and Cultures, 600–1800," and "Modern Issues and Values."

The final course in the sequence was "Christianity and Contemporary Problems," a course first taught at the Philadelphia campus.

Faculty teams devoted prodigious amounts of time and energy in meetings, planning for and developing these courses. In the early years, two weeks of teaching team meetings were devoted in the summer to the planning for each of the new courses, with many faculty serving on two teaching teams, thus committing a month to this background work. The discussions were far-ranging, the meetings often intense, and the results impressive in the scope of material covered. But the sheer amount of material included in these large-group lectures was often a challenge for students.

The philosophy undergirding these interdisciplinary courses, particularly the three historically based courses at the core of the programs, was strongly Reformed (Calvinist) in orientation. Interestingly, an eight-page document, "The Philosophy of Chapel at Messiah College," written in 1972, articulates this orientation well: "It is the responsibility of Messiah College, as a Christian liberal arts college, to undertake the challenge of unifying God-given and man-discerned truth. The insights of all the disciplines, be they those of the natural sciences, social sciences, literature, religion or some other field of study, are to be related into one whole. The work of fusion is never completed and comprehension is gained only in part. Yet, the goal is clear." This statement may well be indebted to Dr. Arthur Holmes, long-term professor of philosophy at Wheaton College, whose influential *Idea of a Christian College* was later used as a text in one of the courses. In any event, whatever the particular source for the Messiah statement on a "philosophy of chapel," the orientation probably reflected more Reformed understandings than it did earlier specifically Brethren in Christ ones. And this Reformed philosophy of the integration of faith and reason, though not often articulated as fully as does the chapel statement, in some ways undergirded the wide-ranging scope of the integrated studies program at Messiah College. The Anabaptist and Wesleyan emphases on reconciliation, community, and societal need were most prominent in the fifth course in the sequence, "Christianity and Contemporary Problems," which was strongly influenced by the six-credit course of that title earlier introduced on the Philadelphia campus by Dr. Ronald J. Sider.

Although there was support from both faculty and administration for this new and ambitious program, there was also the recognition that the sequence needed careful reflection and possible revision. In a February 8, 1972, memo to the faculty, Chamberlain called for a faculty meeting to discuss the freshman-sophomore program. Among other issues which he suggested as topics for discussion were the following:

1. Should the courses pursue fewer topics in greater depth? (For example, should a single pre-Columbian American Indian civilization be examined in some detail rather than examining three as we now do?)

2. Should we continue to include as many disciplines in the team-taught General Education courses as we now do?

3. Should teams remain at their present size or should there be smaller teams and multiple sections?

4. If our calendar in the future provides for intensive [January term] courses, should some of our General Education requirements be met by such intensive courses?

The scope of the new courses was challenging, to say the least. In addition to the more traditional "humanities" components, the sequence of courses included instruction and practice in speech, the visual arts, and music. Thus not only was "freshman composition"— as it was traditionally conceived—taught within these integrated studies courses, but selected courses in the sequence also included oral communications and the arts. Not surprisingly some faculty felt uneasy both in teaching and evaluating disciplines quite outside their areas of professional training and expertise. Few faculty, for example, had significant training in speech communication or the visual arts, and there were only a few historians in the program, despite the historical framework of three of the five major courses. Further, as Chamberlain suggested in his memo, the scope of the early courses was extremely ambitious, making it difficult to provide adequate time for the presentation and assimilation of content.

Within a few years, then, the oral communications courses, as well as art and music studios, were taught in individual courses outside the interdisciplinary sequences. The six-credit courses in the freshman-sophomore program were refined, and for the most part became restructured into four-credit courses largely taught in large lecture classes of several hundred students, and two-credit courses taught in much smaller, more traditional classes with individual instructors. For example, the 1978–80 academic catalog describes the second course in the sequence, Three Ancient Civilizations (which replaced the earlier Ancient Ideas and Institutions) as focusing on "the history and cultures of the Hebrews, Greeks, and Romans [with] special emphasis upon the Hebraic-Christian tradition." Running concurrently with this four-credit lecture class were a number of two-credit "Topics in Ancient Civilizations" courses, which were individually taught and focused on more specifically defined topics, such as ancient art or selected works of Greek and Roman literature. Similarly, the fourth semester in the sequence, Modern Issues and Christian Values (four credits), was taught concurrently with multiple sections of Topics in Modern Ethics (two credits), which addressed a wide scope of philosophical and ethical issues, including medical, environmental, and justice concerns, with these "topics" classes being taught by individual instructors.

Most students found this sequence of courses challenging and sometimes frustrating, though often they became more appreciative of the sweeping overview of world history and culture after graduation. The grading in most of these courses was fairly rigorous and demanding, and these high expectations didn't contribute to the popularity of the requirements.

Faculty also found that the courses required considerable commitment, particularly in the planning for each semester. Especially in the early years of this ambitious program, as we have noted, several weeks of team planning were required each year during the summer as courses were painstakingly evaluated and carefully revised. A considerable benefit of this effort was that faculty who in their graduate programs had focused on fairly specialized academic areas learned much from colleagues in other disciplines. A given course, for example, Modern Issues and Christian Values, might include on the teaching team an historian, a philosopher, a political scientist, an artist, a sociologist, and a literature professor. The interchange was often spirited and stimulating.

Initiated in 1970, this ambitious interdisciplinary program flourished for over 20 years, but eventually the early enthusiasm waned, faculty and administrative support declined, and the courses were mostly replaced by a variety of discipline-based individual courses. A few new courses (for example, Science, Technology, and the World) retained an interdisciplinary component, taught, usually, by a single faculty member, but the large, ambitious program was dismantled. The concept of interdisciplinary learning had been energetically supported by key administrators and many faculty, but a rapidly growing faculty body and changes in key administrators seemed to contribute to a loss of consensus. The sheer size of the program and the logistics involved in the planning may well have contributed to the need for change as well.

The process of moving from the wide-ranging, inclusive "integrated studies" program to (mostly) disciplinary general education courses wasn't done rapidly or capriciously, of course. A large faculty committee, chaired by Dr. David Parkyn, was charged with developing a multi-layered series of objectives, including College-Wide Educational Objectives (later called "CWEOs"), General Education Objectives, and Objectives for Majors. The major support for this broad background study was initiated by the academic dean, Dr. Harold Heie, who came to Messiah College in 1988 after the eleven-year tenure of Dean H. David Brandt, who had strongly championed the interdisciplinary approach to general education, both on theoretical and practical grounds.

Both Brandt and Heie were trained as scientists, though in differing fields, but each was strongly supportive of the liberal arts and the role of general education in the education of all students. Brandt argues that while more professional majors (for example, computer science, nursing, and engineering) were being added to the college, the liberal arts continued to be important: "One of the most gratifying things . . . [about the new majors was] that the traditional liberal arts . . . [still] thrived at Messiah College. . . . In a broader sense Messiah College is still a liberal arts institution at its very heart, and that's an attitudinal thing." Heie just as clearly supported the attitudes of liberal learning and promoted those at the college, but he was more interested in the larger philosophical framework, less in *how* the program was delivered, thus his strong emphasis in having the college spell out in careful detail the College-Wide Educational Objectives (which the Faculty Meeting passed on February 19, 1990). Then the faculty needed to determine *how* and with what set of courses the objectives would be met — an arduous task. As we have noted, the move, then, was away from the wide-ranging interdisciplinary courses to mostly disciplinary courses. Students were given far more choices in the revised program, but there was less coherence in the whole than in the more focused interdisciplinary structure of the previous program. But by the mid-1990s an era had (largely) passed.

As the current provost, Dr. Randall Basinger, says, "When we changed the old . . . [Integrated Studies program], that was a radical paradigm shift." Not only did the changes dramatically affect the general education course requirements for students, but the revised curriculum significantly increased the costs to the college. Reflecting on those changes, Basinger says, "It [the Integrated Studies program] was extremely efficient [and] from an administrative point of view, it was just a wonderful system. Then when we changed that [format], immediately we had to hire, and the student-faculty ratio went way down." In fact, over several years the ratio went from 19 to 1 in the late 1980s to about 13 to 1, with each percentage point reduction costing an additional $800,000, according to the provost. One additional major cost of the new structure was the need for many more classrooms to accommodate the smaller individual sections. In the large-group lecture format through which a substantial part of the Integrated Studies program had been offered, about 10 percent of a student's total required college credits, according to Basinger, had been offered in one large lecture hall (Miller Hall in the Climenhaga Fine Arts Center). Thus, with the more conventional discipline-based courses of 25 to 35 students, the college needed to add substantially more classrooms. But the college had long been accustomed to a growth mode, and the new challenges seemed manageable.

One of the benefits of increasing faculty size was that academic majors could be significantly strengthened, while at the same time the faculty was being renewed and energized by the addition of young faculty. So, for example, the college went from having only one philosopher to having three and eventually four. Similarly, in other disciplines such as history and English, more faculty were needed to teach multiple sections of general education courses. As Basinger says, "It [the new requirements] allowed us to grow programs. . . . The old system [of general education] allowed Messiah to grow professional programs, and we switched it, and then we grew the traditional [liberal arts] programs after that with the new gen ed." Clearly, there were gains in the humanities disciplines by having historians teach history, philosophers teach philosophy, and English professors teach literature. In short, both the content and the methodology of the disciplines could be more effectively taught by persons in the respective disciplines. Further, many faculty would also argue that the new format for teaching was more effective than large-group lectures for classes such as literature and philosophy, which thrive better in a more discussion-oriented setting. At the same time, however, the wide distribution of courses made it impossible to assume that all students, for example, had at least some knowledge of the background of the Protestant Reformation. Nor did the cross-fertilization of ideas across disciplines happen as readily for faculty as they had when they were germinated in the planning of team-taught interdisciplinary courses.

While these changes were taking place in the academic programs, other areas of the college were also affecting the direction and potential identity of the college. To three of those developments we turn next.

Chapter 6

Enlarging the Borders
Grantham and Beyond

Even at a time when the college had a student body of just over two hundred and was not yet accredited, there was discussion of reaching beyond the Brethren in Christ denomination and enlarging the borders. In a memo prepared for the Executive Committee of the Board of Trustees in March 1962, President Arthur Climenhaga argued that the college should consider developing a relationship with the larger community and expanding the mission of the college. The changes would include broadening the student base, enlarging the Board of Trustees, and probably changing the name of the college "to one of a more 'liberal arts' flavor" (Cumberland Valley College, Central Pennsylvania College, and Grantham College were all suggested). Climenhaga concluded his appeal with these words: "I believe we stand at the crossroads and that we must make a vital decision. I see the possibility of moving outwards from, but not away from our present base," language which the next president, D. Ray Hostetter, would use again later. At the time of Climenhaga's appeal, the Executive Committee was apparently hesitant about making major changes; nonetheless, significant changes did come a few years later, though becoming a regional college for the larger local community never caught on in the way Climenhaga imagined.

But the idea of enlarging the borders did fall on fertile soil. As we have seen, one outcome was the development in 1972 of the college covenant, which shifted ownership of Messiah College from the denomination to a self-perpetuating board. Other major developments in the next years included expanding and deepening relationships with other Christian colleges, significantly enlarging the scope of intercollegiate athletic programs, and forging a cooperative relationship with a school in East Africa, three areas which we will explore here.

About the same time as Messiah was establishing a new covenant, the college became a founding member of a consortium of ten Christian colleges, including Bethel (MN), Eastern Mennonite (VA), Gordon (MA), Greenville (IL), Malone (OH), Seattle Pacific (WA), Taylor (IN), Westmont (CA), and Wheaton (IL), none of which had more than 2000 students, and over half of which — including Messiah — had fewer than a thousand. Initial planning by the presidents took place in the spring of 1971, and by July 1, 1971, the new organization was incorporated. "Nationally," they wrote, "a united voice must speak out for the evangelical focus on higher education. A strong committed stance must be articulated, enhancing the opportunity for students to gain the wholistic approach . . . the emphasis on Christian values, the biblical perspective of human history, which is absent in secular universities."

Messiah College, as one of the founding institutions, was both significantly involved in and shaped by this developing cooperative educational venture. One early ambitious goal — a goal which was strongly championed by President Hostetter — was the development of "a university system of Christian colleges" as their promotional brochure described it. This idea never came to fruition, but there were significant interchanges of ideas through meetings of presidents, deans, admissions officers, and financial managers.

For faculty development, though, cooperative ventures were quite successful, particularly efforts "to encourage support for research by Christian scholars to integrate faith and learning." Over a number of summers, primarily during the 1970s, faculty at member colleges were given scholarships to participate in weeklong workshops and seminars, some of them designed for specific disciplines, others being more wide-ranging in scope. Although only three of the founding members were clearly in the Reformed (Calvinist) tradition, the language and methodology of "the integration of faith and learning" were heavily influenced by Reformed philosophy and theology; and the workshops were primarily staffed by faculty from that tradition. At Messiah the Anabaptist, Pietist, and Wesleyan streams of the heritage were not forgotten, but neither were the particulars of that heritage clearly incorporated in the developing focus on faith-learning integration. In retrospect it seems clear that because some of the largest, most influential colleges were in the Reformed tradition, they had a formative impact on the guiding philosophy of the Christian College Consortium.

The shaping impact of Reformed thought, with its emphasis on the unity of all truth, informed faculty discussion on many Christian college campuses. As Dr. Arthur Holmes, professor of philosophy at Wheaton College, argued cogently in his influential book, *The Idea of a Christian College*, "All truth is God's truth." This emphasis on the interrelationship of Christian faith and academic endeavors was incorporated into the promotion and tenure policies for faculty at Messiah. In addition to meeting expectations for superior teaching, satisfactory scholarly work, and effective service to the college, all faculty needed to prepare a coherent "faith-learning integration" paper as it related to their own discipline, with the purpose, for example, of demonstrating how one's Christian faith intersected with the reading and teaching of literature, if one were a professor of English. This paper was presented to the Faculty Status Committee, where it was discussed with the faculty candidate who was applying for promotion or tenure. Only if the paper was judged to be of sufficient merit would the candidate be further evaluated by considering the other criteria guiding promotion policies. In subsequent years the assumptions undergirding the paper have been somewhat adjusted and modified, but for a number of years the "integration of faith and learning" essay (which was largely shaped by Reformed assumptions) played a significant role.

Early plans for expansion of the Consortium by the founding presidents were quite ambitious: from the 1971 beginning with ten colleges and fewer than 12,000 students, they projected by 1975 to include 33 colleges with "50,000 students, faculty and staff." In fact, they added only three more schools to the original ten, because in 1976 the decision was made to create a second organization, the Christian College Coalition, rather than further expanding the Consortium.

The Christian College Coalition, while being more inclusive than the Consortium, described itself as "a cooperative organization of evangelical Christ-centered four year liberal arts colleges and universities," emphasizing biblically centered faith and a hiring practice which required personal Christian commitment from full-time faculty and administrators. Initially, the Coalition was founded with 38 members. Because of some confusion with the original name, the "coalition" has now become the Council for Christian Colleges and Universities (CCCU), which has grown to include 105 member institutions in North America.

The CCCU, with its headquarters in Washington, D.C., has been ideally situated to become a strong advocacy institution promoting and supporting the cause of Christian higher education. Currently representing over 100 colleges with more than 300,000 students and 19,000 faculty, the CCCU has vastly expanded its services from its modest beginnings in 1976. Among other programs, CCCU offers courses and internships in American Studies and journalism (both in Washington, D.C.) and film studies (in Los Angeles). Abroad there are eight "culture-crossing programs," including the Scholar's Semester in Oxford (England), Russia Studies Program (in Nizhni Novgorod), and Middle East Studies Program (in Cairo). Many Messiah College students have had their horizons broadened with study, for example, in the political center of our nation's capital, or in the tradition-rich setting of Oxford, or in vastly different cultures in Russia or Egypt.

In addition, the Coalition (as it was named then) was involved in promoting and funding the publication of a series of introductions to various disciplines. The series, with the general heading "Through the Eyes of Faith," was designed to offer a reasoned approach for students seeking to make connections between their academic studies and their Christian faith. Published by Harper & Row (later Harper Collins), the series included, among others, volumes in business, history, literature, psychology, and biology. Several Messiah College faculty members served on task forces which provided oversight to the various disciplinary studies. Clearly, the impact of the CCCU (and the Christian College Consortium) on Messiah College, while hard to quantify, has been significant, both in terms of enlarging potential study programs for students and in linking the college to intellectual and theological streams outside the tradition. The academic dean during this era, Dr. David Brandt, also notes that Messiah's membership in these organizations was very helpful in recruiting new faculty "because it gave us an identity that could be used nationally." No doubt President Climenhaga could scarcely have anticipated the extent of the changes which the college would experience in the years following his 1962 word on standing "at the crossroads." He envisioned then an enlarged role in "The Place of Messiah College in the West Shore Area of the Greater Harrisburg Community," as he called his paper. In some ways it was a bold vision, but the next decades, as we have observed, would see a movement to a wider arena beyond Grantham.

An additional significant association for the college was a long-term working relationship with Brethren Colleges Abroad, which, many years earlier than the CCCU, provided venues for Messiah students to study abroad in England, France, Germany, Greece, and Spain. Modern language majors at Messiah were — and are — required to study abroad for at least a semester, often for a year, thus vastly enhancing their understanding of the language, history, and culture of their chosen area.

In the cocurricular area as well the college was beginning to move in wider circles. As Dr. E. Morris Sider notes in his history of Messiah College, the founding denomination looked with disfavor on organized athletic competition. Apparently not until the early 1960s did Messiah participate in intercollegiate athletic competition, though as Dr. Douglas Miller, professor of sport and exercise science, notes, President Ray Hostetter "was an athlete . . . [he] played basketball at Messiah, but Ray as president did not talk much about athletics." By the late 1960s a number of sports — soccer, basketball, baseball, and wrestling — were active in intercollegiate competition. The men were, at least in the perception of some, given priority in several areas, including scheduling and funding, and only gradually did women's athletics gain parity, in part, one surmises, because of federally mandated guidelines.

The college became a member of both the National Christian College Athletic Association (NCCAA) and the National Association of Intercollegiate Athletics (NAIA), where Messiah continued until 1981. By that time a number of programs were becoming increasingly successful in intercollegiate competition, especially men's soccer under Dr. Layton Shoemaker, who was head coach from 1974 to 1996. Shoemaker came to Messiah as soccer coach and chair of the Health, Physical Education, and Recreation Department; and then in 1980 he was asked to become director of athletics as well. He reported to the academic dean, Dr. David Brandt, who was an avid supporter of athletics and who with Shoemaker urged changing affiliation to the National Collegiate Athletic Association (NCAA) as a Division III school. As Shoemaker argues, "That was a transitional point for Messiah. . . . In terms of projecting Messiah's growth at that point it made sense because we wanted to become more collegial with liberal arts colleges in our region." At about the same time Messiah also became a member of the Middle Atlantic Conference athletic association and thus moved into a different circle of competition.

In the early 1970s, the soccer program at Messiah had experienced considerable turnover among coaches, and Shoemaker was recruited to help bring stability and continuity. Although many athletic programs — field hockey, women's soccer, women's basketball, track and field, to name a few — have become highly successful and have brought national recognition to the college, men's soccer was probably the first to gain prominence. As Shoemaker says, "I am . . . the first to admit that by the grace of God that happened, and [it required] a lot of sweat, tears, and toil in the process." A significant component of the increasing sophistication and success of the soccer program was recruitment of top athletes. Shoemaker worked hard to be sure the school was a good "fit" for the student athlete and his family. He says, "I was probably one of the first coaches at Messiah who began to do home visits in the recruiting process." In the process the program gained great loyalty from parents. "Parents followed us everywhere," he says. "We took teams to Europe, and parents went with us to Europe. . . . Wherever we went, there were parents with us."

The type of family loyalty to school, program, and coach which Shoemaker cultivated became the norm for a number of other athletic programs as well. Perhaps for no program has that been more the case than for women's field hockey, where head coach Jan Trapp has served for over 35 years, the longest tenure of any coach at

Messiah. Having coached over 700 games with a remarkable record of participating in thirteen Final Four national tournaments, Trapp was honored by being the first Messiah College coach in any sport to be inducted into the national Hall of Fame for coaches.

In a later chapter we will describe in more detail a number of remarkably successful athletic programs at Messiah. Suffice it to note here that the outstanding records in men's and women's soccer, in field hockey, in women's basketball, and, most recently, in women's softball, to name a few sports, have brought national recognition to the college. As Doug Miller notes, "One of the changes . . . I've seen is how athletics is being used to market Messiah. . . . I think it's good to do what we're doing." But he adds, "We have to be careful that we keep it all on balance, and I think Messiah is working hard at that." This word from a teaching faculty member and coach (with fifteen very successful years in two different sports) links academics and athletics without allowing the latter to overwhelm the former. Always there is the temptation to allow success in one area to control the identity of the college in ways which may detract from, rather than contribute to, the long-term core mission of the institution. Affiliations — whether with the Council for Colleges and Universities or with the National Collegiate Athletic Association — do make a difference in the college's identity.

A third area of reaching out in the late 1970s and early 1980s was in some ways the most surprising. After all, association with similarly minded colleges is not unusual, and for a growing college to develop its athletic programs seems an almost routine expectation. On the other hand, for a small college with limited finances to establish a relationship with a small, struggling institution in a developing nation would seem extraordinary, if not foolhardy. But in 1979 the Messiah College Board of Trustees granted a four-month refresher leave for President D. Ray Hostetter, who proposed a trip with his wife Audrey "to see what alumni were doing around the world," as he said. In addition, they planned to see "whether there might be a third-world institution that . . . [Messiah College] could connect with . . . so we visited places in the Philippines, in India, [and] in various parts of Africa to see whether we might make a connection, and we eventually chose Daystar."

Located in Nairobi, Kenya, Daystar Communications, as it was known then, offered a two-year diploma program (which had no official recognition or accreditation) and a masters degree in communication through Wheaton College (in Illinois). According to Hostetter, "I told them that even though they had an institute [which offered short-term courses] and a graduate program that they really needed that centerpiece of an undergraduate baccalaureate degree program, and they agreed." Although the one-and-a-half acre campus was small, it was ideally situated in Nairobi, a city with good communication and transportation links to much of Africa and beyond. Another practical advantage was that, despite being located in a tropical zone near the equator, the climate was temperate because of the elevation of the city.

Besides seeing these advantages, Hostetter was impressed with the abilities of Daystar's executive director, Dr. Stephen Talitwala, a Ugandan, and with the strength of their African board, under the leadership of James Mageria, a Kenyan businessman. "I thought they were exceptional people," Hostetter says, "and that's why we connected with Daystar." The institution was small — only about a dozen students and several of them graduate students — but the Daystar administration and staff were deeply committed to educating African young people from various countries to serve as Christian leaders, many of them pastors. In 1982 Talitwala wrote, "It has been estimated that there are over 200 million Christians in Africa today out of a total population of 450 million. This is good news but at the same time a challenge. . . . The challenge is to the church to train effective communicators of the Gospel." After an appeal for prayer and support by African Christians, he adds, "The available training institutions are too few, poorly staffed and equipped, and . . . [heavily] subsidized from overseas." Thus the administration, including the academic dean, Dr. Josphat (Josh) Yego, and the Daystar Board were strongly in favor of developing a partnership with Messiah College in order to offer a baccalaureate degree. Not all the faculty at Daystar were in agreement, however, and the potential partnership created considerable dissension on campus because some feared that the baccalaureate program would deviate from the original purpose for Daystar as a school for the preparation of pastors and other leadership roles in the church. Nonetheless, the decision, finally, was to move forward to develop a four-year degree program.

At Messiah one might wonder about the commitment from a relatively small college — there were about 1400 (FTE) students in 1980 — to developing a partnership with a fledgling Institute almost half-way around the world in East Africa. Dr. David Brandt, the academic dean during those years, says, "I think Messiah College was far ahead of its time" in its globalization efforts. He recalls a conversation with Hostetter, when he returned from his time abroad, and the president said, "There has to be a better solution to how we help our mission effort to educate people in Africa than to bring a handful of them here at huge cost, and then . . . have most of them never return [to their home countries]." The Brethren in Christ Church, of course, had had a long history of mission work in Zambia and Zimbabwe, which had led to a number of African students coming to Messiah College. Thus it was perhaps not surprising that after discussion with the Board of Trustees, Brandt was sent in February 1981 to help Daystar administrators "establish a structure that looked like a college." So Brandt and his wife Melva spent three busy weeks discussing educational goals and policies and helping to set up some basic committees, including an Academic Policies Committee.

Important to the process was the approval of the Middle States Accrediting Association because obviously this would be a major extension of Messiah College's degree-granting privileges. Brandt recalls that after some initial contacts with the staff at Middle States Association, he and Hostetter travelled to Philadelphia to meet with the head of the association. After the college administrators explained the proposed relationship with Daystar, as Brandt recalls, the Middle States administrator said, "You're crazy, you know, but you're also right." After this discussion, the college was given permission to move forward, even without an on-site visit by Middle States administrators. The doors were continuing to open, but much needed to be accomplished before the relationship could be formalized.

Specifically, someone needed to go to Nairobi to serve for an extended period as the liaison between Messiah and Daystar, and actually help set up an academic program that would be acceptable

President D. Ray Hostetter and Mr. James Mageria, Daystar Board chair,
sign the formal agreement between Messiah and Daystar while Jay Barnes,
David Brandt, Ron Long, and Robert Hamilton look on.

to Messiah (and Middle States) and that would also be suitable for
the East African context. A particular challenge would be general
education requirements, which would be quite unusual in Kenya, a
country heavily influenced by the British academic system. At the
time Dr. Paul Nisly, who at Messiah was chair of a large and diverse
academic department, had applied for a sabbatical. Brandt seized the
opportunity and urged Nisly to take the challenge of helping to set up
this new baccalaureate degree program. In addition to the expected
challenges of moving a young family with three children and arrang-
ing school for them was the major question of the health of Nisly's
wife Laura, who was in the midst of a long regimen of chemotherapy
treatments for cancer. A courageous woman, she determined not to
let her health issues keep the family from travelling. So leaving
Grantham just after Christmas in 1981, the Nisly family was the first
of a number of Messiah faculty families to serve at Daystar. The

institution was on a trimester calendar at the time, and the Nislys served there for two school terms.

In contrast to Messiah College, which, while not large, was a comparatively stable institution, Daystar seemed to survive almost week by week. Among other problems, finances were never assured, and prayer took on a deeper meaning when one heard the fervent, faith-filled prayers of African colleagues on behalf of the struggling institution. Further, the process of developing the new curriculum took considerable patience because the best communication with the States was by telephone or FAX, and actually submitting lengthy documents was often difficult. In writing the proposals there was always the necessity of balancing the requirement of Messiah to have a program with clear linkage to their approved course of study and the needs of Daystar to develop programs which were suited to the African context. Eventually, though, a curriculum was prepared with requirements for general education, only one major, Communication (with several areas of concentration), and a few minors.

In addition to the overall curriculum, individual course descriptions needed to be written and forwarded for approval to Messiah. Finally by November 15, 1982, the curriculum from Daystar was brought to the Messiah Faculty Meeting by the Academic Policies Committee for approval of the general education program, the one major in Communication, and minors in Christian Ministries and Community Development. The recommendation noted that the "program is structured very much like a Messiah degree but is 'Africanized' to a large extent."

Because of the need to negotiate various legal requirements, the actual formal agreements between Messiah and Daystar were not signed by James Mageria, the Daystar Board chair, until February 28, 1983. Originally it was planned that the initial class of baccalaureate students would be admitted in the fall of 1983, but actually the first fifteen B.A. students were admitted in early 1984. Later that same year the institution's name was changed to Daystar University College as the new program was launched. Several years later, in June 1987, with both Dean Brandt and President Hostetter in attendance, Daystar celebrated with great joy the graduation of fourteen young men and

Entrance to the current Nairobi campus of Daystar University.

women with Messiah College degrees, given in Kenya, but with a
Grantham, Pennsylvania address on the diploma!

For her part Messiah College agreed to oversee the academic
program, including the approval of new courses and majors, and to
maintain the permanent file of student academic records. In addition
to these supportive administrative functions, Messiah also committed
to providing a faculty member each year, sometimes for a semester,
often for a year. During the years from 1982 to 1999 sixteen faculty
members — often with their families — served at Daystar. The
impact on their lives is, of course, incalculable, but teaching in an
international setting in an urban environment with students from
many African countries in one's classroom was both a challenge and
a gift. Daystar students tended to be older than their American
counterparts, and they usually saw higher education as a great opportunity which one dared not squander.

Faculty returned to the home campus at Grantham encouraged
and enriched, not least by the deep spirituality of many African
Christians. The name of the college, Daystar, is taken from the biblical
passage in II Peter 1:19, "You will do well to pay attention to the
message of the prophets as to a light shining in a dark place, until the
day dawns and the daystar arises in your hearts." Returning faculty

Messiah faculty member Martha Long with Danisa Ndlovu,
a student at Daystar in 1987, who now is Bishop of the
Brethren in Christ Church in Zimbabwe and current
President of Mennonite World Conference.

often brought back a deepened awareness of African spirituality, heightened appreciation for international education, and enthusiasm for Daystar specifically. Some people jokingly referred to those who had served in Africa as having the "African mystique," at times, perhaps, with a bit of envy because of the enlarged experiences of those fortunate enough to have served at Daystar. A returning faculty member reported, for example, that in a class of twelve, the students came from Ethiopia, Uganda, Rwanda, Malawi, Tanzania, Zimbabwe, and, of course, Kenya — a wonderful diversity of voices and views in one small class. Another faculty member, Professor Martha Long, reflecting on her experience, wrote, "Teaching students at Daystar who are eager to learn and are self-motivated was a joyful experience. What better place is there for non-Kenyan Africans to deal with culture shock as they encounter traditions and mores differing from their own backgrounds."

Messiah College students, too, were involved in an exchange program, and up to six students could go to Daystar in a given semester. At the same time, an agreement had been reached with the other twelve colleges in the Christian College Consortium, who also

Daystar chapel construction at the Nairobi campus in 1982.
Roof beams were set by hand.

After enormous human effort and much physical labor, a completed chapel.

Outside prayer service on the Nairobi campus.

could send students from their institutions. Almost without exception Messiah students returned with deep appreciation for their educational experience, even while being "deprived" of some of the creature comforts assumed essential by their colleagues at home.

Daystar grew rapidly, and in 1994, ten years after the first B.A. students were admitted, the Kenyan government granted a charter to the institution, which now officially became Daystar University. That encouraging development probably contributed, however, to less involvement by Messiah College because only a few Messiah faculty went to Daystar after that time. No doubt the initial enthusiasm had somewhat waned as well, and some more recently appointed academic administrators probably didn't fully share the vision of those who had initiated the relationship.

The growth of the Daystar program meant that the tiny one-and-a-half acre campus in Nairobi became impossibly crowded. After some considerable searching, the Daystar principal, Dr. Stephen Talitwala, located 300 acres of undeveloped pasture as a possible site for major expansion. Funds were always a challenge, as might be expected, so Talitwala knew that he would need help from the States.

President Hostetter joins in planting trees on the Athi River campus.

Campus buildings on the Athi River campus.

President D. Ray Hostetter presenting a diploma to a Daystar graduate.

He contacted some of those who had served at Daystar to be involved in a fund-raising effort at Messiah. He asked Paul Nisly, who had been the first Messiah faculty member at Daystar, to head the effort. A steering committee was set up, and each administrator, faculty, and staff person was personally invited to donate or pledge money toward the $60,000 goal, an ambitious effort in 1989, especially because the college was in the midst of her own campaign for capital funds. Through many generous gifts the Daystar Partners campaign, as it was called, actually raised almost $80,000 by June 1994, with an additional $57, 000 from trustees and other off-campus donors.

The stories from Daystar concerning the giving from Messiah College personnel were most encouraging. Talitwala describes one difficult time when a bank payment of approximately $20,000 (U.S.) was due on a Monday. Not having the money in hand, nor having knowledge of what might be coming, but trusting God to provide, Talitwala asked for an extension and promised to bring payment on Friday. On that Friday in August 1991, he received a Daystar Partners check from Messiah College for $21, 883.91! The check had been sent earlier without any knowledge of the urgent need. The evident faith in God of the leadership at Daystar was an encouragement and challenge for the "partners" at Messiah. Clearly, the vision for service was given a major focus through the relationship with Daystar in a major city eight time zones away from the tiny village of Grantham.

In short, the 1970s and 1980s involved not only enormous growth at the main campus, but it was a time of establishing new associations and affiliations, both academic and athletic, and developing a global vision. The college would continue to grow in the 1990s, but the rate of growth (with a few exceptions) was much slower.

Chapter 7

A Presidential Legacy
Successes and Struggles

Thomas Carlyle, an essayist and biographer in nineteenth-century England, wrote, "Universal History . . . is at the bottom the History of the Great Men who have worked here." Carlyle seems to be arguing that history is fundamentally biography. His statement no doubt is a sweeping over-generalization—and obviously reflects different assumptions about men and women in leadership—yet certain leaders can and do leave a large imprint on the character and direction of an institution. In the case of Messiah College, three men from successive generations, fathers and sons in one family, served the college as president. C. N. Hostetter, the second president of the young institution, held the office from 1917–1922; his son, C. N. Hostetter, Jr., had a twenty-six year tenure as president (1934–1960), in addition to filling an amazing number of leadership roles in the church and in church-related agencies. "C. N.," as he was affectionately known, was preeminently a churchman and cultivated the college's relationship with the Brethren in Christ denomination. Among leadership roles outside the denomination, he served for ten years as president of the World Relief Commission of the National Association of Evangelicals (1957–1967) and for over fourteen years as chairman of the Mennonite Central Committee (a relief and service agency) from 1953–1967.

To discuss or evaluate his presidency would go beyond the scope and purposes of this essay. Suffice it to say that "C. N." was intimately involved in the life and decisions which affected this small but developing college. He was recognized for his strong leadership on and off campus. A long-time faculty member and colleague, Professor Earl Miller, who was the director of the music program and

Sons D. Ray, S. Lane, and C. Nelson join with their father and mother,
Christian N. Hostetter, Jr., and Anna (Lane) Hostetter at
their fiftieth wedding anniversary.

himself a considerable force on campus and in the community and church, said, "I didn't always agree with 'C. N.', but when I walked into his office, I knew I was in the presence of greatness."

While not involved in such a broad array of church-related agencies, Hostetter's son Ray, who became the sixth president, had an even longer tenure with 30 years in office. Those years from 1964–1994 were, as we have seen, an era of significant change and enormous growth at Messiah College. Remarkably, this one family led the college for 63 of the institution's first 85 years. Ray, grandson of the second president and the person who would have the longest tenure of any Messiah president, grew up with intimate first-hand knowledge of the college. In his words, "I moved here [to the campus] with my parents and family in 1934. So I was six years of age when I came to the campus and lived on the campus throughout my childhood and teen years, and then [I] went to the academy and to the junior college, and then returned [after a few years] to teach."

From 1952–55 Hostetter taught history and physical education while his father was president. In fact, Hostetter's life is more intimately intertwined with the life of the college than even these facts may suggest. "I knew all the presidents [of Messiah] but one [the first president, S. R. Smith]," he says. Further, he adds that in the early days of his father's presidency, Ray and his brother Lane lived with their grandparents — thus hearing more stories about the early days of the college — while their father was taking graduate school courses in Indiana.

After his early teaching stint at Messiah, Hostetter left the college in 1955 and "went into private business in New Jersey . . . into the ice cream business, and [I] was there for several years." Meantime his father had resigned the presidency, and Dr. Arthur Climenhaga had been called to serve. Climenhaga's predecessor, C. N. Hostetter, Jr., had himself essentially been the development officer of the college, perhaps because he was an ordained minister and strong leader in the denomination and seemed ideally suited to cultivate contacts with the churches. But Climenhaga, who had less inclination for finances, called on Hostetter's son, who meantime had become a successful businessman, to return to the college for a new office as director of development, a role which subsequently became the vice-president for finance and development. Then after only four years as president, Climenhaga, as we noted earlier, resigned his office, and this third Hostetter, a young man in his mid-thirties, was called as president. Recalling those changes, Rev. Merle Brubaker, a long-term Brethren in Christ pastor and later an instructor of philosophy, says, "In my view, . . . [Ray Hostetter's] leadership was the most important factor in Messiah's growth. And his leadership ability was the result of many factors: the personality he inherited, the information he absorbed growing up in the president's house on campus, the special training he received in his doctoral program [in higher education administration at Columbia University], . . . and the roles he performed at Messiah prior to his becoming president."

In earlier chapters we have observed some of the many changes which occurred during the years from 1964–1994: the more than eight-fold increase in the student body; the thirteen major buildings added; the development of an urban campus in cooperation with Temple University; the linkage with an African institution to develop a baccalaureate degree program through Messiah; the vast increases of on-campus academic courses and majors; the greatly enlarged

President D. Ray and Mrs. Audrey Hostetter (1964–1994).

services in the co-curricular areas. Of course, no one person — or even a family — can singlehandedly develop an institution. Many people at all levels were essential to the growth of Messiah College. But leaders can help focus a vision and establish a climate for significant development to happen.

Most — if not all — of these developments required both astute planning and significant additional financing, and here the young president, who had been both a successful businessman and then, at Messiah, the person charged with expanding the financial base of the college, made outstanding progress. Reflecting on President Hostetter's contributions in the college's growth, Barry Goodling, current vice-president for development, says, "Ray Hostetter . . . was very much the entrepreneur. . . . He thought in business terms and was always looking [for new opportunities] as he was growing the college; and he knew we needed to grow to survive and be successful. He would be looking at programs he thought were coming down the road . . . computer science would have been one of those where he [was] . . . ahead of the curve. [He also] saw a demand for nurses at one point so started a nursing program."

Commenting on Hostetter's astuteness as a financial manager, Galen Oakes, who served a lengthy tenure on the Messiah College Board of Trustees (from 1965 to 2007 with over seven years as Board chair), says, "Dr. Hostetter brought a lot of business people on the Board." Further, he says that the president built "bridges with some of the local people that had the means to be contributors to the college, and he was successful in getting a number of major gifts for buildings. The Kline Science Hall was one of the early ones, and that was significant . . . he was starting to make inroads into the financial community of the Harrisburg area."

Perhaps no single event was more important to the developing of a strong financial base for the college's endowment than a trust established by the funding from the estate of Leonard S. Fry. Mr. Fry had large shareholdings in several coal companies, and he became interested in the mission of Messiah College and another Christian college. His connection to Messiah was apparently through a trustee of the college, Richard E. Jordan. Jordan was himself a very successful businessman, and according to Galen Oakes, Jordan was selling heavy equipment to Leonard Fry. In Oakes' words, "They [Jordan and Fry] were business friends, and . . . [Fry] was doing some planning for his estate . . . and Dick Jordan suggested that he [Fry] might want to remember a little college . . . [which he served as trustee] by the name of Messiah College, and a few years later, Messiah College received a 12 million dollar gift, and that was big in the life of the college . . ."

This summary, of course, simply gives one a quick snapshot of this stunningly large gift to a small college, which had only recently received accreditation. In reality, the actual acquisition of the fund took several years of careful cultivation, many meetings, and probably scores of letters and personal contacts.

Leonard Fry had died in January 1974, and his will instructed that part of his estate be used to fund a trust, with Messiah and another college named as the beneficiaries. A letter to President Hostetter (in September 1974) from an officer in PBS Coal, Inc. suggests something of Hostetter's efforts to establish a credible connection with those involved in the management of the coal company. The officer writes, "Your thoughtfulness in sending the

[Messiah College] Bulletin and the [essay] reprint to me is appreciated for I enjoyed not only the reading of the material but the message it conveys. I feel too many educational facilities are concerned with numbers and they also lose sight of the real values in life. This naturally reminds us of the reason Leonard [Fry] chose Messiah to be a beneficiary of his estate and, at this point, all of us that have worked with you are impressed even though it has been a short time." The overwhelming evidence from the correspondence suggests that Hostetter, with the strong support of Richard Jordan, was able to build on this early good will. Letter after letter indicates the satisfaction of the PBS Coal Company Board and the company's officers with their relationship with Messiah. The other college that had been named in the will apparently took a much more adversarial stance, and over time the PBS Board's relationship to them became quite contentious.

The prodigious efforts by Hostetter and others led, as we have seen, to a successful conclusion, and on July 1, 1977, the president reported to the Board of Trustees that the "court has approved the petition for Reformation of the Trust, and therefore, it appears that the sale of Messiah College's interest in the coal companies of Leonard S. Fry is approved." The total of $12,273,242.50 was to be paid over four years, with the fourth payment to be over 8.6 million dollars. In a letter dated August 15, 1977, the attorney representing the college wrote in his letter to Hostetter, "I attended the settlement of the Fry coal company stock on Monday, August 8, 1977. Settlement with regard to the Messiah Trust went off without a hitch in an hour and a half. Settlement for . . . [the other college's] stock took $9\frac{1}{2}$ hours." The money was held in a trust fund for eighteen years by Waynesboro Bank Trust Department, with earnings available to the college.

One might imagine that the college would spend considerable amounts of these earnings, but, in fact, as Glen Raser, who was the financial controller from 1979–2006, explains, the president and Board took a very conservative approach. He says, "The approach taken by the trustees [was] to spend very, very minimal amounts of that for several years. The expenditures out of the earnings . . . [in the early years] was limited to . . . $110,000. . . . That's a tiny, tiny bit of earnings on 12 million. So the rest was just plowed back in. So not only do we have the Trust which was growing over the years by market appreciation, but we have the significant earnings … which were not being expended. . . . So of our 127 million [in endowment in 2007] … you can trace about 85 [million] of that to the Fry [Trust]."

In short, the combination of a major gift, prudent investments, and very conservative use of the earnings all contributed to enviable growth of the endowment funds, which provided financial stability for the rapidly growing institution. Again, as one would expect, no one person was responsible for the success. In addition to President Hostetter, Dr. Robert Hamilton, as director of business and finance (later vice-president for business and finance), had a significant role in the expanding financial base. Hamilton notes that having a much larger endowment made it possible to get more favorable terms for borrowing money for the many building projects, which were seemingly always in process during those years. As he says, "It is pretty important in college finances to be able to have unrestricted funds to back up your borrowing. So to have that kind of [endowment] money available to us gave us some leverage in borrowing." This favorable financial rating was significant, because during Hamilton's fourteen years at Messiah (1972–86), he was involved with a major addition to the library; significant renovations of Old

Before this library was built in 1958, the library was housed in Old Main.

Note the massive wooden beams in this major addition to the library.

The completed Murray Learning Resources Center (1977).

Main; the building of five residence halls, the Climenhaga Fine Arts Center, and the Sollenberger Sports Center; and a number of other renovations and additions.

Although the Fry Trust money was not fully available, the impact on the college was enormous, and may, in fact, be considered another "watershed" in the history of the college. The academic dean during those years, Dr. David Brandt, says, "The wonderful Fry Coal Mine gift . . . was profoundly changing for this institution . . . not only because of its size, but because of the timing and because of the spin-off effect. . . . I remember how worried . . . [the president] was early on that the gift would decrease future [additional] gifts, but in fact the opposite happened . . . it was stimulating instead." As it happened, during those years interest rates were extremely high. The controller, Glen Raser, reports that certificates of deposit "were paying 15 percent up to as high as 20 percent."

The student body was increasing yearly, many faculty were being hired, the endowment was growing rapidly, buildings were being added almost annually: the late 1970s and early 1980s were heady days at Messiah College. Some have even referred to those years as the "Golden Age" because of the pervasive spirit of hopefulness. Little Messiah College was coming of age. One concrete embodying of the growing maturation of the college, as well of the esprit de corps of faculty, staff, and student body, was the "Book Walk Day" held on March 2, 1977 (and organized by librarian Mike Brown) to carry tens of thousands of books from the cramped rather ordinary library to their magnificent new home under a splendid vaulted ceiling with enormous wooden beams. Even the pretentious, trendy name (Learning Resources Center) didn't detract from the excitement and camaraderie of the day, which was complete with pep band and fanfare. A local newspaper reported, "Television crews and other media reporters added to the excitement of the festive occasion which included continuous refreshments, pep music, and prizes. The average trip took about six minutes and there were almost 10,000 trips." Another cause for rejoicing was that the three million dollar goal for the library building campaign was reached three months ahead of the deadline set by the Kresge Foundation in order to qualify for their $100,000 challenge grant.

"Book Walk Day," moving books into the new library.

On this celebratory day in March 1977 the academic life of the college was receiving major focus. Although the campaign for the library had been named "Beyond Books," this day made clear to all that books and printed journals were still key in the academic center of the institution. And, at the same time, Hostetter and other college administrators were working carefully, quietly, and effectively behind the scenes with the Fry Coal Company officials to receive the largest bequest (or series of bequests) ever made to the college. In retrospect, 1977 was a special year — and these several years might well be characterized as "golden."

But not all efforts at expansion would come to such satisfying conclusions. In the early 1980s President Hostetter became convinced of the importance of Messiah College's establishing a full-scale retirement community on part of its 300-acre, scenic campus. Although there may have been discussion of the idea earlier, the concept was initially presented to the Executive Committee of the Trustees on February 7, 1983, where it received a favorable hearing. Then in the May meeting the full Board of Trustees affirmed the approval of a new corporation which was being formed under the name "Grantham Woods." The proposed legal relationship between Messiah College and Grantham Woods included the following clarification: "It has been determined that a separate non-profit corporation should be formed to maintain separate balance sheets and liabilities. The purposes declared in the articles of incorporation would provide for the permissible transfer of funds from Grantham Woods to Messiah College as deemed appropriate." As it would turn out, the flow of finances would be altogether in the opposite direction, but the administration's hopes and dreams were that the retirement community would not only be self-supporting but revenue-enhancing for the college. In fact, in the June 1984 *Bridge* an official announcement of the new Grantham Woods initiative described the plan: "The good news is that a funding campaign will not be required since the [retirement] center will be self-financing now and in the future. While it will be necessary to have start-up capital, such advances will be repaid relatively quickly."

The newly named Board of Grantham Woods moved expeditiously, meeting seven times in the next six months, and as they reported to the October 18, 1984, meeting of the Board of Trustees, they had hired a director (Dr. James O. Banks), selected a build-design team, and developed marketing plans. They were also preparing to request land to be transferred from Messiah College. The plans were ambitious: 300 residential units in four phases, with 70 units and a central facility to be built in the first phase. The Board of Trustees in that fall meeting authorized a loan for the "capital required for the project, not to exceed . . . $1,500,000."

The president argued that having this residential community close to the college would provide benefits to both communities. For the college, the retirement facility would offer opportunities in areas such as nursing, recreation, and the behavioral sciences. For the retirement community, there would be available an array of educational, recreational, and cultural opportunities. In addition, the college might expect to cultivate friendships with persons who could potentially be encouraged to contribute significant funds to the college.

By May 1985 twenty-six people had signed contracts with Grantham Woods, assuming that the project would go forward. But there were significant hurdles to be overcome: a few local neighbors were passionately opposed to the project; the land would need to be re-zoned from agricultural to institutional; and to comply with regulations, Grantham Woods was obligated to acquire a Certificate of Need, a Certificate of Authority, and building permits. But first they needed zoning approval—a process which became entangled in hearing after hearing. The October 17, 1985, Executive Minutes report the effect of these delays: "Twenty-four apartments are currently committed for. We have lost six residents during the delay period. . . . We are likely to lose more future residents if we do not soon gain zoning approval." A year later (October 16, 1986) Executive Committee Board member and chair of the Grantham Woods Board, William Woods, "regretfully reports that zoning legal wranglings continue." Grantham Woods expenditures then totaled $950,000.

The college administration continued to press forward. (By this time Dr. Kenneth Martin was the vice-president for administration and finance; part of his role was to work on zoning issues.) In his fall 1987 presentation to the Board, Hostetter acknowledged the difficulties which the retirement village project had confronted, but he still believed the venture to have good potential: "While I am confident that the project will be sound business-wise, it should not be described as an unrelated business activity since, from the start, educational motivations have been part of the aspirations in its development." Some on the board were apparently voicing reservations by this time, however, because in the previous spring meeting of the Trustees College Advancement Committee (May 14, 1987) there is concern that there may be problems with a new capital campaign. Among other reasons, "Board of Trustee enthusiasm may be diminished as a result of Grantham Woods difficulties . . ." But in the fall meeting the reservations seem to have been sufficiently met so that the Board gave authorization to increase the line of credit to Grantham Woods from $1.5 million to $1.75 million.

In the spring 1988 meeting, five years after the initiation of the project, the Board of Trustees requested a thorough review of Grantham Woods, including the past experience and the possibility for future success. The review, dated October 14, 1988, provided a candid assessment of the problems and delays, noting, among other factors, that "throughout the initial planning stages, there was little awareness of the negative feelings that the township residents closest [in proximity] to the college held toward Messiah." In addition to the external opposition, there was limited enthusiasm among faculty, many fearing that needed funding for academic programs more central to the college were being encumbered by the funding needs of Grantham Woods. The report to the Board offered four options: (1) "continue the project as it is"; (2) "drop the project and swallow our losses"; (3) "move the project to another contiguous site"; (4) move the project to an off-campus site. Those writing the report urged the acceptance of the first option, and the Board despite some questions affirmed continuing "as it is," while realizing the protracted legal struggles.

To be brief, the "legal wranglings" did continue over the next several years, and more money continued to be spent in the hope of moving the project forward. The May 7, 1992, meeting of the Executive Committee of the Trustee Board approved the motion to "increase the authorization for Grantham Woods from $2,250,000 to $2,500,000." Although some approvals were granted, there seemed to be no clear end in sight.

The retirement of President Hostetter in 1994, and the beginning of a new administration, left the project in limbo. In a lengthy memo to the Board, dated August 9, 1994, the new president, Rodney J. Sawatsky, noted that the Grantham Woods project was "an issue which I have inherited." He raised questions and asked for counsel from the Board, but he acknowledged that "the market and financial studies would need to be very convincing with the feasibility of this project for one to be comfortable about proceeding." In the October 13, 1994, meeting of the Executive Committee, members approved a motion "to put the project on hold indefinitely and to review the project periodically." With that action the eleven-year-long process came to a conclusion, albeit not the one which the earlier administration had hoped for.

In retrospect one can say that the process consumed much administrative time and energy, as well as significant college finances, and some loss of local community goodwill. Should the process have ended earlier — at the time of the 1988 comprehensive report, for example? Probably. But vision is never perfect—even in the most astute managers. And the hope for long-term goodwill was very high as the 1988 review argued: "When operational, Grantham Woods will be home to a host of friends, both old and new, who, because of their close proximity to the college, will come to appreciate Messiah in a deeper way than is now possible." That dream was a worthy one.

As the story of Grantham Woods was being played out during the 1980s, many other developments were continuing to shape the institution. Among the many new and revised academic programs, two—nursing and engineering—deserve particular mention because of their potential cost and impact on the college. Although the college had never been a purist liberal arts institution, these two majors would add a strong professional component to the curriculum.

For a number of years the college had offered a Bachelor of Science in Nursing degree, but it was described in the college catalog as a "degree program specifically to upgrade academic preparation for the practice of nursing. It is not be confused with programs designed to prepare teachers and administrators for schools of nursing . . . [nor] as a foundation for graduate work."

In the late 1970s, however, a decision was made to develop a full-blown baccalaureate nursing program. Dean David Brandt recalls that in the first year of his tenure at Messiah (1977–78), President Hostetter asked Brandt to come to his office and told him, "'I really want a nursing program at Messiah. . . .' [But] he didn't give me a lot of detail, and what I quickly discovered [was] that the state of Pennsylvania . . . had a moratorium on new nursing programs." So with his characteristic determination Brandt entered, as he describes it, "a new culture that I had never entered before, the . . . world of nurse education, and it was fascinating." Thus, although the Pennsylvania Board of Nurse Examiners had placed a moratorium on new nursing programs, Brandt worked in concert with other institutions; and by 1980 the moratorium had been lifted, the college had hired a nursing chairperson, Dr. V. Elaine Gallaspy, and the nursing curriculum was approved. By the fall of 1981 the first pre-nursing students were admitted, with the first class graduating in May 1985. During that fall the Pennsylvania State Board of Nurse Examiners completed their site visit to the college and recommended full approval of the newly developed program. Later the National League of Nurses also recommended approval; the young program was off to a solid beginning of what was to become a significant major at the college.

The administration had not forgotten Messiah's earlier focus on education in the urban setting, and during the following summer (1986), Dr. Dorothy Gish, then an assistant dean, together with Dr. Donna Dentler, director of career development and cooperative education, helped plan and initiate an educational program for urban youth in Philadelphia. In brief, the intensive four-week residential program, which was housed at the Messiah College Philadelphia campus during the month of August, was designed to "help minority students gain admission to the college of their choice and to maximize their chance of succeeding there." A master of the acronym, Gish called the program STEPS, Skills and Techniques for Experiencing Personal Success. In her report to the Academic and Faculty Affairs Committee of the Board in October 1986, she reported, "Fifteen minority students . . . began and completed" the program under the direction of Messiah faculty member Steve Hayes, working with four other "highly qualified black faculty members." As Donald Wingert, long-term director of the Philadelphia campus, recalls, the program was primarily altruistic in purpose. In essence, according to Wingert, Messiah said, "Let's provide this service, and hopefully we might get a few students with it."

Besides the four-week summer school, the college also sponsored a school-year tutoring program for the high school students, pairing each one with a Messiah College (Philadelphia campus) student. Although not a major goal, the implicit hope was that this intensive program — in addition to providing good educational benefits — might lead to recruiting more students from diverse backgrounds. Under a new administration, however, these programs were reviewed and ended. With some sadness Gish says, "I think for me . . . as a dean . . . probably my biggest disappointment was that I had to close the STEPS program [after about ten years]. . . . I really feel that was a loss for the college." Although the program may not have had the positive results that one might have desired for recruitment, it would seem that the financial commitment was justified as part of the educational mission of the college, particularly when one considers the early goals of the Philadelphia campus.

The same fall (1986) that the Academic and Faculty Affairs Committee of the Trustees received the report on the initial STEPS courses they also considered the possibility of adding an engineering major which could be completed on the Grantham campus. At the time, an engineering technology degree was available through a cooperative arrangement with Temple University. Students in the major would study at the Grantham campus for their first two years and then complete the major in Philadelphia during their junior and senior years. But in a pattern that became common to the college, there was strong interest in "bringing the major home" to the Grantham campus.

After completing an "engineering feasibility" study, the administration recommended that "Messiah College plan for an Engineering Department offering a Bachelor of Science in Engineering (B.S.E.) degree with concentrations in electrical and mechanical engineering." The Academic and Faculty Affairs Committee of the Board noted the following concerns:

1. That the addition of engineering will hasten the need to expand facilities in service areas, e.g. library, dining, etc.;
2. That engineering will increase the pressure to increase all salaries;
3. That engineering is a high-cost program in capital expenses;
4. That engineering not be pushed until everyone is ready for it.

Nonetheless, the committee recommended to the full Board the continuation of campus-wide discussions on implementing the new major and supported the hiring of an engineering chairperson for "fall of 1987 pending faculty approval." The Executive Committee (in the same fall 1986 meeting) recognized the need for a major capital campaign, with the campaign being launched in the spring of 1988, fund-raising to be completed in 1989, and the new building ready for use in the following year.

The faculty had vigorous debate concerning the addition of the engineering major at the Grantham campus. Questions were raised about the potentially significant expenses of purchasing and maintaining the necessary equipment and about the impact of the major on the liberal arts character of the college. But in the spring of 1988 faculty voted in favor of developing the four-year engineering major, and by that fall Dr. James T. Scroggin had been hired as chair of the newly created department.

During that same year a campaign, "Shaping the Future," was initiated to fund the new building, purchase necessary equipment, and provide endowment for some of the on-going expenses. In 1988 the goal of $16,400,000 — about twice as large as the previous campaign — seemed ambitious, but the college raised $15,137,000, not quite reaching the goal, yet strongly supporting the building project. Thus in 1991 the new Frey Hall, which housed engineering, business, mathematics, and an expansion of the visual art program, was dedicated. This major campaign would be the final large campaign of President Hostetter's lengthy tenure.

In his 1987 paper, "A Common Agenda for the Future," which Hostetter presented to the Board, he wrote, "As Christians we are faced with the need to deal intelligently, responsibly, and in a Christ-like manner with this age. We must prepare our students to assess the moral and social implications of our technology. . . . Engineering is one curriculum which will allow Messiah to have part in preparing men and women for the challenges of the future." He argued further from a pragmatic basis: "The Christian market for engineering education is good — little is being offered in the way of engineering at Christian colleges, and for good reason — most Christian colleges would not be able to accommodate [financially] such a program." His confidence was well founded, and we will return to later developments in a subsequent chapter.

Such assessments reveal Hostetter's astute reading of potential growth areas. But during his tenure he faced challenges, particularly during a difficult late period in his presidency. But, first, some context may be helpful. During his thirty years as president, six deans successively served as the chief academic officer at Messiah. The first, Dr. Carlton O. Wittlinger (1961–68), was already the academic dean when Hostetter was named president. Although he continued to serve as dean for four more years, Wittlinger yearned to return to his first love, the teaching of history. As we have noted earlier, Dr. Daniel R. Chamberlain (1968-76) was recruited from his administrative post in the New York State University system, where he had served as an assistant to Dr. Ernest L. Boyer, who at that time was himself a dean (later the chancellor). A talented, forward-looking administrator himself, Chamberlain — much to the sadness of many at Messiah — after a few years was called to be president of Houghton College (NY), where he served for many years until his retirement. Chamberlain had led several significant initiatives, including the Temple University–Messiah College relationship and a complete revision of the general education program.

His resignation was a significant loss to the developing institution, but Dr. D. Wayne Cassel, who had already served as an assistant dean and who had been named registrar, agreed to serve as interim academic dean for a year (1976–77) to provide continuity. His leadership in developing the computer services of the college was of inestimable help. During the year a search committee was formed, and Dr. H. David Brandt, who was teaching at Gordon College (MA), was recruited as academic dean (later also named vice-president for academic affairs). In addition to his leadership in curricular development, Brandt was convinced that faculty salaries needed to be more competitive. As he says, "We managed significantly to increase remuneration, and that was . . . incredibly important in establishing Messiah as a legitimate player on the Christian college scene." And because of the rapid growth of the college during the years of his deanship (1977–88), Brandt was involved in the hiring of almost 75 percent of the faculty by the time of his resignation to become the first provost at Bethel College (MN). Brandt was an effective and strong leader — though some had differences with him — and his leaving once again left vacant a major academic post.

Although it seemed unlikely that another qualified dean could be found late in the hiring cycle for the next academic year, a search committee was named, announcements were published, and a number of potential candidates responded. The committee worked expeditiously, and after interviewing a few candidates, Dr. Harold Heie, who had been dean at another institution, was invited to be the next chief academic officer.

During his tenure he led the hiring of engineering faculty and the development of the engineering major and, perhaps more importantly, orchestrated a complete revision of the general education program (as we have seen earlier). Heie pushed the large Committee on General Education to go to first principles, beginning with agreed-upon College-Wide Educational Objectives (affectionately called CWEOs), and from those deriving large sets of curricular and cocurricular principles. The dean's Reformed background no doubt helped shape his insistence on an orderly, coherent, defensible model.

In addition to the curricular revisions and additions, Heie helped to initiate a major review of college governance, a committee which was led by Dr. Randall Basinger (who was later to become dean of curriculum and then provost). The college had grown rapidly, with significant additions to the faculty and staff, and as a result a number of policies were *understood* as part of earlier campus practice without being clearly defined and written. Again, Heie took major responsibility to codify and bring coherence to practices that had been flexible, for example, in matters relating to faculty rank at the time of employment at the college. Further, as Heie says, "When I came to Messiah . . . there was real lack of clarity as to who decides what. And there wasn't the clear delineation of where faculty responsibilities and administrative [decision-making] responsibilities [lay] . . ." Faculty valued the emphasis on collegiality of process, of sorting out these procedural issues, but they sometimes wearied with the number of meetings and extended time commitments that the work required. Heie himself was indefatigable in his efforts to help Messiah become a first-rate academic institution. Among his strong initiatives was providing more release time for faculty to pursue scholarly research and publication, a goal that would both significantly impact faculty scholarship and increase college costs.

But behind the scenes all was not well. So it was that on August 13, 1993, President Hostetter met with Dean Heie and the chair and vice-chair of the Board of Trustees in the president's office, and the dean was told that his employment was being terminated. What exactly the president intended to communicate is not entirely clear, however. Hostetter's memo to "Faculty, Staff, and Administrators," dated August 23, notes that the meeting had taken place "to inform ... [Dean Heie] that his employment contract would not be renewed beyond the academic year of 1993–94," leaving the impression that the dean might continue to serve during the year. On the other hand, Heie in his memo on August 24 to Hostetter and the Trustee Executive Committee writes, "It was clear to all present at the August 13 meeting that the President was not extending to me the option of working at Messiah through my signed 1993–94 contract." So whatever the intent of the meeting, the contract was not to be renewed for the following year; and Heie's understanding was that at most he was being given a few weeks to conclude his work at the college.

Even the language used to describe what happened affects one's perception: the President wrote that the "employment contract would not be renewed." In the chapter titled "Fired" in his book, *Learning to Listen, Ready to Talk*, Heie writes, "At the level of feeling, I was devastated. I felt violated without any warning (one of my faculty likened my dismissal to a drive-by shooting) and believed that a great injustice had been done to me. I was never given a welcoming space to explain to anyone at the college why I felt this way."

In his letter to faculty, staff, and administrators, Hostetter wrote, "The reasons for this decision are that the Board and I have had continuing fundamental disagreement with Dr. Heie about administrative style, institutional decision making, and working relationships." In his September 2 memo to the faculty and Board of Trustee representatives who would be meeting on September 15, Heie wrote, "I think it is fair to say that the biggest difference between President Hostetter and myself revolves around the category of 'administrative style' or our differing concepts of what constitutes effective 'leadership.'" Both statements note that there were basic — and as it turned out unresolved — differences in the perception of the roles of president and chief academic officer. Some of the specific areas of difference included the adult degree completion program, faculty term-tenure policies, faculty-administration governance issues, and the major revision of the general education curriculum (which required the hiring of additional faculty). But more fundamental were issues concerning *how* decisions were made and where the authority lay for those decisions.

In any event, where one stood made an enormous difference in one's response: many faculty were outraged by what they perceived as a major injustice and lack of due process; one response was the formation of a chapter of the American Association of University Professors (AAUP) on campus, a first for Messiah College. Some faculty believed this to be a necessary response while others had significant hesitations about the appropriateness of this organization for the college. The trustees, however, supported the decision to release the dean as being necessary. In the October 22, 1993, "Response of the Board of Trustees to the Faculty," the Board wrote, "The Board takes seriously the fact that the Faculty remain unconvinced regarding the President's rationale for non-renewal. As a result, there was significant discussion of this issue in a special executive session of the most recent Board meeting. The expressions were unanimous that the reasons and the decision for non-renewal were appropriate and were affirmed in that meeting by the entire Board."

Future historians will have further distance and, one imagines, more clarity to discern these issues. What is clear is that in addition to the personal pain experienced by the two principals, the campus was charged with emotion. The scheduled fall faculty retreat (the theme: "Celebrating God's Grace") was cancelled, and a faculty meeting was called with Niles Logue, faculty chair, presiding. This was the first of numerous meetings, leading to a joint meeting of selected departmental representatives (17) and trustees (16) with two additional support persons, who took minutes, and an external mediator, John Paul Lederach, who observed. At the meeting both the trustees and the faculty read prepared statements, followed by questions from the faculty and responses by the trustees. Although the meeting was a good-faith effort to improve mutual understanding, the chasm between Board and faculty still seemed large by the end of the meeting. According to the recorded minutes, the meeting concluded with these reflections: "Niles Logue [faculty chair] stated that a number of issues have surfaced that will need attention in the future. Galen Oakes [Board chair] stated that we must work together to communicate better and that we will try to build bridges no matter how deep the water that needs to be spanned. We are on one team and let's work together as a team."

In his "observations" on the meeting, John Paul Lederach, the outside mediator/observer, made a distinction between the "text" and the "subtext" of the situation. He wrote, "It seems to me that the text, the content or presenting issues are the concerns around Dean Heie's dismissal, term tenure, [and] details/facts around recent decisions and policies. The subtext, the emotional process or relational concerns, are the areas related to identity, community, interdependence, and power. These latter areas are not easy to define or measure; they seem more related to feeling than pure fact, to perception and even fear more than empirical evidence. They seem to grapple with questions like who are we, where are we going, are we going there together, and do our various voices have a place and are they counted?" Lederach may have somewhat underestimated the importance of the dismissal of the dean, but his perception that there was a "subtext" to the current situation surely merits consideration.

During the thirty years of Hostetter's presidency, the college had grown unprecedentedly. This third Hostetter president came to the office when the college had fewer than 300 students, a college where "everyone" knew everyone else, an institution where the president was the one whose hand guided every major decision. No doubt his view of the presidency was strongly influenced by observing the long, effective tenure (26 years) of his own father in the office. But changing times brought changing expectations. Already in 1972 the Middle States Association evaluation team had made the following observation about the governance structure of the college: "From an organizational standpoint Messiah is a 'tight-ship,' with authority and decision flowing from the top down, specifically from and through the President and the Dean. It is because of this forceful and efficient direction that the College has been able to keep its programs on target. . . . Every area of the College's life shows evidence of the strong leadership and direction by the Administration, and there is little resentment of this."

After offering these assessments, the team writes about a future direction: "Almost inevitably and properly the next few years should see some abatement of this 'from the top down' pattern. Faculty and students should have a larger role in developing curriculum and academic policies. Policy determination and initiation of programs by administrators may have been necessary in the early days of the institution and its march toward accreditation. But in the academic community to which Messiah now belongs, Faculty and Students increasingly are sharers in these policy functions." In fairness it should be noted that over the years President Hostetter did accept a number of changes. For example, in 1972 the president, among many other responsibilities, would have chaired both the Faculty Meeting and the Faculty Status Committee (which made recommendations for faculty promotion and tenure), and he later relinquished both of these important posts in the governance structure.

But in the twenty years following this Middle States report, the college had grown and changed enormously. Questions of identity surfaced in multiple areas. If Messiah was no longer in 1993 a college primarily serving a small denomination, neither was it an independent Christian college without historic ties to the Brethren in Christ. If Messiah was no longer an intimate small college, neither was it a large multi-faceted university. If the former governance patterns seemed too paternalistic, what should the new patterns be — and who would decide? In short, the college faced significant questions of identity and direction, and the conflict between the president and dean was a significant highlighting of some of those areas of concern. Both men, no doubt, wanted the best possible outcome for the good of the college and its future direction.

Meantime, the college struggled with what to do in the immediate future. There were strong faculty voices insisting on the reinstatement of the dean; others felt that on all sides such a "solution" would be problematical. At the same time there was hesitation about moving to appoint an interim dean. Eventually, though, a multi-stage nomination process was set in motion, and after several faculty votes, three persons — two of them faculty members, and a third an off-campus candidate — were selected and vetted. No clear choice emerged, and near the end of the fall semester no dean had been named, leaving a significant gap in academic leadership. Ultimately, Hostetter asked Dr. Dorothy Gish to serve as acting dean, and on December 13, 1993, the president sent a memo informing the faculty of his recommendation and requesting response to an affirmation ballot. In her December 16 memo of acceptance, Gish wrote, "I am amazed and humbled by your strong affirmation of me as Acting Dean. . . . My original decision not to allow my name to be included among the nominees was based partly on my concern over the events which led to our leaderless state. The response to that situation led me to believe that I could best serve in my role as Associate Dean of the Faculty [for faculty development]." Having served previously in an interim role as dean of students, Gish had no illusions that her task would be easy, nor that the healing necessary for the college would automatically follow the naming of a dean. But she worked extremely hard, and because of the difficulty in naming a new dean, she served for five years as dean and vice-president for academic affairs until her retirement in 1998.

The naming of an acting dean was a positive step forward, but campus turmoil continued with unresolved governance issues. A long-term president was retiring, a search committee for a new president was seeking suitable candidates, and the acting dean didn't feel fully empowered. So the questions loomed: who were we, and where were we going? Who had the authority to lead? What was the role of the president, the vice-presidents, the faculty, and the Board of Trustees? Trust is a fragile plant, and when it withers, restoration to health takes a long time.

So 1993–94 seemed longer that the usual academic year, which often seems to fly from late August to May. The year was difficult for Dr. Heie: he had lost his deanship; the year was difficult for Dr. Hostetter: his thirtieth and final year was marked with conflict and mistrust. Was it a "watershed" time for the college? In retrospect, perhaps not, but certainly it was a deeply unsettling time. Because of the events of the year, the president didn't receive the accolades and the warm farewell that his long, effective service deserved; nor did the dean receive the public hearing which he desired. For the trustees, too, the climate was difficult and the outcome unclear. After a special meeting on May 11, 1994, of the Academic and Faculty Affairs Committee of the Board, Dr. Mark Garis, the chair, wrote, "The discussion [in the committee] began with a look at what the [committee's role] . . . should be. The more we discussed this issue, and the more we discussed the total structure and functioning of the Trustee Board, the more we felt uncertain about our role. . . . There was a sense that we need to seize this opportunity to make adjustments or changes which will begin to restore trust and place us on a course in which some of the experiences of the past are less likely to reoccur."

Not all things were disrupted, of course. Classes were still being taught; student services continued to be offered; the structures had not collapsed. This was the inaugural year of the newly (and completely) revised general education program with the first offering of the Freshman Seminar required of all new students. Life for students on campus probably seemed quite normal. Many faculty were committed to providing the best educational possibility for students, whatever their own sentiments were regarding the administrative difficulties. So the long difficult year finally came to an end, though with limited positive conclusions: the tangled skein of strained relationships was not untangled, despite some good-faith efforts by trustees, faculty, and administrators. And the long-term president had a sad final year in office.

In the heated atmosphere that marked the end of President Hostetter's tenure, it was perhaps difficult at times for members of the campus community to recognize their common concern for the well-being of students, a concern shared by almost everyone, staff, faculty, and administration. A story from the president's early years: Melinda Fisher Nowak, an English major alumna, offers this intriguing personal insight, "In 1972 Eisenhower [Campus Center] was just being finished, and so we were still eating in the old dining hall [in the Alumni Auditorium] which was down a flight of steps. . . . And it was my first night there, my first evening meal; and I remember going to the top of the stairs, and I was in the wheel chair because of the distance . . . from the dorm. I used my [non-motorized] wheelchair frequently at the college because of the distances. . . . I remember sitting at the top of the stairs thinking, 'Well, this is great,' because I knew Eisenhower [Campus Center] . . . [would be] accessible . . . and that was one of the selling points for Messiah . . . and someone came up behind me and asked if he could help. And [he] recruited another person, and these two people took me down the stairs; when we got to the bottom he introduced himself. And it was Ray Hostetter, and I asked him what he did at the college, and he said, 'Oh, I'm the president here.' . . . and that's all he said; he

Located near the current Eisenhower Student Center, the Alumni
Auditorium was begun in 1933 during the Depression and housed
the college's kitchen and dining room in the lower level.

welcomed me to the college, said he hoped that I'd enjoy dinner
and went on his way. And I never forgot he did that."

A man who often operated quietly, behind the scenes, Hostetter's
achievements might be taken for granted. Now with the (still limited)
perspective of fifteen years since his presidency, one sees the remarkable eight-fold increase of the student body during his tenure with
the commensurate growth of faculty, staff, and administrators; one
recalls the far-sighted initiatives of programs such as the Philadelphia
Messiah–Temple urban campus in 1968, and the international connection with Daystar Communcations (later Daystar University
College) in Nairobi, Kenya, in the early 1980s; one reviews the single
largest endowment gift of the Fry Trust in the 1970s and 1980s, a
fund with an enormous impact on the financial stability of the
college. Scanning the 2009 aerial campus photo taken for the
centennial year, one is stunned at the physical growth: Kline Hall of
Science (1969), Eisenhower Campus Center (1972), Murray Library
(1977), Climenhaga Fine Arts Center (1981), Sollenberger Sports
Center (1984), Frey Hall of Science (1991), plus ten large residence
halls of various types. A time of growth, a time of challenge, a time
of change. The legacy of one family on Messiah College, one can
safely assert, will never be duplicated on this campus.

Chapter 8

A New Presidency
Roads Taken and Not Taken

In a commencement speech on June 25, 1998, to the graduates of W.C. Miller Collegiate in Altona, Manitoba, Rodney J. Sawatsky reflected on choices which we make and situations which we don't choose: "I did not choose to be born in Altona, to be raised in Altona, to love the smell of the sunflower plant. Perhaps my parents didn't really make this choice for me either. We were products of decisions others made for us. . . . Much of our road is given to us; we do not choose the path we take." But then Sawatsky adds, "Even if we do not choose this road, we can choose how we will respond to what has been given to us. . . . Forget the 'what ifs'! Celebrate the road already given to you. But now that you are graduating, you do have choices, big choices, important choices!" He concludes his address at his early alma mater with these words: "The full and abundant life is not lived selfishly, it is lived for others. Where you live your life of service [in this small town of Altona or elsewhere] is less important than that you live such a life."

Although he is addressing graduates, Sawatsky's return to his hometown no doubt led him to reflect autobiographically. Without fully exploring the various turns in his own "road," he does strongly hint that after an early lack of direction—even after receiving his baccalaureate degree—he took a road "less traveled by, / And that has made all the difference." That road led him from a small town in Manitoba to a college in Winnipeg (Canadian Mennonite Bible) to a college on the plains of Kansas (Bethel) to two major universities (Minnesota and Princeton) and finally to a Ph.D. in religion. After short teaching stints at two different colleges, he and his family moved to Waterloo, Ontario, in 1974, where he was professor and academic dean at Conrad Grebel College until 1989, when he was named president, a post which he held until 1994.

The 1993-94 academic year at Messiah College was marked with considerable turmoil, as we have seen, with the non-renewal of the academic dean's contract and the planned retirement of the long-term president. But life in academe rarely stops, even during times of swirling currents, and a presidential search committee was named with Galen Oakes, the Board of Trustees chair, serving as chair of the Search Committee. Members of the committee included other Trustee Board members, representatives of the Brethren in Christ Church, administrators, two faculty members, and a student. After receiving and reviewing applications from over forty candidates and selecting those who seemed the strongest, the committee gathered to make a final selection. After much discussion the committee had selected four candidates and stood to leave the meeting. As Galen Oakes recalls the meeting, "As we were screening these candidates, we dropped the name of Sawatsky [as a finalist]; we didn't know much about him and . . . Dr. [Ernest] Boyer . . . said, ['We] need to take another look at this man. He's a Princeton graduate, and we're interested in improving our academic standards and our academic reputation'; and by his asking for another review of him, I've always given Dr. Boyer the credit for the selection of that president." In recommending a further look, Boyer also noted his favorable response to Sawatsky's thoughtful theological reflections in his application.

A few weeks later the Search Committee met in Philadelphia for interviews with each of the five candidates and their spouses. With Dr. Ernest Boyer chairing the sessions, the committee had inter-viewed four couples and was very favorably impressed with one candidate. Dr. Rodney Sawatsky and his wife Lorna were the last of the five presidential interviewees at the end of a long, intense day. But according to some participants, the tiredness seemed to fade, the committee was energized by the interchange, and they recognized that they now had a second strong candidate.

For their part, as Sawatsky recalled, "We had no plans of making a move at this time. I think I had once perhaps gotten a little restless where I was; it was a momentary kind of thing. . . . Lorna and I both

President Rodney and Mrs. Lorna Sawatsky (1994–2004).

... took it [the interview] a little bit as a lark ... why not do this?"
After the interview, though, they were very favorably impressed and
inclined to come to Messiah, if chosen. The committee brought the
two candidates to the Executive Committee of the Board for final
recommendation to the full board. The recommendation to offer the
presidency to Dr. Sawatsky was a significant break from tradition: the
Board invited a Canadian, a man who was not an alumnus, nor a
member of the Brethren in Christ denomination (though he was a
Mennonite, a sister denomination), nor a person with family connections in the denomination, to be the seventh president of this
growing college. Among other things, this choice made apparent at
the top level of administration that the identity of the college was
continuing to change and the borders were being enlarged. For his
part, in a formal interview in August 1994 with *The Bridge*, Sawatsky
said, "What I like about Messiah is that it has not remained narrowly
sectarian. I prefer a community where a variety of Christian traditions are represented. I find variety to be enormously enriching. If I
was to move anywhere, I was looking for a place that was embracing."
Whether he quite realized it or not, he was already sounding a word
which he was to use often later, "embracing" evangelicalism, as his
vision of one aspect of the college's identity. In a similar vein as his
predecessor, D. Ray Hostetter, Sawatsky avoided narrow sectarianism.

Another theme, academic excellence, was given clear voice in his inaugural address ("Renewing Our Minds; Transforming Our World") on November 19, 1994. "Educating the mind, renewing the mind is our Christian vocation. Our gifts, whatever they be, need to be developed and utilized to their fullest measure. Accordingly Messiah College must strive for academic excellence. We must be the very best we can possibly be in every department, every discipline." Excellence in the classroom, the music hall, the art studio, the science laboratory, the athletic field: *excellence* was to be a major theme. Further, he argued that "Christian liberal arts colleges should place much more emphasis on research and published scholarship. At Messiah this is true for our professional as for our liberal arts and liberal sciences programs." Whether in the classroom or in other professional or scholarly venues, Sawatsky would urge the importance of excellence as part of one's Christian vocation. Although he said that in his first year he intended to do much listening, clearly the new president was not going to remain on the sidelines, quietly.

An early initiative for a significant administrative restructuring was Sawatsky's decision to create the position of provost, with the provost replacing the vice-president for academic affairs. A December 21, 1994, memo to the Community of Educators outlined his plans with the vice-president for student development and the academic dean reporting to the provost. Although the plans were still in process, the faculty didn't feel that they were adequately consulted about such a significant change in the administrative structure. The faculty were particularly sensitive about being left out of the process because of the events of the previous year. The February 6, 1995, Community of Educators minutes report that "President Sawatsky began with a reference to his sore shins—not as a result of an old hockey injury—but from what he said was well deserved feedback regarding the manner in which the communication concerning administrative changes [including a vice-president for community relations] have been handled." Despite the early reservations about the process, faculty did accept the president's recommendation, and by February 17 the Board's Executive Committee had approved both the position of provost and the process for selecting the person to fill the role, with the intention of naming a provost during the summer of 1995.

The initiatives from the president's office were coming in other areas as well. Indeed by February 6, 1995, three major new ad hoc committees had been named and given a mandate for review of quite disparate areas of the college: the Philadelphia campus, the "Adult Degree-Path Programs," and potential graduate study programs. Some of the areas would take much more extended time for review than others, of course. The potential graduate programs to be considered were in education, nursing, and religious studies. After several meetings the committee on April 24 decided to put further consideration "on hold" for two reasons: (1) the primary mission of the college was undergraduate education and many—on and off the committee—felt the college was not ready to embark on a significant new area of expansion, and (2) because there was a search for both an academic dean and a provost there was a need "to attend to personnel appointments in the academic office" prior to curricular expansion. The other two committees—particularly the committee reviewing the Philadelphia campus—needed more time to bring recommendations to the Community of Educators (which included teaching faculty, curricular administrators, and cocurricular educators).

The search committee for the provost reported on April 24, 1995, that they had reviewed 50 candidates' applications at the first stage, 14 at the second stage, and they hoped to narrow the field to four applicants and be ready to recommend a candidate by mid-June. On June 15—during the summer break—the Community of Educators did meet to hear a report and have further discussion, but the search had not achieved the hoped-for results. No provost would be named for 1995. Meantime Dr. Dorothy Gish was asked to continue as academic dean, as well as carry other responsibilities that might have been given to the provost, had one been named.

At the same time other administrative changes were being announced: Ron Long, vice-president for admissions, financial aid, and communications, resigned after over twenty years of tireless work. As part of a restructuring move William Strausbaugh was named to serve as vice-president for enrollment management. Dr. Jay

Barnes, vice-president for student development, resigned after fifteen years of effective work to become provost at Bethel College (MN). John Addleman was appointed to a half-time position as acting dean of students for the year. By the following year (March 1, 1996) two new search committees had been named, one for an academic dean and the other for a dean of students, with the goal "To have a candidate named for each position by the end of the academic year."

In addition to these three ad hoc committee reviews and several academic searches, an Institutional Identity Committee had been initiated by President Hostetter, and that committee under the leadership of Trustee Board member Dr. Donald Minter (a medical doctor) had its first meeting in May 1994. Besides Minter, the committee included three other Board members, four faculty members, a staff member, two administrators, and a student. Dr. Minter recalls that when President Hostetter, who was a long-term friend, asked him to chair the committee, he had many questions: "I went to his [Hostetter's] home, and we spent an hour and a half [with] my asking questions, mostly about what the intention was. And I was still trying to pick up enough wisdom to know [whether] I could be aware that . . . [the committee's work] could be either a divisive thing or it could be a thing that brought cohesiveness. And it would be a tragedy if it was divisive." His hesitation was a reasonable one because the faculty climate in 1993–94 was quite sensitive to possibilities of divisiveness. Trust was not available in large quantities. As he recalls, Minter pressed the issue of intent: "I needed to know whether this was an honest searching or whether the answers [to institutional identity] were already there, and they just needed to fill in the blanks. . . . [Hostetter] assured me that this was open-ended."

Minter became convinced that the process was going to be open, with faculty members chosen by affinity "cluster" departments. After the nominations were received, he requested and then read essays from each of the applicants, which gave him insight, he says, "that I could never have gotten any other way." Having had this written introduction to the potential committee members, Minter then went to each of their offices. As Dr. Douglas ("Jake") Jacobsen, professor of church history and theology, recalls, "Don [Minter] went around and talked to each of us individually before we could be on the committee." With the chair of the committee taking his work so seriously, and the committee members becoming convinced that the process was to be an unbiased one, the door was being opened to a potentially positive process. In the initial meeting of the entire committee, Minter expected to spend some introductory time getting acquainted, but in fact, "We spent two and half hours at that first meeting [getting to know each other] . . . and the bonding that took place [was remarkable]." That initial positive experience served the committee well: Minter recalls that for the first year and a half with long meetings two or three times a year, they had "100 percent attendance."

In that initial May 1994 meeting, the committee agreed that the study of institutional identity was particularly timely, given the significant transitions which the college was experiencing administratively. According to Jacobsen's May 16 letter to the faculty, they also "agreed that there should be a sense of congruence between the identity we claim as an institution and the identity we embody as an institution." As part of their background work the committee sent an "opinion survey" to faculty, focusing on a number of key documents, including the college's philosophy statement, the college's statement of faith, the community covenant, the College-Wide Educational Objectives (CWEOs), the Church-College Covenant, and the college's "Guidelines for Promotion, Tenure, and Dismissal." Of the 153 surveys that were distributed, 90 were returned for a 59 percent response rate. In their November 1994 update, Minter and Jacobsen reported, "While we do seem to be agreed on the basic ideals of the institution, we seem to be having some problems translating those ideals into the way we actually live."

Although the committee acknowledged problems in "institutional identity," they suggested that their "preferred approach would be positive — trying to help the college do a better job of living its ideals, rather than trying piecemeal to solve a variety of particular problems." The new president, Rodney Sawatsky, as a church historian, was keenly interested in the committee's work and was invited to join the committee in its deliberations. In the fall of 1994 the committee projected the hope of completing their work by October, 1995 — presumably in time for the fall Trustee Board meeting — with a plan to draft a succinct "mission statement" for the college community's response.

An important issue became the relationship of Messiah College with the larger evangelical movement in the United States. As Jacobsen recalls the discussion, "The dynamic that emerged . . . was, are we going to identify ourselves . . . simply as an evangelical college . . . ?" Ultimately, the committee decided to reaffirm the Brethren in Christ origins of the college with three particular emphases: Anabaptist, Pietist, and Wesleyan. The mission statement, though brief, went through many revisions as the committee drafted a version, took it to various constituent bodies, and then further revised and refined. Minter recalls taking what the committee thought were virtually completed documents, "And then when we thought we had it all put together — it was after two years — we came to the Board . . . and it [the prepared statement] wasn't going anyplace. . . . So I went out and whispered in an ear, 'Why don't we back off for a year?'" But Minter adds, "We had the good fortune of having Ernie [Dr. Ernest Boyer] this last month be able to join us in our Board meetings. . . . [He addressed the mission and identity issue] in his hoarse and husky ill voice . . . maybe twenty minutes to half hour, and he is the one that brought in the vocational part . . . into the mission statement." Although the mission statement was not completed at this time, the eventually adopted statement reads: "Messiah College is a Christian college of the liberal and applied arts and sciences. The College is committed to an embracing evangelical spirit rooted in the Anabaptist, Pietist, and Wesleyan traditions of the Christian Church. Our mission is to educate men and women toward maturity of intellect, character, and Christian faith in preparation for lives of service, leadership, and reconciliation." In addition to Boyer's emphasis on calling, on vocation, one recognizes Sawatsky's theme of an "embracing evangelical spirit."

Besides this mission and identity statement, the committee refocused five ideals which summarized Messiah's definition of its expression of the Christian faith: (1) unity of faith, learning, and life; (2) importance of the person; (3) significance of community; (4) disciplined and creative living; (5) service and reconciliation. Each of these core values was then described in a carefully crafted paragraph. Perhaps most distinctive to Messiah College was the fifth foundational value with its affirmation: "Central to the Gospel is the work of reconciling individuals with God, with each other, and with all of creation." Perhaps nothing was unexpected in this reaffirmation, but there was a renewed clarity of call to a particular response to the Gospel.

In addition to these two documents, the committee also drafted and circulated a new Confession of Faith. Less a creedal statement than a series of doxological affirmations, the "confession" includes a litany of responses beginning with these words: "God creates, God speaks, God forgives, God bestows, God calls, God gives, God instructs." The Confession of Faith concludes with this response: "We praise the one God, our Creator, Redeemer, and Sustainer — who has called us to personal faith and new life in Christ and to so order our lives that they may demonstrate the truth of our confession." Clearly, the completion of the three documents was important to clarifying the identity of Messiah College, but perhaps almost as important was the open, collegial process. As Jacobsen recalls, "I think the documents are much, much better because of the feedback we received from on-campus and off-campus. . . . We modified and modified and modified until we got the documents." Not only were the documents improved, there was an increasing sense of ownership by the campus community, as well as by the trustees. In addition to the college's own new faith statement, Messiah College also affirmed the use of the Apostles Creed as part of her official faith commitment.

All of this work took extended time commitments. After the initial action of the Executive Committee of the Board of Trustees in January 1994 to constitute an Institutional Identity Committee, the plan was to have recommendations prepared for Trustee Board action by October 1995. In fact, there were reports to the Board at several points, including a major summation in October 1996, but the final recommendation to the Board came in May 1997, over three years after the beginning of the process. But the cooperative efforts of faculty, staff, administration, and trustees helped restore a greater sense of trust and mutuality. Reflecting back on the events, one can sense the importance of President Hostetter's initiating the process for this review of the college's identity. His initiative came during the difficult final year of his presidency. Perhaps the process wasn't carried forward as far as he had hoped during those several months, but that extended timing also allowed for the significant involvement of the new president to contribute to the rethinking and reformulation of these key documents.

While the college was working hard to clarify and redefine its identity and relationship with the founding denomination, the new administration also needed to work with the local Brethren in Christ congregation, which was located at the heart of the campus. The new president was a strong supporter of the congregation — and indeed he and his wife joined the Grantham Church — but he was concerned that the planned expansion of the church's facilities on campus would be problematical for the college. In his May 12, 1995, report to the Trustees, he notes his concern: "Last fall as we began to envision future campus developments . . . a potential conflict area quickly became apparent. How would the College's plans and developments over the next decades coincide or compete with the plans and developments of the Grantham Church located at the center of our campus?" He noted the long-planned-for $1.5 million addition to the rear of the current church structure. Although he wrote appreciatively of the mission of the church, "Yet the College's primary constituency is our students. . . . We are committed always to cooperate with the Church, but when the development of these two distinct institutions compete, those responsible for the College must give the College's concerns precedence." For their part the Grantham Church was dismayed at the obstruction in their long-planned expansion. Writing for the Church Board, senior pastor Dr. Robert Ives laments, "I think it would be a fair summary of the Board's response to say that it falls between the extremes of anger and wanting to cry."

The Trustees' Executive Committee "appointed a committee of three — Dr. Harold Engle, Mr. Clyde Horst, and Mr. Ben Rooke — to discuss the situation with three people appointed by the Church." The ad hoc committee was empowered to negotiate an offer with the church to buy the on-campus property and provide college land across the railroad tracks for a building site. Part of the process would also be providing for the relocation of the Thompson family, whose house would need to be demolished to make room for new construction. The decision facing the Grantham Church was not easy because the study and preparation for expansion had taken years, and to some the college's sudden intervention seemed heavy handed and ill timed. Nonetheless, the church did eventually accept the offer of the college, which many agreed was a generous one. The ultimate outcome was a splendid new Grantham Church building, far larger than would ever have been possible at the former location at the heart of the campus. There were losses as well, and some alumni lament the loss of having the "campus church" at its traditional, symbolic, heart-of-the-college location. On balance, though, the resolution of the college-church discussion of facilities seems to have been satisfactory on both sides.

In the same May report to the Board, Dr. Sawatsky noted beginning to discuss the feasibility of a large campaign to fund a chapel/convocation center (sometimes called a Great Hall), an early, keen interest of the president's, particularly because of his dual interest in worship space and a large music hall with excellent acoustics. Another facility, a major addition to the Kline Hall of Science, Sawatsky reported as being further along in the planning process. That addition would house a natural science museum, expanded science laboratory and nursing facilities, and provide classrooms and offices.

The final major item in his eleven-page report was to update the full Board on the search process for the provost, the position having been approved by the Executive Committee the previous February. The plan was still in May (1995) to have named a provost by early summer, though as we have already noted, that plan was not realized, and the position was held open throughout the next academic year. Dr. Donald B. Kraybill reports that in the fall of 1995 Dr. Sawatsky "started talking with me [about the position], and I met with the Search Committee . . . and then in December . . . [I] agreed to take the position." In a January 17, 1996, memo to the Community of Educators, the president reported, "At the conclusion of an extensive and what we felt was an exhaustive search, the Provost Search Committee is very pleased to announce that we have found an exceptional candidate. . . . Unfortunately in spite of your strong encouragement and our best efforts, we are not in a position to present several candidates for your consideration."

So it was that a search which had been initiated in November 1994 was concluded over a year later with the introduction and subsequent confirmation of Dr. Donald B. Kraybill as the first provost of Messiah College, a position which would become more fully defined through the actual experience of working within the new administrative structure. Kraybill formally began what would be a four-year tenure as provost on July 1, 1996.

In his January memo announcing Kraybill's candidacy, the president also announced the search for both an academic dean and a dean of students. Neither Dr. Dorothy Gish, who was serving as academic dean, nor Dr. John Addleman, who was serving as interim dean of students, desired long-term appointments to those positions. After reviewing a number of applicants for the academic deanship, the Search Committee invited two candidates for on-campus interviews in May 1996. The campus community gave mixed reviews to each candidate, neither receiving strong support. Thus Donald Kraybill, the provost-elect, requested that Dorothy Gish, who was scheduled to have a sabbatical year, continue as academic dean in 1996–97 in the new administrative structure. With her continuing commitment to serve for the good of the whole, Gish accepted the appointment and agreed to postpone the planned sabbatical.

The Academic Dean Search Committee, under the leadership of Dr. David Parkyn, considered nearly 95 nomination and applications and conducted off-campus interviews with six semifinalists. As the committee reported on February 17, 1997, "Three of these semi-finalists (one woman and two men) were deemed viable candidates and invited for a campus visit. Only two of the three finalists were able to accept the invitation for a campus visit." The two candidates visited the campus in the next weeks, but again neither was judged to be a good fit for the position. Thus, once more Dr. Gish was asked to continue her service for an additional year as academic dean.

The third finalist the previous spring had been unable to come to the campus because of family commitments, but in September 1997 the Search Committee announced the campus visit of Dr. Kim S. Phipps, who, the committee wrote, "brings a variety of gifts, strengths and experiences that make her a strong and viable candidate for the Academic Dean's role." And this time the campus community strongly supported the recommendation — and Dr. Phipps was appointed as academic dean to begin serving at Messiah College on July 1, 1998. So the lengthy search process — after several years and three interview cycles — finally came to a highly satisfactory conclusion. And the campus community shared a collective sense of relief.

Meantime, the Dean of Students Search Committee, with Donald Kraybill serving as chair, had recommended two finalists for on-campus visits in January 1997. In their memo the committee noted the selection of these finalists "after considering nearly 50 nominations and applications and after conducting off-campus interviews with four semifinalists." Minutes from a February 10 Community of Educators Open Hearing report the outcome of those interviews: "After careful consideration, there was unanimous agreement on the committee NOT to invite either candidate [to serve as dean of students]." The committee further noted that John Addleman, while willing to continue service on an interim basis, "prefers not to be a candidate for the permanent position." The search for a dean of students "will continue immediately." The searches did continue, and finally that fall the college was pleased to name Cynthia Wells-Lilly as dean of students (and later vice-provost). Her appointment began in July 1998 and continued for five years until her transition to the Ernest L. Boyer Center in 2003.

Far more than administrative searches were happening on campus, of course, and some of the ad hoc committees appointed earlier were bringing their work to completion. The March 25, 1996, Community of Educators (COE) minutes report that the Ad-hoc Committee for Review of Adult Degree Programs recommended that no new programs be offered "at the present time," and that the current Business Administration cohort of students be the last one. On the other hand, at their April 29, 1996, meeting the COE "gave unanimous support to the future of the DegreePath Nursing Program," which at that time had a total of 48 adult students enrolled in four cohorts. For the moment, at least, the prospects for this program were hopeful, but the future was not assured. In the following years as the strategic plan for the future was revised, the adult degree program was phased out when the last cohort of students graduated in 2000. As Dr. Carolyn Kreamer, chair of the department of nursing reports, "The official rationale for the closure of the program was that the College's new strategic plan intended to focus resources on the traditionally aged student (18–22) and predicted enrollment growth of that demographic cohort." During its somewhat limited lifespan, the Nursing DegreePath had eight cohort classes and a total of 95 graduates.

The third of the major ad hoc committees appointed in 1995 was the Committee for Review of the Philadelphia Campus. Of the three committees (the other two were the adult degree completion program and potential graduate studies), the review of the Philadelphia program was perhaps the most inclusive. Under the leadership of Dr. David Parkyn, who at this time was executive assistant to the president, the committee ranged widely in gathering information. Giving able assistance was the director of the Philadelphia campus, Donald Wingert, who welcomed and encouraged this thorough review. During the review process the committee surveyed many alumni from the program; these persons who had experienced the challenges and benefits of living in an urban context and taking courses in a major university, while at the same time being connected to a small-campus living community, were almost without exception extremely positive about their experiences. No doubt part of the reason for their favorable response to living at the Philadelphia campus was the dedicated leadership of Donald Wingert, who in 1980 was invited by the college administration to serve as director of the campus, a position which he initially thought he might hold for two years. In fact, he and his family lived at the center for many years, and he served as director for 23 years (and for a total of over 30 years at Messiah in various roles).

As part of the review process the committee went to the urban campus and interviewed key staff members, as well as engaging five consultants who also visited the campus and gave oral and written responses to the program. Finally, the committee wrote a revised and expanded mission statement, which then helped shape the further review of the program. In their February 1996 report to the COE, the

Messiah students eating dinner with Philadelphia
Mayor W. Wilson Goode in the dining room.

committee wrote, "We believe [that] the Philadelphia program is
one of the unique dimensions the College offers the world of higher
education in general and the Christian college community specifically. . . . The Review Committee enthusiastically endorses the continued life of the Philadelphia Campus and believes the College
should revitalize its commitment to this program." The committee
brought a series of recommendations, which they labeled as Tier
One, Two, Three, or Four, with the first tier being foundational to the
others, and the next tiers becoming increasingly more expansive and
costly. The faculty approved the statement of mission and purpose
and recommended a continuing advisory committee to assist the
provost "in matters related to the implementation of the recommendations as approved by the Community of Educators."

Receiving this positive review assured the continuation of the
Philadelphia campus beyond its initial 25 years, but recruiting
students would always be a challenge. Some faculty were more enthusiastic than others in encouraging their students to study in Philadelphia; no doubt some administrators were more convinced of the
importance of the program to Messiah College than others; sometimes parents were very concerned about the potential dangers of the

urban setting for their children. So for a number of complex reasons, growing academic programs that required study at Philadelphia for several semesters were often brought back to the Grantham campus. Nor has the Philadelphia campus been as successful in recruiting urban students to this major city campus as those who established the program in 1968 had hoped. One of the initial faculty members, Dr. Ronald J. Sider, had dreamed of establishing "the first black evangelical college, using the Philadelphia campus . . ." But Sider left to teach at a seminary, and that dream never came to fruition. One wonders whether it could have been possible.

Regarding the present-day prospects of the Messiah Philadelphia campus, current program director and professor of urban studies, Dr. Timothy J. Peterson, says, "Prior to 2003 students were coming pretty much because it was required of their major to take courses at Temple. . . . We certainly still have that in certain majors-theatre, journalism, broadcasting-those all require a semester here. But [now] . . . every semester we have a good third to 40 percent of our students taking an internship . . . and we have a database of over a 1,000 potential internships." At the same time, Peterson argues that in order for the Philadelphia campus to be financially and program-matically sustainable, there need to be connections made "between particular departments — if not every department — and Philadel-phia." Thus he would like to encourage more faculty visits to the urban campus, and he would also urge some faculty to take their sabbaticals at Philadelphia. In short, continuing institutional con-nections and commitments will be essential for the Philadelphia program's long-term viability and vitality.

A loyal friend of Messiah College and no doubt her most famous son, Dr. Ernest L. Boyer, Sr., was one of the three educators who had dreamed together about the potential of a Christian college relating to a major urban university. Dr. Boyer and (now former) President D. Ray Hostetter, two of the three dreamers, were long-term friends and graduates of the same junior college class of 1948 at Messiah. Both were deeply committed to education, but where one committed over 30 years to one institution, the other served in a variety of highly visible roles, among them being the chancellor of the New York University system and then later becoming the U.S.

Dr. Ernest L. and Mrs. Kathryn (Kay) Boyer.

Commissioner of Education under President Jimmy Carter. Finally, Boyer served for sixteen years as the president of the Carnegie Foundation for the Advancement of Teaching.

Dr. Boyer continued to be a friend of Messiah College, serving on the Board of Trustees from 1968 until his untimely death from cancer in 1995. Despite his extremely demanding schedule, he served as chair of the Board of Trustees from 1982 to 1987. He played a key role in the invitation to Rodney Sawatsky, and he contributed meaningfully to the mission and identity statement of Messiah College. Because he was such a wonderful friend of the college, some of Messiah's senior administrators cultivated a relationship with the Boyer family, suggesting the possibility of an Ernest L. Boyer Center for Advanced Studies, a center which could house the vast amount of Boyer materials on education.

A memo from Provost Kraybill to the Boyer family in late 1996 was well received, and on January 31, 1997, the Board of Trustees authorized "the [Messiah College] administrative staff to proceed with plans to establish an archival collection of the Ernest L. Boyer, Sr. papers in cooperation with the Boyer family and officials of the Carnegie Foundation . . ." The collection was to be as comprehen-

Boyer Hall, the newest academic building, was dedicated
on October 17, 2003.

The Ernest L. Boyer Center is near the entrance of Boyer Hall.

sive as possible, housed in professional archival facilities, accessible to scholars, and "incorporated into a larger center of scholarship." President Sawatsky made the announcement on campus on February 3, 1997, along with Mrs. Kathryn (Kay) Boyer, who made a wonderfully winsome presentation regarding her late husband and his desire to remain connected to his roots. In a letter she noted that her husband's "family roots are in the Brethren in Christ Church. . . . He always honored and cherished this heritage. . . . His grandfather, William Boyer, started a Brethren in Christ mission in the poor section of Dayton, Ohio, during the depression years. Grandfather pastored that mission work for over forty years. Ernie grew up in Dayton where his family faithfully attended and supported this work. Grandfather Boyer was his hero and was perhaps the strongest influence on his life."

The receiving of the legacy of an outstanding educator and leader was welcomed with great appreciation by the Messiah College community. Originally it was planned that the college would receive only copies of originals, and a major commitment was made to copy the vast quantity of material. However, in August 1998, Kraybill received word that the Carnegie Foundation would be "delighted to provide you with the original of the documents which the Center has previously copied." The legal agreement between Messiah College and Mrs. Boyer was signed on December 19, 2001, donating the Ernest L. Boyer, Sr. materials to the Boyer Center.

The initial "Boyer Center" at Messiah was located in the Schrag house, which was significantly remodeled to provide a suitable home for some of the materials, with Dr. Charlotte Kroeker serving as the first director. The location was adequate, but hardly ideal, for this major center; and in a few years plans were developed for a much-needed academic building, an enormous and elegant four-story facility, Boyer Hall, which housed not only the Boyer Center but 20 classrooms, four seminar rooms, a language lab, two computer labs, a cinema, and 90 offices. The college was enriched by the accession of a vast amount of Boyer materials, which included not only printed and video documents, but many pictures and other artifacts from a wide range of sources, both from the United States and from countries as distant as China and Japan. And Boyer's influence on education would continue to have a living legacy through the Boyer Center and the faculty who were "Boyer Fellows," as well as from the seminars, workshops, and other programming that would be initiated by the Center.

Having the Boyer Center at Messiah supported President's Sawatsky's emphasis on "excellence," which became something of a mantra during his tenure. Already in his Inaugural Address (on November 19, 1994), the new president, as we have seen, sounded this call: "Educating the mind, renewing the mind is our Christian vocation. ... Accordingly Messiah College must strive for excellence." Then at the end of that first academic year in his report to the Board of Trustees, he wrote about his hopes for the new mission and identity statement which was in progress. "I am confident," he wrote, "that these statements once approved will reemphasize Messiah's commitment to be academically excellent — even premier — and unapologetically Christian in the Brethren in Christ tradition." Later, the statement would morph into the tag-line which appeared in many college promotional materials: "Rigorously Academic, Unapologetically Christian." The college catalog for 2000–2001 first included that identifying phrase on its back cover, and the president's "message" to students that year sketched the advantages of the distinctives of the college and asserted, "By concentrating our energies on these priorities we can pursue educational excellence." Later in the letter, he adds, "We prepare students to excel in their chosen discipline and profession."

An important aspect of this emphasis on excellence was the recruitment of highly qualified students. Again in his first year-end report to the Trustee Board, he noted his plan "to maximize our financial aid to gain the desired admissions results. To this end we have shifted more funding toward merit-aid and away from need-based aid." Thus it was not surprising that the administration on October 13, 1997, recommended to the Community of Educators a College Honors program with its own director and several courses which were specifically designed for and limited to honors students. Among the first goals listed for the College Honors Program were (1) to "attract students of high academic ability to the College"; and (2) to "challenge students with exceptional intellectual abilities."

The students who were able to meet the rigorous admissions standards for the honors program were eligible to receive significant scholarships — including four full-tuition scholarships — regardless of financial need. Many faculty were supportive of the new initiatives, though some were concerned lest the college become too elitist in orientation. One may ask to what extent the shifting of more money to merit-based rather than need-based students reduced Messiah's accessibility to those with more limited financial resources. Further, how has the College Honors Program affected the recruitment of a student population with a wide range of giftedness and academic backgrounds? The president may have added to those concerns with his expressed wish that "Messiah become the Harvard of Christian colleges." In some ways the college was continuing to discover and develop her identity. No longer a small college serving a specific denominational clientele, nor, on the other hand, a selective liberal arts college without Christian commitments, Messiah had developed a mission and identity statement, but that, in itself, still left much to be worked out in the shaping of the institution.

One of the major initiatives was the development of a new strategic plan, which was first mentioned to the Board of Trustees in January 1998. In anticipation of a new century and Messiah College's own centennial ten years hence, the senior administrators of the college and the Executive Committee of the Board had the first formal discussion of the strategic plan, which led to the writing of the document, "A New Vision for a New Century." This completed document was then presented to the full Board in January 1999 for discussion of the whole and approval of three specific initiatives. In the executive summary of "A New Vision" the introductory section affirms, "We must balance continued faithfulness to essential commitments with changing expressions of educational mission." The document further affirms the particular educational "niche" for Messiah: "to promote meaningful and successful learning by students of traditional ages in a residential setting and Christian context." Neither of these statements would have been surprising to the Community of Educators, but the three initiatives approved by the Board — without prior discussion by the COE — did generate much intense discussion on campus.

The three approved initiatives were (1) "To adopt a university structure for our academic programs comprised of multiple schools and a Core College"; (2) "To review the College's curricula with a renewed commitment to student learning, and consider a reconfigured course-load for both students and faculty"; and (3) "To review the College's cocurricular programs with a renewed commitment to student learning." The third of the Board approved initiatives was probably the least controversial, but the first two with a proposed a new administrative structure and significant curricular revisions were a great surprise to the COE when the proposals were presented on campus on February 8. The document had been prepared with few on campus being aware of the contents; and with trust only gradually being regained between faculty and administrators, these major initiatives presented to and passed by the Board seemed ill timed to many.

In the description of the first initiative, the new academic structure is further described: "The Core College will be the integrating center of the University's academic program. The Core College may be the home of the University Core Curriculum and the University Honors Program." "Core College . . . University Core Curriculum"? Surely these were matters on which the faculty should have been consulted, many believed. Further, there was discussion of a possible name change for the college, perhaps "Grantham University," a name which might suggest change on a number of levels.

Initial meetings on campus were followed by an open hearing for the COE. In the meeting Provost Kraybill acknowledged that in recent weeks "the trust has been tattered somewhat" and apologized for his "part in rupturing trust." A few days earlier the campus chapter of the AAUP (which had been initiated during the earlier controversy surrounding Harold Heie's contract termination) had sent an open letter to the COE and the Governance Review Committee with these observations: "When we as the local AAUP chapter look at patterns of practice that prevail at Messiah College, we see a marked lack of timely, open and honest communication." On a somewhat different level, three full professors from different departments prepared a lengthy letter, which was then signed by a number of faculty, raising questions both about the process and content of the initiatives. In particular the letter raised questions about using "university" as a description and about (potentially) losing the historically important "Messiah" nomenclature.

Off campus the response of parents and alumni was enormous and largely negative. In conversation years later Kraybill wryly notes, "It's the first time I learned how powerful the internet could be. Because ... [the] internet was fairly new ... somehow the idea [of the name change] got out to some alumni, and they started sending emails all around the world . . . and it just created an enormous outcry from some alumni." For many of these concerned alumni the key question was *identity*: Was Messiah College signaling a move away from her Christian commitments? Many asked, "Are you ashamed of your Christian identity?" With some hyperbole one person wrote, "I can't think of anything more controversial and divisive that the college could do in one simple act." Because of the prevailing negativity, a number of rumors and half-truths were also circulated, some of which seemed to develop a life of their own.

In their May 1999 meeting, the Executive Committee of the Board of Trustees discussed the proposed name change. Acknowledging that they had not "extensively consider[ed] the question of the benefits and liabilities at its January meeting," they noted that "this has been raised as a significant question in the broader constituency discussions.... The Board will need to be aware ... of the strengths and limitations associated with the College's name." Years later, reflecting on those intense discussions, President Sawatsky said, "The name change [of the college] ... I don't think we had really thought it through that well." In time the proposed name change was dropped, but the costs to the college in good will were probably larger than those suggesting a possible change could have imagined. The senior administrators, and especially the president, spent considerable time assuring their off-campus publics that the basic mission and identity of the college were not in jeopardy.

On campus, too, there were a number of efforts to help restore trust and facilitate communication and increased levels of co-operation. A committee was selected to bring a recommendation concerning the potential restructuring of the college into several schools, each with its own dean. The Academic Restructuring

Advisory Committee, co-chaired by Dean Kim Phipps and Provost Donald Kraybill, met seven times throughout the summer, first to consider feedback to a questionnaire which had been distributed, and then to work on a number of models, ranging from two schools to six schools — and every level between the two. The committee solicited feedback from faculty and administrators, eventually recommending a five-school model to the president.

A number of questions were raised about the costs of the new structure, which included four additional deans, with their support staff, plus more department chairs, since significantly more disciplines would now be housed in individual departments. With the president's strong recommendation and solid faculty support, the five-school model was eventually recommended to the Board, though it did not include the Core College which "A New Vision for a New Century" had featured as a key component in the original proposal. Some faculty continued to be concerned about the budgetary effect of adding this large administrative layer to the governance structure.

In addition to the search for new deans for the five schools, there were additional administrative changes. Provost Donald Kraybill announced that he wished to resign his office in order to pursue his scholarly interests, as well as to focus more time on teaching and supervising several "centers" on campus. The president on August 12, 1999, announced that he planned to appoint Dr. Kim Phipps, the academic dean, to serve as provost, beginning July 1, 2000.

Meantime President Sawatsky prepared a new ten-year vision statement, which he sent to college employees on September 28, 1999. No longer "A New Vision for a New Century," the new document was rather more modestly named, "10 Years to 100." The paper was first distributed on campus for discussion and feedback in preparation for the Board of Trustees meeting later that fall. In the introduction the president emphasized his desire for a broader constituency for the college, as well as his continuing focus on excellence: "Established in 1909, Messiah has been built on several hills, yet in 1999 it remains too hidden. Its excellence is known by too few. In turn it is not the salt and light that it could be and ought to be. But in ten years, at the time of the college's centenary, Messiah will have progressed significantly towards becoming the *premier comprehensive, undergraduate, residential Christian college/ university* we believe it was called to be."

Among the many resources which would be needed to support this vision are the students who "will be chosen from a vast pool of applicants who say: 'My first choice is Messiah' [and who] are among the best and brightest Christian young people from the U.S. and abroad." The plan called for an enrollment of approximately 2,750 students through the 2002–2003 academic year; then "beginning with 2003–2004, student enrollment will be gradually increased, reaching approximately 3,050 students in 2008–2009."

The emphasis in the new vision statement was not primarily on buildings, but "through 2009, several new facilities will be constructed . . . " including a "new Chapel/Concert Hall/Convocation Center [which] will . . . feature an acoustically excellent 'Great Hall' designed to be the college's primary chapel and performance venue for music." Other major additions included a new academic building, a new student union, an athletics field house, new student residences, and a pedestrian bridge over the railroad track, "linking with the main campus near the entrance to the Eisenhower Campus Center." That the "Great Hall" was mentioned first in the president's list was not incidental: this major building was still an important part of Sawatsky's vision for the physical development of the campus. Indeed, the Board of Trustees' minutes for October 21–22, 1999, record a motion supporting "a campaign planning study" with a possible goal of $50 million, including $25 million designated for the proposed "Great Hall." As it turned out, the academic building (later named Boyer Hall) would receive higher priority, and the chapel/convocation center would be postponed, as were a number of other major potential projects.

Funding for significant new initiatives is always a challenge. A few years earlier Messiah College — along with many other colleges — had been invited by Mr. Jack Bennett, Jr., to place money with the New Era Foundation with the promised return of matching funds. After careful investigation of the offer, Messiah College invested $2 million with the fund. Some colleges did in fact receive additional returns on their investment, but the New Era Foundation was based on shaky footing, a Ponzi-type scheme that eventually imploded,

Jordan Science Center, dedicated in October 1999.

with Bennett declaring bankruptcy in 1995, and leaving many non-profit institutions a legacy of much embarrassment and frustration — but little money. Messiah College enlisted the help of a legal firm, Rhoads and Sinon, and eventually was able to recover most of the money. The New Era Foundation had seemed too good to be true — and it was. President Sawatsky's candor in confronting the losses and explaining the situation to both on-campus and off-campus publics served both him and the college well and avoided the blaming and accusations which might otherwise have followed.

Major financial resources, it was again abundantly clear, needed to be raised in more conventional ways through hard work and personal contacts. In 1996 a new initiative was announced, a "Campaign for the Sciences" with a goal of $10 million, its purpose being the renovation of Kline Hall of Science and a significant addition to the building, which would house nursing facilities and an impressive natural history museum. The Jordan Science Center and the Oakes Museum received significant support, and the campaign exceeded its goal, raising $12,679,000. The attractive, functional building with its lovely brick patio was dedicated in October 1999.

The next major campaign, "To Serve and to Lead," initiated in 2001, was to be the last one under President Sawatsky's leadership.

The campaign was multi-faceted with a large academic building (as we have seen) receiving top billing, followed by a student union building, endowment funds, and scholarship funding. By far the largest campaign to date, the initial goal was $40 million, an ambitious goal when one realizes that the largest previous campaign raised something over $15 million.

Adding to the challenge was the financial slow-down in the larger economy. In a December 10, 2002, memo to the college community the president addressed the changing fiscal climate: "The current recessionary economy is placing an enormous burden on virtually every college and university in the country. . . . In order to maintain our positive momentum toward increasing educational excellence, the College will be required to exercise unusual budgetary restraint and cost saving initiatives." The tone of the memo is, however, characteristically positive, and the president concludes on this hopeful note: "Messiah College is very strong and will become even stronger despite these considerable challenges."

Other challenges of a very different nature — challenges of which he could not have been aware — would soon loom large in the president's life. Just over a month later in January 2003 the president sent a memo of announcement and condolence upon receiving the sad word of the death of a 2002 graduate of Messiah, Hannah Showaker. Hannah, who had been teaching English in an elementary school in Indonesia, had been caught in a flash flood in a mountainous area in Java. "Now that Hannah's life has ended so prematurely," he wrote, "we join her family in mourning the loss of this gifted, loving young woman." The untimely loss of the young, particularly those who have focused on serving others, is always heart wrenching.

In retrospect, an additional poignancy of the president's memo is that he himself would in a few short months confront his own mortality. In late March 2003, President Sawatsky was attending a conference in California; while there he told a friend confidentially that something was wrong because he was having some troubling physical symptoms. A memo from then-provost, Dr. Kim Phipps, to the Messiah College community explains the situation: "On Monday, March 24, 2003, President Sawatsky returned to Pennsylvania following a meeting with the Christian College Consortium presidents.

While on the trip he began to experience discomfort in his neck, and so on returning he met with his family physician on Tuesday morning. The physician scheduled additional tests and examinations by a specialist for Wednesday morning. These exams indicated the diagnosis of a serious condition that must be treated immediately. President Sawatsky will undergo surgery on Monday, March 31, 2003 to remove a brain tumor."

The surgery (which was actually a week later on April 7) at Johns Hopkins Hospital in Baltimore went well, but the surgery also confirmed the diagnosis of a very serious problem. On April 10, the president sent a message to all employees and students: "Today my family and I are full of gratitude. Thanks be to God and to an excellent surgical team that my surgery seems to have gone well, and I am resting comfortably at home with more care than anyone deserves. I have no doubt that your prayers were answered. I literally felt enveloped by love and compassion, especially as I awoke from my sedation." Always having a hopeful outlook on life, Sawatsky nonetheless did not deny the seriousness of the situation. "We have begun what is likely to be a long journey with this cancer in my brain," he wrote. "We have already experienced miracles, and we pray for many more." A deeply committed Christian, Sawatsky believed in prayer, but he had no illusions that we always receive what we earnestly desire and pray for. In an address on prayer to the Harrisburg Kiwanis club at their prayer luncheon on May 10, 2001 — two years earlier — he had said, "Prayer is very central to who I am as a Christian, not least as a Christian leader." But he also believed, as he said, that prayer "doesn't come with guarantees. Even righteous people get sick and die. . . . Prayer can be answered even if no healing happens. . . . Prayer for me is not a scientific matter to be proven or disproved. . . . Our lives are prayers — they are our response to God for God's goodness to us."

As might be expected, the Messiah College community was strongly affected by this difficult time in the life of their president and the president's family. In turn, the Sawatskys communicated regularly with their friends, who cared deeply and prayed fervently. On April 24, Lorna Sawatsky, speaking for her husband, who was there, and who had prepared the talk, addressed the gathered community at chapel. She acknowledged both the difficulty of the experience and the continuing sense of God's presence: "There have been few times in our lives when we have felt God's presence so literally. Perhaps recognizing our complete helplessness and weakness and our dependency upon God is essential to letting go and allowing God to be fully and completely who God is—a God of love and compassion. A primary way God loves us and cares for us is through other people."

In their chapel address Mrs. Sawatsky acknowledged that "the prognosis is not good," but that the doctor had encouraged her husband to return to work later as he was able, despite the major time and energy commitment in travelling to Baltimore for six weeks of daily radiation treatments. "We will seek to live each day fully and to take one step at a time in this strange journey. We are living in a spirit of hope, confident that God is ever with us and that He cares for His children." Powerfully moved by the health crisis of their beloved president, students rallied to support him and his family with prayer and personal messages.

As would be expected, the president's schedule and his ability to respond to the demands of his position were strongly impacted. In his May report to the Board of Trustees, he acknowledged that "a life threatening illness is preoccupying my thoughts, influencing my work schedule, and potentially challenging my role and future at this great college." Other senior administrators—particularly Provost Kim Phipps—accepted additional shared responsibilities to accommodate the new realities confronting the administration. Although the president struggled to spend some time responding to the needs of his office, increasingly it became apparent that the load was too much to handle. Thus, that fall he requested and was granted a medical leave for 90 days in order to focus his energy on recuperation, and Dr. Phipps accepted additional responsibility in the leadership of the college.

Although there was a measure of recovery, by January President Sawatsky sent a letter to Eunice Steinbrecher, the chair of the Board, saying he needed to retire from his position on June 30, while acknowledging that he had hoped—and earlier planned—to continue as president for some years (no doubt at least until the centennial celebrations at Messiah in 2009–2010). Ever concerned about how his progress—or decline—would affect others, particularly students, he wrote in his letter to the campus, "We want to be very sure that all of you who have prayed for us so faithfully do not read this decision [to resign the presidency] as indicating a loss of hope." But with a voice of realism, he added, "Many people of faith and hope, despite their trust in God and despite being surrounded by prayers, do die of cancer."

Three months later, on April 16, 2004, the president sent another e-mail to all students and employees with a difficult message: "We are now at a new stage in my journey with brain cancer. . . . My tumor has reappeared somewhat larger than the first time." He reported that the initial round of chemotherapy was ineffective and surgeons were proposing a second surgery, a year after his earlier surgery.

Often his messages included a pastoral word, and this sobering letter again expressed his deep faith. "Actually," he wrote, "we refuse to give this cancer charge of our lives. Surely it will continue, as it already has, to influence us profoundly, but ultimately God is in control and will care for us no matter what comes. The abundant life is defined by its quality and not its quantity. In that spirit we seek to live each day as fully and joyfully as we can in spite of the uncertainties we face. We remain deeply grateful for God's active and continuing presence in our lives."

That spirit of hope and joy was also reflected in a writing project that continued to occupy his thinking. Collaborating with his good friend, Douglas (Jake) Jacobsen, Sawatsky was working on a book, *Gracious Christianity: Living the Love We Profess*, which was organized around the eight clauses of the Messiah College Confession of Faith. As Jacobsen describes the process, they would talk "for hours before we would write any of these chapters." Then Jacobsen would write a draft, Sawatsky would scribble notes on the draft, and then they together would revise. A number of readers at the college then read the manuscript, and (in Jacobsen's words) they "just tore it apart." So the authors did a thorough rewriting of the chapters, even continuing after the Sawatskys had moved back to Canada that summer. There is a poignancy in the effort to write this book about some essential qualities of the Christian faith, even as one author is dying of cancer. As Sawatsky had written in 2002 in a Lenten sermon, part of which is quoted in *Gracious Christianity*, "The incarnation means that God in his very own body knew what it meant to be human, to be limited, to be broken-to be with us. . . . We are here because we humbly know we are a broken people and because we thankfully know that God in Jesus was also broken with us and for us." Sawatsky's personal experience of brokenness no doubt contributed to a strongly pastoral tone in *Gracious Christianity*. Not designed for a scholarly audience, the book is characterized by a warm, invitational tone. Facing his own intimate confrontation with mortality, Sawatsky experienced grace and offered a "gracious" view of the Christian faith.

Before the Sawatskys permanently returned home to Canada to live near their three daughters and many friends, Messiah College planned a major celebration evening on June 13, an evening which included many tributes, both from colleagues and from persons in the greater Harrisburg community. The Sawatskys' pleasure in and support of the arts was strongly in evidence with original visual art and music both featured. A bitter-sweet, accolade-filled time, the evening essentially marked the end of Rodney Sawatsky's presidency. The pernicious disease had taken its toll: no longer did the president have a booming voice and a larger-than-life stage presence — but the inner vitality remained. Ever gracious, always elegant, deeply spiritual, Lorna Sawatsky was an integral part of the presidential team, becoming even more public in her role during the illness of her husband.

The Sawatskys returned to Ontario, where they lived quietly among family and friends, experiencing life deeply, and yes, preparing for death. On November 27, his beloved wife Lorna's birthday, Rodney James Sawatsky passed from this life to a new realm of existence. In her moving eulogy, President-elect Kim Phipps concluded with her personal word about her last visit with her friend and mentor. She recalled her anger as she said, "I don't understand how any of this can be part of God's plan for you or for Messiah." After a pause he had responded, "Sickness and death are not part of God's plan, but they are part of this imperfect world. Why should I be spared from the scourge of cancer?" Although he loved life, loved people, loved God, he refused to wallow in self-pity.

Now only several years later, how does one summarize his legacy? A few words, perhaps, though future historians will have much more perspective from which to make assessments. Among many positive achievements one should note his emphasis on excellence: excellence in academics, in athletics, in scholarship, in facilities. Anything worth doing deserved being done well; shoddiness was not worthy of a Christian. Sawatsky also championed an "embracing evangelicalism," a "gracious," hospitable Christian faith, as identified particularly in *Gracious Christianity*: "Graciousness is how we externalize to others the grace we have internalized from God" (p. 18). In his own life he was gracious to others, whether speaking to a leader in the Harrisburg community or meeting a beginning, timid student. His support of the revision of Messiah's mission and identity statements contributed to a greater sense of the historical roots of the college. At the same time he was able to reach out beyond the college. Galen Oakes, chair of the Board for many years, says, "I think the greatest contribution that Dr. Sawatsky made to this college was the tie to the Harrisburg community. . . . He made the college part of mainstream Harrisburg community."

No one can do everything, of course, and sometimes areas of strength can lead to concerns in other areas. The president's emphasis on excellence—a strong theme—sometimes may have led to a neglect of considering the full implications of the financial cost. For example, the added personnel costs of the move to a "university model" with five schools, each with their own dean and other support staff, was probably underestimated rather significantly. Two major new buildings, the Boyer Center and the Larsen Student Union, were wonderful additions to the campus, but the increased debt load for the buildings plus the significantly larger utility expenses were probably not fully considered nor adequately prepared for. Future administrations in all likelihood will need to husband finances more carefully.

The emphasis on being a welcoming ("embracing") community, one which accepts considerable diversity of Christian expression, contributed to greater hospitality and openness. Some, however, both on and off campus, worried that at the same time there might be a weakening of core commitments, a view perhaps exacerbated by the discussion of a potential name change for the college. Clearly, we were more diverse religiously: could the core commitments hold the college together? These questions, of course, are on-going. No president, no matter how dynamic, will provide definitive answers. At best a president can help set a tone, suggest a direction for the future.

Perhaps the most profound impact of President Sawatsky on Messiah College came from his weakness in body and his wonderful strength of spirit through the last 18 months of his life. As Kim Phipps said in her eulogy, "In my judgment, one of the most significant contributions Rod made to Messiah, to the broader community of Christian higher education, and to me personally was his consistent teaching and modeling of the gospel as a faith-filled hope. . . . [He] not only preached that message, but also lived his life rooted in a promise of hope." Perhaps more important than his focus on "excellence," more central, even, than his emphasis on an "embracing" faith, was his emphasis on the hope in Christ which alone can sustain life.

Chapter 9

External Programs

Extending the Academic Table

In his inaugural address in 1994, President Rodney Sawatsky spoke about the need to reach beyond the local and parochial: "The bridge-building metaphor is very appropriate to Messiah's roots in the Anabaptist, pietist, and holiness [Wesleyan] traditions. Christian faith for all these communities includes reaching out to our neighbors in mission and service. . . . Christian college education . . . is by definition interracial, interethnic, and international in scope and purpose." Messiah College was from its inception in 1909 as "Messiah Bible School and Missionary Training Home" conceived as an institution where young people would be schooled for missions and service. Education, although regarded with suspicion by some church leaders, was intended, as the original charter stated, "to educate men and women for home and mission or evangelistic work; for . . . Christian spiritual training . . . and to give men and women an opportunity of preparing themselves in secular studies for future occupations, especially for religious work."

Deeply rooted within the Anabaptist tradition is an ethic of service, of taking seriously Christ's mandate to care for the needs of the poor, the outsiders, the powerless. In his gospel, Matthew quotes Jesus' word on judgment day, a dividing of "sheep" from "goats" on the basis of feeding the poor, giving water to the thirsty, clothing the naked, caring for the sick, visiting those imprisoned; that instruction was understood by Anabaptists as being normative for the believer. And within the Wesleyan tradition there was in the nineteenth-century a strong emphasis on social reform with a particular commitment to the abolition of slavery and to the improvement of conditions in prisons. Although the impact of Wesleyanism on the Brethren in Christ denomination varied somewhat depending on geographical region, the Wesleyan impulse to change may have moderated a more separatistic strain in Anabaptism. Again quoting Sawatsky's inaugural address, "The Brethren in Christ who founded Messiah College . . . [sought] to foster . . . a holistic vision of the Christian personality and of the Christian church."

In short, it's fair to say that the "new" mission statement of the college, adopted in 1997, was not a deviation from the heritage of the college and her founding denomination, but a fresh "revisioning" of that tradition: "Our mission is to educate men and women toward maturity of intellect, character, and Christian faith in preparation for lives of service, leadership, and reconciliation in church and society." As we have seen in earlier chapters, this service impulse was reflected in establishing an urban campus in north Philadelphia and later in supporting the development of a baccalaureate degree program in East Africa, both rather surprising efforts for a small Christian college located in a tiny village in south-central Pennsylvania. In other less public ways the ethic of service was deeply ingrained in the DNA of Messiah College in various ministries in the local community, in services ranging from tutorials to income tax preparation to ministry in nursing homes to assisting with refugee services.

Thus the developing emphasis on what was nationally being called "service-learning" was more a movement to incorporate service within the curriculum itself rather than going in a new direction. Dean Harold Heie was keen on placing more curricular emphasis on service, and in the summer of 1992 he, with a team of four faculty members, attended a summer seminar on service-learning. Upon their return they worked to develop a plan which would incorporate service-learning across the curriculum. One result was the offering of a two-course sequence, Studies in Service-Learning I and II, with the first course being offered each spring to prepare students to engage in a summer service project. Students then served in a variety of locations, stateside and abroad, with many receiving some stipends or grants to assist with fall tuition payments. Following the summer service activity, students were expected to enroll in the second semester course (offered in the fall), with this course primarily focused on students' reflecting on and evaluating their experiences. Among other topics, students considered "the distinction between individual and systemic change relative to the communities served." The relationship between addressing social needs one person at a time or focusing energy on effecting systemic change is, of course, not an issue that admits to easy resolution.

To give formal, structured leadership to the developing service-learning program, Vern Blackwood was appointed in 1991 and was allocated a half-time academic load as the first director. Then in 1994 Dr. John Eby was recruited for a faculty position in sociology and the directorship of the service-learning program. Eby brought a wealth of background in voluntary service leadership, academic administration, and international experience to the position. In Eby's view, service-learning has three essential components: (1) authentic service; (2) a solid academic component; and (3) significant formal reflection. For any academic program to thrive, faculty must be convinced of the integrity and merit of the work, and Eby, with the capable assistance of others such as Cindy Blount, worked to bring service-learning to a new level of academic recognition.

The program developed significantly under strong leadership, and in 1998 service-learning was given a much more visible space on campus with a home — which serves both the curricular and cocur-ricular areas — in the ideally located and newly renovated Hostetler house in the center of the campus. Dedicated in November 1998, the house was appropriately christened the "Agape Center," a name chosen from several possibilities and finally selected by Dean Dorothy Gish. "Agape," of course, suggests the self-giving service motivation of Jesus, the Messiah, and is a highly visible reminder of the central impetus for service on a Christian college campus.

To increase awareness of service-learning and to help solidify the academic component, Eby organized a national Service-Learning Conference for Faith-Based Colleges and Universities. The first con-ference met in June 2000 and featured several nationally recognized authorities in the field, as well as offering a number of seminars and workshops. The biannual conferences grew in scope reaching a peak attendance in 2004 with nearly 150 faculty members from 70 colleges and universities participating.

In Eby's view the Agape Center needed a full-time director; but when the college chose not to make the directorship a faculty position, Janell J. Patton, an English-major alumna from Messiah, was recruited as the director in 2002. A high-energy leader, Patton moved to integrate service-learning more fully into the curriculum. Through her urging, a Service-Learning Faculty Dialogues Project was inaugurated in 2003. Goals for the project involved efforts to broaden the conversation (by including faculty from each of the five schools), to enlarge the definitions of service-learning, to support those faculty who were incorporating service into their courses, and to determine how the Agape Center could support the five schools in further developing service-learning.

One major outcome of the Dialogues Project was the bringing of a series of proposals to the Community of Educators Senate in April 2007 to formalize service-learning at Messiah. The Senate voted to approve the creation of a standing COE Service-Learning Committee, which would include representatives from each school, in addition to several administrators. This committee would serve to give on-going visibility and direction to service-learning at Messiah. Service-learning is one important way of extending the academic table, of inviting a broader understanding of the relationship of academics, service, and (at a Christian college) Christian vocation. As Evie Telfer, the associate college pastor, says, "Stepping out of our ordinary time and space to travel across town or around the world opens us to see in new ways and be changed. This is what education is about — not a head full of knowledge, but new eyes with which to see the world, to make new connections, and to imagine new possibilities. . . . This is why we do service-learning at Messiah — because changed people change the world." The successes of the program have been recognized by others: in 2007 Messiah received the highest distinction from the U.S. Department of Education by being placed on the President's Honor Role for Community Service; and in 2008 the college was given a special classification by the Carnegie Foundation as a Community Engaged Institution.

Over the years the Agape Center has continued to develop and expand its ministries into other service areas which are not part of the service-learning program. Rebecca Owen, who was the local community director until April 2009, has coordinated three major "Service Plunge Days" each year, days which include a wide range of activities. Each fall all first-year students are involved in the "Into the Streets" program, part of a nationally recognized effort by many colleges. At Messiah this program is connected to the academic curriculum in that the groups serving together are sections of the First Year Seminar, often accompanied by their instructor for the course. The service experience helps to form bonds between students and instructor. The hope, of course, is that this one-day introduction will lead to more extended community service. As Dr. Mary Ann Hollinger says, "Into the Streets . . . helps students . . . to define . . . the boundaries of their college experience well beyond the boundaries of the Grantham campus." Indeed, throughout the year in 2008, 768 students were a part of outreach teams, many of whom went weekly to places such as Big Brothers, Big Sisters; Habitat for Humanity; Saint Barnabas Center for Ministry; and many others.

Each spring a service day has now been incorporated into the academic schedule with all classes cancelled and students, staff, and faculty encouraged to participate. First-year students in the core course, Created and Called for Community, are required to participate, and the experience is the basis of subsequent class discussion. The largest single event of the day is "Special Olympics," which in 2008 involved 516 student "buddies" and 128 employees. That same year, the twentieth year of participation, Messiah was honored as the 2008 Olympics School of the Year in Pennsylvania. An even larger number of participants served off campus in a wide range of projects from clean-up in inner-city Harrisburg to stocking food pantries to construction work. Although the service is encouraging to community partners, participants often gain as much as they share.

The third one-day "service plunge," the Dr. Martin Luther King Community Engagement Day, has not been as successfully incorporated into college programming. There are probably several factors that affect participation, perhaps most significantly the date in winter, which is not as inviting as the spring service date. And the King *holiday* is seen *as* a holiday with many students and faculty travelling off campus, though recently there has been an increasing level of involvement. The goals of greater awareness; deeper understanding; and a life-time commitment to peace, justice, and reconciliation are certainly worthy, though the "Engagement Day" itself has had more limited success than one would desire at the Grantham campus, and one hopes to see participation continue to grow. At the much smaller Philadelphia campus, however, 32 students and three faculty members joined their neighbors in 2008 to clean up Fisher Park, which is located several blocks from the campus.

Another significant component of the Agape Center is the Office of National and International Service and Mission, which is coordinated by Matt Hunter. A number of students participate in one or more of three annual service opportunities during the fall, January, or spring-term breaks with 203 total participants in 2008. The largest of these is the spring-term service with 94 students involved in ministries in eight states from Mississippi to Illinois to New York. Service and mission partners included, among others, Koinonia Farms (GA), The Pittsburgh Project, and Remote Area Medical (VA). Also during the spring break four groups travelled to international service sites in Northern Ireland, El Salvador, Dominican Republic, and Mexico for eight days. One can reasonably ask whether the significant expense for these short-term (usually eight days) service and mission assignments can be justified. Chad Frey, the full-time Agape Center director, who himself has gone on at least seven trips to Northern Ireland, says, "I've seen personally the impact that a short-term trip has had on students and how it has really reshaped the way that they think about reconciliation. [For example] many times in the States we think about reconciliation in terms of black and white [racial] issues . . . But [in] Ireland, it's a theological kind of reconciliation." Frey argues further, "There's . . . a developmental model we're trying to cultivate. And as a result . . . some students may go into overseas or international service for years." In fact, Frey notes, a Messiah graduate has moved to Northern Ireland and become the youth pastor at a church where Messiah College teams have served for eight years. As one might expect, during the summer students are typically engaged for longer terms, usually from a minimum of two weeks to over a month. In 2008, for example, several students and alumni spent 35 days teaching English in China.

Whether stateside or international, relatively short-term or for longer periods, the mission and service goals embody important distinctives of college identity. Frey acknowledges that Agape Center "distinctives are really taken from [President Kim Phipps]: 'excellence, hospitality, engagement, and hope.' . . . My vision for the Center is that we're able to embody those distinctives in an experience or pedagogy that really meaningfully contributes to the church and society."

Other aspects of "extending the table" in the Agape Center include World Christian Fellowship (WCF) and Human Rights Awareness (HRA), both of which work primarily on campus but often focus on issues of national and international concern. A major effort of WCF is the organizing of an annual week-long missions conference in November. In 2008 WCF arranged for and hosted 40 representatives (from 25 different organizations) who set up display tables in the Howe Atrium in Boyer Hall and met with many students in both formal settings (such as chapels or classes) and informal times in the dining hall or residence hall. Other events sponsored by WCF include "Salt and Light Chapels" and "Ignite Prayer Conference," the latter a weekend prayer emphasis which brought together representatives from a number of area schools. Human Rights Awareness, as the name suggests, advocates for justice issues in many parts of the world. HRA includes four student organizations: Amnesty International, International Justice Mission, Children's Issues, and World Diseases. Through meetings, displays, e-mails, and fund-raisers these organizations — and others — attempt to educate and persuade wider involvement in a world of need beyond the campus. Issues of peace, justice and reconciliation are clearly linked to the historic identity of Messiah College, especially in her Anabaptist roots.

Cooperating with the Agape Center on certain projects, though under its own structure and management, is the Collaboratory, which is housed in the School of Mathematics, Engineering, and Business. The Collaboratory developed from an earlier name, the Greek phrase, *Dokimoi Ergatai*, which means "approved workers," and is taken from the Apostle Paul's letter to Timothy, "Do your best to present yourself to God as one approved, a worker who does not need to be ashamed and who correctly handles the word of truth" (II Tim. 2:15 TNIV). In brief, the Collaboratory is a broad organization of service projects which are integrated with the academic curriculum and seek to apply academic learnings with practical applications in a wide variety of settings. According to Dr. David Vader, professor of engineering and since 2004 half-time director of the Collaboratory, the more recent name is a word first used by computer scientist William Wulf, who coined the idea of a "collaboration laboratory." At Messiah the collaboration with other disciplines has become much more extensive as the program has developed.

The initial impetus had its "genesis" when Dr. Donald Pratt suggested that his Introduction to Engineering classes might consider the possibility of building — and perhaps eventually racing — a solar car. The prospect seemed daunting, but engineers (and engineering students) relish confronting challenging opportunities. By January 1994, 40 students joined Pratt in working on a proposal for Sunrayce '95, as the national project was called. The competition — the third national collegiate solar car race — included highly recognized engineering programs such as the University of Michigan (which had won the first two races), MIT, the University of Pennsylvania, Yale, and many others. Newly appointed in July 1994, President Sawatsky soon became an enthusiastic supporter and promoter of the project, obviously relishing both the challenge and the potential publicity which the solar car could bring to Messiah College. The engineering program had only recently received full ABET accreditation, and the budget for the new car was a modest $60,000, minuscule compared with Michigan's $2 million. The odds were formidable. But Pratt and the students persevered; innovative designs sometimes failed, sometimes succeeded; and after much concentrated effort the "Genesis" car was completed and in the summer of 1995 entered the race at Indianapolis. But problems continued, both during the qualifying heats and during the race itself. The tough persistence in responding to multiple technical difficulties impressed others, and the Genesis team received the "Missouri Mule Award" for teamwork and determination. The team finished 22nd out of 38 competitors, as well as winning the Innovation Award for the design of the solar

Messiah College's entry in the 1999 Sunraycc.

array. A young engineering program and a small Christian college
were in the news.

The success encouraged the student engineers and their advisor,
Don Pratt, to redouble their efforts in preparation for Sunrayce '97.
The nine-day race from Indianapolis to Colorado Springs led to an
exciting 12th place finish in a field of 36 competitors. Again the
team won the Renaissance Innovation Award, usually given to one of
the larger, more recognized engineering programs. And also, as were
the first Genesis "racers," the team was welcomed home to Grantham
with a celebratory rally.

In the following year Harsco Corporation under CEO Derek
Hathaway entered a partnership with Messiah College to support the
next model solar car. Making the announcement in September 1998,
President Sawatsky said, "In today's competitive, changing world,
there are many times when your success depends on finding the
right partner, working together with others who share your same
goals and values." The support of Harsco Corporation included not
only financial support but the opportunity for students to learn

from other professionals in the field. After successfully designing and building a new car — this one with four wheels, as now required for greater safety, rather than the three of earlier models — the Genesis '99 team finished seventh among 29 competitors, its first top-ten finish, though inclement weather slowed all contestants.

As it turned out, the 1999 competition from Washington, D.C. to Orlando, Florida was the last "Sunrayce." The 2001 event, appropriately named the "American Solar Challenge," covered the most difficult course yet, beginning in Chicago and finishing in Los Angeles and featuring major "challenges," including hot desert temperatures and dangerous mountain terrain. Racing more than 2,300 miles, the Genesis team placed 13th in a field of 30 competitors. For the third time a Genesis team won the top technical honor with the Technical Innovation Award. But the dangers that the race had posed raised questions about the safety of the race format. As Don Pratt notes, "With student lives at risk . . . [we] decided that the team would no longer build and race solar cars." With this era now ended, the Genesis team has turned to building solar boats, no doubt a worthwhile effort, but one which has generated much less publicity.

The Genesis solar cars were possible because several faculty, particularly Donald Pratt, and later, Timothy Whitmoyer, contributed untold volunteer hours; and students, similarly, committed themselves far beyond any ordinary expectations for out-of-class work. In addition to learning engineering theory and practice, they experienced the importance of team-work and commitment to common goals. And the cooperative work included disciplines besides engineering: the '99 Genesis team, for example, included majors as diverse as theatre and business, as well as mechanical engineers. Working to tap into the enormous resources of the sun's energy contributed to focusing attention on the potential of solar power for energy needs in many different areas, whether or not solar cars would ever become practical for general use. "Genesis" clearly extended the academic table.

But as interesting and publicity inspiring as the Genesis project had been, there were other possibilities for service which perhaps more directly connected to the college's identity and desire for service. Speaking of his coming to Messiah in the fall of 1993, David

Vader says, "I came here [to the college] with this vague notion that engineering work should be more than just about paying the bills, the mortgage, and buying the groceries . . . , that Christians in engineering should be involved in service." Thus about the same time that the Genesis project was germinating, other possibilities for the engineering program were developing. Several faculty went to Charlotte, NC, to talk with representatives of Serving in Mission (SIM); and with their encouragement, that summer Vader, John Eby, and Cindy Blount (who was director of student outreach), and two students went to West Africa for a site visit. From that visit came an invitation to build a solar electric power plant to supply electricity for a medical clinic. Vader's initial invitations to students to work on the project were unsuccessful, but finally two students, David Owen and Greg Holmes, joined him, as well as engineering staff member John Meyer. So, as Vader describes the process, "We designed that power plant here, worked for over a year on that, put a team together, travelled back to Burkina Faso . . . and installed that system. And the night before we installed our system, they delivered some babies by flashlight, and the next night they actually had electric lights for nighttime delivery!"

Thus began a long-term relationship with the Handicap Center in the village of Mahadaga in Burkina Faso. As alumnus Joseph Longenecker describes the beginning efforts, as the first solar implementation team was installing the electrical system, "They observed needs for water pumping and irrigation at the new Handicap Center. . . . Two years later another implementation team returned to do pump and irrigation work. This team observed the hand-powered tricycles used by many of the handicapped people and decided to improve them. The *Dokimoi Ergatai* organization was started for the Mahadaga teams (solar, tricycle, pump) to bring coherence to the partnership with the Handicap Center." Among those who have served there extensively are Matt and Julie Walsh and Dale and Florence Johnson, each of whom put in untold hours of work in the early years of the solar, pump, and tricycle projects. And these couples are now serving in long-term missions in Mahadaga, continuing among other things, as Longenecker notes, "to advance the work of the Collaboratory there."

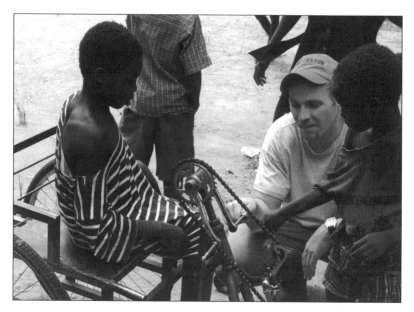

John Meyer, mechanical engineering technician at Messiah, demonstrates to children in Burkina Faso, West Africa, how to use a hand-powered tricycle.

Soon a number of projects developed, including additional solar power projects, but also expanding to work in other areas such as clearing land mines in Nicaragua, a project which Don Pratt developed. Eventually, Vader says, "We began to work in multiple countries, and we realized [that] engineers can't do engineering on their own. We need people who know how to write and tell the story and take videos . . . , [who] can do accounting . . . [and] who know about leadership."

When Dr. Ray Norman became dean of the School of Mathematics, Engineering, and Business in 2002, he was impressed with the quality of the faculty and the quantity of work being accomplished: "I found a lot of energetic people doing a lot of different things — solar cars, land mines in Nicaragua . . . urban gardens in Harrisburg. But there wasn't any cohesion." Further, he says, there was significant faculty burnout because the various activities were not integrated into the curriculum and thus faculty were not receiving academic load credit for their major responsibilities and time commitments outside the classroom. To bring various activities together, Norman,

Messiah student Elizabeth Ball works with a woman in Choma, Zambia, demonstrating how to make paper from harvested local grasses.

Pratt, and Vader in 2003 proposed a center, which became the Collaboratory, initiated in the Engineering Department but soon to have a school-wide focus—and eventually to involve other disciplines and departments outside the school.

In subsequent years the faculty and students of the Collaboratory have drafted and affirmed core purpose statements. Defining their identity, they say, "We aspire to fulfill Biblical mandates to foster justice, empower the poor, reconcile adversaries, and care for the earth in the context of academic engagement in the disciplines of our school." The mission statement includes the goal of partnering with others, serving the disadvantaged, and developing "our members' abilities and vocational vision for lifelong servant-leadership, and [fostering] the courage to act on convictions." As Deborah Tepley, the full-time manager of the Collaboratory, says, "Dr. Vader . . . wanted [the program] to be holistic . . . to incorporate all aspects of our students' and members' lives, and to not just be doing work to serve the poor, but also to really engage, as Christian disciples, how does this intersect with my faith . . . what does it mean to be a disciple . . .

[how can I] critically analyze the American Dream . . . [how should I] live my life . . . [after] college?"

To help accomplish those ambitious, wide-ranging goals, students and faculty meet regularly for 40 minutes each Monday evening with over 100 students, faculty, and staff advisors attending regularly. The Monday night meetings provide a regular venue for presentations—followed by later discussion—of core values and key goals of the Collaboratory. Important to the work is the model of shared leadership through which, as Tepley says, "Every project and team and group has both a student leader and either faculty, staff, or community advisor, who work together in tandem." Sharing leadership means that student leaders have the privilege and responsibility to make decisions and even the authority "to make mistakes and fail."

Much of the design work, planning, and experimentation is done on campus, though the most visible aspects are the various trips to international sites during the January term or summer. In the summer of 2008—an unusually busy summer—seven teams went to many different locations, among them Burkina Faso, Zambia, the Congo, Mali, and Honduras, as well as to Educational Concerns for Hunger Organization (*ECHO*), in Fort Myers, Florida. Their projects ranged widely from working to develop better hand- and electric-powered tricycles in Burkina Faso, to exploring biodiesel production in the Congo, to building new latrines in Mali, to continuing water purification systems in Honduras. Often the work is done in collaboration with other agencies already engaged in community development. In Mali, for example, the Collaboratory is working on a three-year project funded through World Vision to help provide potable (drinking) water, as well as sustainable water supplies for irrigation.

As we have noted earlier, a long-term relationship has been fostered with the small village of Mahadaga in Burkina Faso with multiple on-going Collaboratory projects. In January 2009 a team of 13 students and faculty—one of the largest and most diverse ever—were engaged with six different projects, including math and literacy education at the local center, which enrolls approximately 200 students with physical and learning disabilities. Under the guidance of Dr. Angela Hare, the math team contributed to teaching mathematical concepts with the use of various games. In a previous year they wrote and distributed a French counting book. A math education alumna, Katie Patton, writes, "in my classes [at Messiah] we talk about foundational math concepts. . . . In the Collaboratory, we are developing tools that emphasize these basic principles to children so that they will have a strong mathematical understanding that extends to their lives outside the classroom."

The literacy team created a book using photographs of life in the village and then inviting young students to create the story that went with the pictures. Because of using local scenes in their stories, the children were able to see themselves in new ways. Dr. Anita Voelker, associate professor of education, says, "We didn't do anything amazing. . . . Being salt and light doesn't mean you're changing the world; it means you're changing that moment of the world."

Learning, of course, is multi-directional, and the Collaboratory regularly emphasizes the value and importance of learning from others. Reflecting on her service trip to Burkina Faso in January 2009, biology major alumna Julie Longenecker writes that the trip "was one of my most valuable college experiences. It showed me what life is like for some of the poorest people in the world, but at the same time it showed me a beautiful culture that survives, and indeed thrives, in poverty. This experience was important to me because it gave faces to the idea of 'poor people,' and it showed me that they are not necessarily sad faces. . . . Although we went with the purpose of serving, we were served just as much by our Burkinabe brothers and sisters." Her perception that in serving others, we ourselves are also served, embodies a mature grasp of the goal of Messiah College to educate men and women for lives of service, leadership, and reconciliation.

Messiah College, of course, is not a mission agency, nor a non-governmental organization (NGO), nor a church. The college is an *educational* institution, and the Collaboratory exists, in significant part, to expand the definition of education. One visible on-campus application of educational theory was the development and installation in 2008 of 16 solar panels in four arrays. Located near the Frey Building, the solar panels were in the planning and production

The Collaboratory's Solar Scholars team poses in front of the newly installed solar electric power generation facility at Messiah College.

process for almost three years before installation. A part of the Clifford L. Jones Solar Scholars Pavilion, the panels do provide three kilowatts of electrical energy, but the major purpose of the installation is educational, both for student groups who visit the campus as well as for Messiah College itself. Educating for more sustainable energy use must become a greater part of Christian stewardship, and this on-campus project offers one visible — albeit modest — contribution. As David Vader says, "We don't simply do. We do and we reflect on what we are doing. We want to make sure we don't have the experience and miss the message. . . . [We want students] to have an opportunity to engage these fundamental questions of what does it mean to be a steward for God . . . over my potential in the material market place."

This understanding of our responsibilities is not easily accepted in a culture that values material goods so highly. "The shortage," Vader says, "is not projects [for the Collaboratory]. We have many people banging on our door now. The shortage is not even money. . . . It is people. . . . There are times when I have a project . . . [and we need] someone here to care enough to invest some of their time and energy and talent to help meet a need, and we cannot find students or faculty to work on that; and it breaks my heart. But we have also had many students who have been transformed." The program has gone well beyond the Engineering Department and includes, among others, computer science, mathematics, business information systems, education, communication, marketing, international business, and Christian ministries. Thus despite limitations and occasional frustrations, hospitality continues to be extended: the table is being enlarged.

Another important area of extending the academic table is off-campus study. In the early 1970s Messiah College in conjunction with Brethren Colleges Abroad (BCA) offered study opportunities in England, France, Spain, and Germany. Modern language majors were required to study abroad for at least a semester, and they often enrolled for two semesters. Although the program in England was open to other majors, the most common participants were English majors who wanted to study and travel in the United Kingdom. Gradually the international studies program grew, and by 1994 a focal point was needed for the gathering and disseminating of information and the "EpiCenter" (Experiential Programs Information Center) was formed. But in addition to her EpiCenter responsibilities, the new part-time director, Wendy Lippert, also provided support service for the internship center and the service-learning program. That first year, Lippert reports, there were 32 students in semester-long study-abroad programs. By 2005–2006, a decade later, 241 students studied abroad for at least a semester. The exact number varies from year to year, but the strong possibility of international study has become a much greater part of student culture at Messiah. Students can study at approved universities and study centers from Australia to China, from Russia to Egypt, from Ireland to Thailand, from Belize to Greece, as well as many other sites, including the earlier BCA programs. Recognized by the Institute for International Education, Messiah ranked 11th in the nation among baccalaureate colleges for sending students abroad. Their 2008 report indicated that 61 percent of Messiah's students had participated in credit-bearing international programs.

The EpiCenter provides both pre-departure orientation and re-entry programming. In preparation for international study, students are offered sessions in health and safety issues, cross-cultural adjustment and communication, and reflections on faith develop-ment while studying abroad. Upon return from living and studying in an unfamiliar culture, students are offered three additional opportunities to reflect on their experiences with sessions on reverse culture shock, civic engagement, and career development.

Alongside the numerous semester-long international programs are three-week January- and May-term cross-cultural courses through which students can fulfill one semester of their language requirement. Taught by Messiah faculty, these courses range widely: in the 2008–2009 academic year, courses were offered in Costa Rica, South Africa, Ghana, Germany, Zambia, Turkey, Albania, Thailand, New Zealand, Mexico, Greece, and the French West Indies. A ten-week study/travel program in Europe and Russia is offered each summer as part of the International Business Institute. This summer IBI program is complemented by a required experience in a developing country. Other international credit-bearing courses include intern-ships and practica in places as diverse as England and Zambia.

Off-campus internships and other professional development experiences are also available in the United States, most, of course, being in Pennsylvania, with many being in the greater Harrisburg area. The Internship Center, under director Mike True, actively seeks to link students' academic interests with appropriate work sites. The 2008–2009 internship profile lists 188 student placements through-out the year, with students representing 35 academic majors. These students worked at 157 internship sites in a wide range of business, medical, and educational professions. In addition to options in central Pennsylvania, nearly 1,000 possible work sites are now available through the Messiah College Philadelphia campus as arranged by Deborah Petersen, the Philadelphia coordinator. Thus in the last five years approximately 100 students have participated in an internship, with most of the work focused in North Philadelphia or center city. Internships there range from small community-based nonprofit organizations to government offices to some international businesses. Whether initiated at Grantham or Philadelphia, all

Messiah's Harrisburg Institute is located a few blocks from
the state capitol building.

internships require students to write reflective essays on their work
experience. As past dean of external programs, Mary Ann Hollinger,
says, "One of the challenges ... in experiential learning pedagogy ...
[is to provide opportunity] for students to make meaning of their
experience and consider what its long-term impact would be on
their lives."

Another recently expanded opportunity for students' educational
growth, especially in urban studies, is the Harrisburg Institute,
located only a few blocks from the state capitol and a dozen miles
from the Grantham campus. To a significant degree the Institute is
the result of the passion of the former dean of the School of Education and Social Science, Dr. Joseph Jones, who told Messiah's
president and provost that he "would only be interested in coming to
the college if they [the administrators] were interested in being more
engaged [as a college] in Harrisburg." Both president and provost
were keenly interested in developing more effective connections with
the Harrisburg community, thus making Jones an excellent fit for the
position. After his coming to Messiah, Jones explored with faculty in
his school to see "how we could actually enhance our scholarship and

engage our students more actively in researching community service, [and being involved in] experiential learning. . . . Harrisburg Institute . . . emerged out of that kind of collaboration [between college, local communities, and agencies]."

The vision of developing an institute which could contribute to serving the local urban community, while at the same time providing educational opportunities, led to finding dedicated space in Harrisburg. With the collaborative efforts of the Harristown Development Corporation and the R.S. Mowery Construction Company, the college was able to renovate an older laboratory building. The newly renovated building provides residential facilities for 25 students and one professional, as well as providing office and classroom space.

The first director, Dr. David Hietala, was a specialist in urban studies who, in addition to his work as administrator, taught one course each semester. Messiah College has written grant proposals through the Institute; and from the office of Juvenile Justice and Delinquency Prevention Program in Washington, the college received two grants for a total of $888,000. In the fall of 2007 the college received an additional grant of $630,000. One of the major projects has been the youth empowerment initiative, which has focused on alternative middle school and high school educational programs. According to Hietala, three community groups involved with William Penn School, a school for students who were experiencing some academic difficulties, invited Messiah College students to assist in various artistic performances, which as Hietala says, were to engage William Penn students, increase their school attendance, and enhance their academic performance. The program was largely successful, and the school changed from a focus on remedial instruction to "looking at the arts as a window to student engagement and ultimately student achievement."

Another successful project has been headed by two English professors at Messiah, Dr. Helen Walker and Dr. Jean Corey, who have been involved with some entrepreneurship classes at William Penn. Kazuri beads from Kenya are shaped into beautiful jewelry by William Penn students working alongside Messiah students. The proceeds from the sale of the jewelry are returned to Kenya, where the money is used to care for babies orphaned by poverty and HIV/AIDS. The project is committed to developing partnerships, locally and globally. Organizers of the project cite the Swahili proverb, "If you want to go fast, go alone; if you want to go far, go together." The partnership of young Harrisburg students, some of whom are already young mothers themselves, with Messiah College students and faculty, linked with a worthy international project, fosters local cooperation and global awareness. One hopes that participants will indeed go far, together.

Another way that Messiah College is extending the academic table is through the Hoverter Course in the Humanities, which is housed in the Center for Public Humanities. A dream of Dr. Joseph Huffman, past dean of the School of the Humanities, the Center for Public Humanities sponsors a number of programs, including the Hoverter course, which is designed for mature students who have received a high school diploma or a G.E.D. certificate, but who have not taken college courses. The Hoverter Course offers instruction in five humanities disciplines — writing, communication, critical/ethical thinking, creative arts, and history/civics — in seven months with twice-weekly classes. Upon the successful completion of the course of study, students receive three academic credits. For the first two years, classes were held in rural Perry County; in the 2008–2009 academic year, classes were moved to the Harrisburg Institute. Through the generosity of the Hoverter Foundation, the course is offered free and includes books and other reading materials, as well as providing money for transportation and childcare expenses, if needed to make possible the completion of the course.

In 2009 eleven students completed the program and celebrated their achievement with a ceremony in the International House in Harrisburg. Graduating students praised the faculty and the program. One graduate, Michael Grant, said, "I had lacked the confidence to pursue my education, but this course has opened doors for me. What a blessing and learning experience!" Reflecting on the recently opened door, Diane DeRosa said, "I can look forward to a new beginning that I never thought possible. I have learned that I am capable. I am creative, and I'm ready to start a new life." The number of students may not be large, but the growth, the enlarged vision, the dreams, of these students who have completed this interdisciplinary humanities course must be encouraging to Joseph Huffman, who fostered the initial idea, and to the Hoverter Foundation, who funded it. One hopes that in fact students will be encouraged to continue their growth in succeeding years in various types of educational opportunities. And not only the students have been changed; faculty who have participated in the teaching of these courses have often found themselves challenged and invigorated as they have seen the course materials through new eyes, eyes which have differed from those in the "regular" Messiah classroom.

Perhaps the door has just been nudged slightly ajar for these Hoverter course graduates. For the four-year Messiah graduate one hopes for doors swung wide open, for new paths leading to lives of service. And, indeed, the Messiah College Career Center is dedicated to helping baccalaureate students make the transition to the next phase of life, whether that be graduate school or the beginnings of a new career. The Career Center for Vocation and Development — to cite the full name — has identified its mission "to assist students in discerning and pursuing meaningful careers which demonstrate a mature integration of faith and lifelong learning." The development model which the Career Center has adopted gives attention to each year of the student's academic program, beginning far earlier than the "placement office" view of earlier expectations. Already in the early 1980s Dr. Donna Dentler, the director of Career Development and Cooperative Education, was working to bring a more holistic and developmental approach to the program. A person with enormous energy, Dentler brought a new level of professionalism to the office. As Deborah Reid Snyder says of her mentor and predecessor, "Donna [Dentler] was a person who had a lot of vision for career development . . . and [the passion] to make it happen here at Messiah."

The philosophy of the Career Center grew and matured during those earlier years. Deborah Snyder, who began working at Messiah in the area of career development in 1981, later becoming the director in the mid-1990s, speaks of her desire that students "think much more holistically about who they are in relation to the church and in relation to God. . . . Vocation is about [the] . . . calling to follow Christ. . . . The way we follow him is through various roles of vocation, and one of those roles happens to be work.... [Other roles] you play [are] in your family, in your church, in your community."

Obviously, the Career Center still assists students in practical matters such as providing various assessment tools for undergraduates, critiquing resumes and cover letters for upperclassmen, and maintaining an active database of job postings. The Center sponsors a variety of career-related programs including an annual Career and Graduate School Expo, Teacher Recruitment Day, Accounting Night, Nursing Fair, and other employment opportunities. The Center also cooperates with the Office of Alumni and Parent Relations to set up contacts with alumni in a wide variety of service and business professions.

Some videos and transcripts of conversations with alumni working in a range of occupations can be accessed on-line. Cindy Smedley, who lives in Uganda and works in education, offers this word: "I think the over-arching advice, if you gave me just one minute to talk to students . . . would [be to] tell them to remember that life is bigger than themselves, that their vocation can be used for a lot of good in God's kingdom on earth, and sometimes it takes being intentional to think about that.... Take time to really consider your faith and how it informs your vocation." Reflecting on his time as a student at Messiah, Ryan Keith says, "I think at Messiah there is a huge emphasis on the integration of your faith with your vocation, and you don't really see it.... But in those moments when you see God right there in front of you . . . you really need to seize [the moment and the opportunity] because God will take care of it."

Without directly citing the Anabaptist emphases on service and reconciliation, both comments suggest that some of the ideals taught and modeled at the college have been incarnated in their life and practice. Through the many and varied outreach functions of Messiah College — the Agape Center, the Collaboratory, the Harrisburg Institute, the Epicenter, the Center for Public Humanities, the Career Center, and more — the academic table continues to be extended and enlarged. Messiah College invests significant resources of time, personnel, and money in these expanding opportunities. In short, the college's fundamental ideals continue to provide vision for current practice.

Chapter 10

Academics and More
Campus Life Outside the Classroom

As we have seen earlier, during President Sawatsky's tenure, Messiah College adopted, as a succinct statement of her core mission, the goal "to educate men and women toward maturity of intellect, character, and Christian faith in preparation for lives of service, leadership, and reconciliation in church and society." To educate "toward maturity of intellect" clearly implies the importance of the academic enterprise. Without that academic core — the life of the mind—an institution of higher education would have scant reason to exist. At the same time, much that is important in holistic education takes place outside the classroom. Over time the language at Messiah has shifted from "extra-curricular" activities to "cocurricular" activities with a conscious effort to forge an approach to education that blends life in and out of the classroom.

At Messiah College many people have supported this emphasis on holistic education, but Jay Barnes, dean and vice-president of student development (1980–1995); David Brandt, academic dean and vice president for academic affairs (1977–1988); followed by Harold Heie, also academic dean and vice-president (1988–1993); each contributed significantly to the conversation. A major governance study in the early 1990s, chaired by Dr. Randall Basinger (then professor of philosophy, currently provost), revisited the entire governance structure. Even the definition of "faculty" is not as obvious as one might imagine, because some who have academic degrees and faculty rank do not teach. Others may have some teaching responsibilities but find their major identity in areas other than the classroom. Earlier we observed the rapid growth of a small, intimate college in the early 1970s, which became a much larger, more complex institution by the 1990s. Thus even the "simple" question, "Who has voting rights in the Faculty Meeting?" was no longer easily answered. Over a period of some three years the Governance Committee grappled with the structural complexities of governing a larger institution. The December 7, 1992, Faculty Meeting minutes record the discussion of how "faculty" should be defined. Dean Heie proposed categories of curricular educators, administrative educators, and cocurricular educators, in addition to "ranked faculty." In the February 15 meeting, a few weeks later, the language of "Community of Educators" was used, that term being inclusive of both curricular and cocurricular educators. And by the 1994–95 school year the Community of Educators became the dominant "faculty" decision-making body, one that included both curricular and cocurricular educators. Although the Faculty Meeting was retained — with a further distinction being made between "ranked" and "non-ranked" faculty — there appears to have been a very limited agenda for the Faculty Meeting, in contrast to the expansive and inclusive agendas of earlier practice.

The acceptance of a "Community of Educators" model may have been a more significant change than many would have imagined. As the current vice-provost and dean of students, Dr. Kristin Hansen-Kieffer says, "I continue to see efforts [to support] curricular and cocurricular bridges. . . . The switch [from a faculty meeting model] to a Community of Educators model has really helped forge some partnerships." In his reflections on the developments of those years, Barnes, who was himself involved in the transitions, says, "The philosophical emphasis on educating the whole student became more of a reality during those years as campus ministries and student development came into their own." Another shift was the establishment of the provost's position in 1995, with the first provost being named in 1996. Both the academic dean and the dean of students then reported to the provost, a move having both symbolic significance and practical consequences, because two of the major components of campus life were now — at least on certain systemic levels — viewed as equal partners.

Change did not happen overnight, of course, and as Barnes suggested, the development of campus ministries was important to that maturation. A key person in that growth was Eldon Fry, who came in 1984 as the director of campus ministries. His was a new position for the college, and his responsibilities included on-campus student ministry (primarily a chaplain's program for the various floors of residence halls), off-campus outreach ministries (particularly with Gospel Teams, which supported smaller churches and which provided a tangible, hands-on way for students to explore their sense of mission and calling), and international ministries (through World Christian Fellowship).

Although Fry did not come as chaplain with responsibilities for overseeing the twice-weekly required chapels, in his second year (1985) he was asked to assume the chaplaincy and thus had a major public role in the development of spiritual life on campus. Over time more options for chapel attendance became available for students with many alternate, specialized chapels added to the large-group chapels. In part this was a decision based on the pragmatics of space limitations for the large gathering in Brubaker Auditorium; another reason for providing more options was the desire of students to have a greater variety of programming. With students coming to the college with widely differing experiences of gathered worship, providing a greater diversity of style and format seemed one tangible approach to responding to the felt need. Over the years the weekly Tuesday chapel has become the common chapel experience with an attempt to focus on certain major themes throughout the semester; on Thursdays more varied options are often available.

Reflecting on the changes and challenges of ministry with a more religiously diverse student body, Fry, who has the benefit of a wider perspective because of having served at Messiah during two periods—first from 1984 to 1997 and then again from 2005 to the present—says, "We come from this sense of a variety of streams of [religious] experience . . . maybe [it's] a mosaic that comes together." Thus, fostering spiritual formation is amazingly complex, in part because of the multifaceted "mosaic" of student experiences. Some students in Fry's observation, for example, "may come in [to the college] with a great deal of international experience and a fairly developed view of social justice. We have others who have never

heard of [the] social justice message.... Part of what is motivating me
[is] that I realize sometimes 'discipleship' was used ... [in a narrowly
defined or] legalistic way as opposed to thinking formationally."
Some students come to Messiah with deep roots in their church;
others have very little experience in a grounded Christian environment. Some know the biblical story well; others have only a sketchy
knowledge. The challenge, then, of effective public religious programming is formidable. Spiritual formation can be nurtured in
many ways, of course, and chapel is just one such venue, albeit a
significant one.

To accommodate some of the diverse needs and expectations of
students, College Ministries schedules elective chapels, with those
chapels usually meeting once or twice a month. In 2008–2009 four
elective chapel series were offered, one focusing on contemporary
worship and teaching; a second "seeking Jesus Christ through a
variety of worship styles"; a third attempting to "enact what it truly
means to live [faithfully] as Jesus lived"; and a fourth series featuring
"relevant preaching focused on God's Word to us." In addition, a
number of alternate chapels are approved on a wide range of
subjects. The challenge of having such a plethora of possibilities is
locating a core of commonality, a center which provides some
coherence and identity to the whole, which is one of the goals of the
Tuesday chapel series.

Smaller venues can be useful for discussion and relationship
building. One such possibility has been the weekly meeting, "Who's
Zooming Who?" a regular Tuesday evening Bible study and discussion group in "Issachar's Loft," a place and structure that began in
1991 and was, indeed, housed in a loft in the Climenhaga residence
on campus for a number of years. Eldon Fry, Jay Barnes, and others
were involved in the planning for this informal Bible study/discussion
group. In contrast with other similar functions, the Loft has never
applied for nor received alternate chapel credit; nonetheless, in the
early years as many as 120 students were involved in this volunteer
group. The identifying name was taken from I Chronicles 12:32 —
the people of Issachar "understood the times and knew what they
should do." And the "loft" of the initial location stayed in the name
even after the relocation to the "Martin" house on campus.

"Understanding the times and knowing what they should do" has always been central to the group according to Jeff Rioux, who was involved as a student in the initial group and has continued his interest. Deliberately in "Who's Zooming Who?" the Loft has attempted to link the study of Scripture with application to contemporary issues such as pop culture, racism, and global warming. Rioux says that student leaders are "formed in non-traditional ways." For example, when the group considered global fair-marketing practices, they began lobbying the college to use fair-trade coffee — and successfully persuaded appropriate college administrators to use alternate sources.

Staffed by persons from the Coalition for Christian Outreach (CCO), the Loft also incorporates Adventure Education into its programming. Canoeing, rock climbing, backpacking, and other physically challenging activities contribute to developing leadership skills and Christian character. Another important — though quite different — goal is to provide a safe space where students can come and feel at home as they confront and discuss some of the challenges — intellectual, social, or spiritual — which they face. Issachar's loft, while clearly not part of classroom life, helps students develop holistically at Messiah. Particularly in "Who's Zooming Who?" issues and questions are focused concerning the mission and identity of the college and students' developing identity formation.

Various "centers" on campus contribute to the core values of Messiah, among them the Boyer Center, which is, appropriately, located in a prominent location in Boyer Hall. Named for perhaps the most distinguished alumnus of Messiah College, the late Dr. Ernest L. Boyer, Sr., the Boyer Center has as its vision the goal of "nurturing the educated imagination." Earlier we noted the impressive gift of the Boyer papers, books, speeches, letters, and videos to Messiah. Dr. Boyer, who graduated from Messiah in 1948 (when it was a junior college) and served on the Board of Trustees for 22 years, was passionate about improving education in the United States at all levels — from early childhood through college. The Center is dedicated to promoting Boyer's legacy, both on campus and nationally.

Dr. Richard T. Hughes, who came to Messiah in 2006 as distinguished professor of religion and senior Boyer fellow, has, with Dr.

Donald Murk and Dr. Cynthia Wells (both Boyer fellows), set an ambitious agenda which includes the Ernest L. Boyer Center Annual Distinguished Lectureship; national conferences; smaller seminars for educators, clergy, and civic leaders; the coordination of "Basic School" initiatives; and a project in Harrisburg that promotes "Conversation on Education and Race." In his view of Boyer's legacy, Hughes, as director, argues that while Boyer was concerned for educational renewal, "He was [also] very concerned for issues like justice and peacemaking and addressing poverty . . . and [I believe Boyer] saw education as the way to address these larger issues. . . . All [this] is very much in sync with the mission of the college: a school that is committed to promoting justice, to community development, to peacemaking, to taking seriously the poor."

In Hughes' understanding, Messiah College will continually need to nurture the several theological streams — the Anabaptist, Pietist, and Wesleyan streams in her heritage — in order to fulfill her distinctive educational mission. "We're defined by these three traditions," Hughes says, "And what do these three traditions share in common? They share in common a heart of compassion for the poor and dispossessed . . . a passion for community building . . . a passion for peacemaking and for doing justice. . . . I think we can draw on those three traditions in a holistic and unified kind of way."

Part of Boyer's emphasis on holistic education has found a particular home in a course which is now required of all first-year second-semester students. This common "core" course, "Created and Called for Community," was designed in part because of President Kim Phipps' keen interest and desire to have students experience a common learning experience, one which would focus on some key themes which each Messiah student would be encouraged to consider and evaluate early in his or her academic career. As the title of the course suggests, the major subjects of the course include creation, community, and calling (vocation). The central text for this common course is Douglas Jacobsen and Rodney Sawatsky's *Gracious Christianity*, a book discussed earlier as responding to key faith commitments as articulated at Messiah College.

Although the course is not specifically sponsored by the Boyer Center, Cynthia Wells, a Boyer fellow, is currently serving as director of the core course, with Dr. John Stanley, professor of New Testament, having served for several years as the initial director. Certainly the course is influenced by Boyer's emphasis on the values of holistic education and on confronting issues that affect the way one lives. As Boyer said, "The goal [of education] is not only to prepare students for careers, but also to enable them to live with dignity and purpose; not only to give knowledge to the student, but also to channel knowledge to humane ends." Particularly in the third — and final — unit of the course, the goal as defined in the syllabus is to "develop a working definition of Christian vocation as it relates to reconciliation, service, and leadership." The intent is to engage students in thinking about their "Christian vocation" early in their academic career as a foundation for future reflection and commitment.

While the Boyer Center has been significantly engaged in focusing Boyer's vision, both at Messiah College and in the larger educational community, much more remains on the agenda for the future. One notable effort to encourage young, developing scholars is the annual recruitment of approximately twenty students who have already exhibited "exemplary scholarship, leadership, and service during their college years." Eligible students are invited to apply to be named "Boyer Scholars"; then a committee screens and makes recommendations to the provost, who makes the final selection. In addition to receiving possible research scholarships, Boyer Scholars have the opportunity to meet and converse with lecturers such as Jonathan Kozol, Naomi Tutu, and Beverly Daniel Tatum. Another academic scholarship, the Ernest L. Boyer Education Award, is given annually to a student who is identified as having the characteristics which Boyer believed essential to good teaching. The 2006–2007 recipient, Kristine (Harvey) Frey, writes that Dr. Boyer "challenged me to view teaching not as a means . . . to produce soulless compliance in students, but rather as an opportunity to creatively seek new ways of realizing justice, reconciliation, and a deeper understanding of what exists inside and outside of the individual." One is encouraged to think that these young scholars and award recipients will be particularly motivated to respond positively to Boyer's own passionate reminder of a life well lived: "The tragedy of life is not death; it is destined for us all. The tragedy of life is to die with convictions undeclared and service unfulfilled."

The Center for Public Humanities, which is also housed in Boyer Hall, supports this holistic vision as well. The mission of the Center is "to bring academic, civic, and cultural communities together in a collaborative advancement of culture and learning, and to contribute to the College's intellectual and cultural climate by stimulating debate and exchange on contemporary issues of significance, both on and off campus." The vision for the Center was initiated through the work of the past dean of the School of Humanities, Dr. Joseph Huffman, who envisioned the Center as both a place for the humanities to flourish on campus and as a venue for civic engagement and outreach to the community outside the academy.

The work of the center is now sustained under the leadership of a director — Dr. Bernardo Michael is the designated director, with Dr. Norman Wilson serving in an interim role in 2008–2009 — with the guidance of the Executive Committee of the Center, which includes faculty from each of the departments in the Humanities School. In a previous chapter we noted the annual Hoverter Course in the Humanities as one of the programs designed to reach a non-traditional clientele. Another program designed for a larger public is Teachers as Scholars, a program designed for secondary teachers in history/social studies, English/language arts, communication arts, and world languages/cultures. This program, taught by humanities faculty, focuses on content for secondary school teachers, not on pedagogy, and takes place on two days, usually at two-week intervals, the additional time allowing for completion of assigned readings. Among others subjects, the seminars in 2008–2009 included "The Holocaust," "Using Documentary Film in the Classroom," "Abraham Lincoln and American Nationalism," and "Reading the World through Slave Narratives and Spirituals."

Both the Hoverter Course — which as noted earlier — offers college credit, and the Teachers as Scholars Seminars, which do not, are fully endowed through the generosity of the Hoverter Foundation. Thus these courses are offered to students and to active teachers without fees. The Center also received a $200,000 matching grant from the National Endowment for the Humanities and is currently working to complete the challenge grant. The funding has been essential to the on-going viability and success of the Center.

In addition to the off-campus programs are several on-campus programs sponsored by the Center for Public Humanities. The week-long Humanities Symposium, which is offered each spring, focuses on one large topic; and faculty and students, both in the Humanities School and throughout the college, are invited to propose lectures, panels, films, or other presentations related to the topic. Past topics have included Culture, Community, and Belonging (2004); The Power of Human Imagination (2006); Eyes Wide Open: Engaging Technology with Our Humanity (2008); and Faith in the Public Square (2009). Each symposium also features a keynote speaker such as the American historian David McCullough; media critic Dr. Jean Kilbourne; or political scientist Dr. Alan Wolfe. Not related to the symposia, but sponsored through the Center is the annual American Democracy Lecture Series, which brings to campus distinguished professionals in both politics and history, including, among others, Jean Bethke Elstain, E. J. Dionne, and Peter Onuf. The various on- and off-campus activities of the Center for Public Humanities focus on the meaning of humanities in a baccalaureate program, and more specifically on the relationship of the humanities to the particular tradition of Messiah College.

Linked even more explicitly to the founding denomination, the Sider Institute in its various programs explores the relationship of the three major theological streams feeding into the Brethren in Christ denomination. The Sider Institute for Anabaptist, Pietist, and Wes-leyan Studies was established in 2000 on the occasion of the retire-ment of Dr. E. Morris Sider, professor of history for 37 years and prolific author, including being the writer of the 1984 official history of Messiah College. The goals of the Sider Institute, as described in the "Founding Document," are two-fold. First, the Sider Institute "encourages scholarly research and interpretative activities that promote understanding of the three primary theological streams of the Brethren in Christ Church, which founded Messiah College. Second, it articulates and explores contemporary expressions of those theological traditions . . . giving priority to projects promoting Brethren in Christ Studies."

The Institute thus is the primary research unit for the Brethren in Christ denomination, as well as serving in a continuing interpretative role on campus. The Institute has had a series of directors — first Dr. David Weaver-Zercher, then Dr. Eric Seibert, and recently Dr. Jay McDermond, followed in 2009 by Dr. Luke L. Keefer, Jr., retired professor of church history and theology from Ashland Theological Seminary — who serve to coordinate the various aspects of the Institute. One of the programs designed primarily for an off-campus audience of pastors and lay persons is the annual fall Brethren in Christ Study Conference. Recent themes have included "Salvation: Exploring the Meaning of Conversion" (2006), "Salvation: Exploring the Holy Life After Conversion?" (2007), and "Salvation: The Church's Role in Christian Experience" (2008). These three themes focused, respectively, some of the distinctive emphases of each tradition, Pietist, Wesleyan, and Anabaptist. Each spring the Institute sponsors the Schrag Lectures on Anabaptism, lectures which typically include a college chapel address and an evening public address. The Schrag Lectures are named in honor of Dr. Martin Schrag, articulate promoter of Anabaptist ideals for 30 years as a professor of church history at Messiah, and Mrs. Dorothy Schrag, who taught music at Messiah for almost as long.

On campus the Institute sponsors the Wittlinger Chapel Series, a series of three chapels required for first-year students with three themes addressed: holiness, reconciliation, and peace, thus introducing students early in their career to some of the distinctive emphases of the Messiah College heritage. This series is named for Dr. Carlton O. Wittlinger, administrator and professor of history at Messiah for 36 years, as well as the author of the definitive history of the Brethren in Christ Church, *Quest for Piety and Obedience*. There is both an appropriateness and a poignancy in this named chapel series because Dr. Wittlinger had just delivered a major chapel address in Brubaker Auditorium on October 1, 1979, a sermon he had been pondering and planning for months. Leaving the auditorium, he collapsed with a fatal heart attack, leaving, understandably, a major impact on students and faculty.

In addition to the chapel series, the "Wittlinger Programs" account sponsors several sizable scholarships, including an Anabaptist student research paper competition and a senior honors project. The several components of the Wittlinger program are fully funded with an endowment of approximately $400,000, most of which was contributed by a generous anonymous donor.

Another program under the Sider Institute's umbrella is the Peace and Conflict Studies Initiative, which both sponsors an annual lectureship and provides the academic "home" for the Peace and Conflict Studies minor. Dr. Sharon Baker, the current director of the program, plans the annual spring Peace Lectures, which in the past have been funded through the generous support of the Lilly Foundation. In 2009 the Peace Lecture featured an inter-faith dialogue on peacemaking with representatives from the three major Abrahamic faith traditions sharing the evening, a first at Messiah College.

Although the Peace and Conflict Studies minor is not large, its contribution to the continued exploration of this important part of the college's heritage is significant. As Kimberly MacVaugh, a 2008 graduate, has written, "The peace and conflict studies program helped me explore the ways in which I could live out the biblical call to seek peace and justice in our broken world. It wasn't about meeting requirements to earn another minor — it was about finding out how I can best use my gifts to serve those in need." John Michael Pickens (2009) says the minor "has given me the skills to engage the broken world we live in." One hopes that this program under the Sider Institute can grow and flourish.

Finally, the director of the Sider Institute is responsible to oversee the archives, located in the basement of the Murray Library. The archives, under the direction of the curator, Glen Pierce, serve as a repository of material both for the college and the Brethren in Christ denomination. In the public display area are featured many artifacts from an earlier era in the college and church's history, and many thousands of items from the denomination and the college are filed and available upon request. Unfortunately, multiplied thousands of additional items have not yet even been catalogued — Pierce says there are over 500 "banker's boxes" stored elsewhere and unfiled — because of the limitations of available staff time and adequate space.

In short, the Sider Institute sponsors a variety of programs: a chapel series, two annual lecture series, a pastors' study conference, an undergraduate essay contest, a scholars program for senior honors students, and the college and denominational archives, in addition to the Peace and Conflict Studies Initiative, which sponsors the minor. With the multi-faceted dimensions of the Sider Institute, and its relevance to the faith heritage of the college, one hopes that the Institute will receive on-going adequate funding and endowment to realize its potential.

Not connected to the Sider Institute, but another lectureship with significant potential for reflecting on the role of faith in our contemporary world is the annual Religion and Society Lecture Series. Initiated in 1986, the lectureship began with a flare on February 18 with President Jimmy Carter as the inaugural speaker, addressing the audience on the subject of "Religion and American Foreign Policy." Interestingly, in his address he observed that the subject is one about which he has often thought, "but one I have never talked about before." He observed that in his view, Christians are called to the ethic of love, a standard not applicable to a nation: "What Christ was talking about was *agapé* love, sacrificial love, love for another person without getting anything in return. . . . As we shape our nation's foreign policy . . . however, there is an inherent difference . . . . A nation is not able to exhibit that kind of a calling. A nation cannot demonstrate sacrificial love." At the same time, he argued that the United States should as a first principle "*exhibit a constant and clear commitment to peace*." Hearing President Carter's thoughtful reflections on the role his faith played in his own decision-making stimulated good conversations at the college.

In his comments on the new lecture series, President D. Ray Hostetter wrote in the April 1986 issue of *The Bridge*, "President Carter's thoughtful analysis of religion and American foreign policy provided an excellent beginning for continued discussion of the topic. . . . It is most appropriate that Messiah should promote ongoing dialogue on the ways religion ought to impact society." The series was the result of a dream of Dr. Douglas Jacobsen, at the time assistant professor of church history, to bring significant spokespersons on the theme to campus. Following the inaugural lecture by President

President Carter with Ernest Boyer and Boyer's grandaughter, Leah Reed.

Carter, Dr. Martin Marty, a major authority and writer on religion in American, gave the first annual lecture. In later years Dr. James H. Cone, a leading African American theologian lectured on Martin Luther King, Jr. and Malcolm X (1991); and Dr. Robert Bellah, the noted sociologist who coined the phrase "civil religion," lectured on individualism and community in America (1990). In recent years the Religion and Society Lecture, while an on-going series, has had a much lower profile on campus, in part, no doubt, because in other venues there are more eminent lecturers invited to Messiah than was true in the past.

One notable event, quite outside the usual types of lecture series, occurred on April 15, 2008, during the extended Democratic primary campaign for president when Senators Hillary Clinton and Barack Obama came to Messiah College to participate in a "Compassion Forum." The Republican candidate, Senator John McCain, had also been invited, but he declined the invitation. Mr. D. Kelly Phipps, presidential spouse and adjunct professor of business law, had a major role in bringing the Compassion Forum to Messiah College. In fact, Phipps travelled to Washington, D. C., where he met with persons representing the Compassion Forum and persuasively made

Barak Obama shakes hands with Jon Meacham, while
Hillary Clinton and Campbell Brown look on.

the case that Messiah College was an appropriate venue for this
national event. Sponsored primarily by Faith in Public Life in
cooperation with The One Campaign and Oxfam America, the Compassion Forum brought unprecedented national media coverage to
the tiny village of Grantham, and, specifically, to Messiah College. For
weeks the college prepared for the coming of these two candidates
with an intensity that probably only those with primary responsibilities fully appreciate. Among others, Carla Gross, the director of the
office of marketing and public relations, and Kathie Shafer, vice-
president for operations, were responsible for coordinating major
aspects of the event, including making the physical arrangements and
preparing for the surge of media personnel.

When the day finally arrived, the weather was damp and drizzly,
but the atmosphere was charged with high-voltage expectancy.
The forum itself was not structured as a debate; rather the two
moderators, *Newsweek* editor Jon Meacham and CNN anchor
Campbell Brown, along with selected guests, posed questions to the
two candidates sequentially, with Senator Clinton responding in the
first hour, followed by Senator Obama, who was not present for

Clinton's discussion. Questions ranged from the trivial ("Do you have a favorite Bible story?") to the imponderable ("Why does a loving God allow innocent people to suffer?"). Although there were the expected questions about the candidates' views on abortion, the questions were not confined to a narrow band of concerns, but included many issues related to compassion: poverty, Darfur, torture, HIV/AIDS, and climate change, among others.

With CNN providing live national coverage and many other networks and agencies also reporting on the event, Messiah College was able to demonstrate that a small college with continuing church connections could help enlarge the conversation to include more than one or two polarizing issues by focusing on a whole range of concerns which thoughtful Christians should consider when they evaluate the positions of political candidates. Obviously, the forum helped students and educators on campus as well to think in more informed ways about the issues. Probably few in the audience of some 1,200 persons knew — or recalled — that 22 years earlier a former United States president speaking on the Messiah College campus had also addressed issues relating to religious commitments and public life. Still as pertinent in the 21st century as in 1986 is President Jimmy Carter's challenge: "There are still things to be done. There are wrongs to be righted. There are causes to be championed. In a great learning center like this . . . we should reach for the highest standard of life."

One reflects that the founders of Messiah Bible School and Missionary Training Home could hardly have imagined that a forum for major political candidates could ever be hosted on this campus. At the same time, one may think that they would have been encouraged by the level of ethical reflection which the event generated. The identity of the college was continuing to be shaped.

Via various media, particularly television, the Compassion Forum brought national attention and a national audience to Messiah College. On a very different level — and probably to a somewhat different audience — some recent athletic achievements have brought national attention to the college. On May 18, 2009, for example, the women's softball team won the NCAA Division III national championship with a victory that capped a remarkable season with a win-loss record of 43–4. Adding to the special drama of this first national softball championship was the added pleasure for Amy Weaver of her 300th victory as head softball coach at Messiah. As the local newspaper proclaimed, there may be no athletic win quite as sweet as the *first* national championship. Having played softball as a Messiah student, Weaver became assistant coach 17 years ago and head coach five years later. Although there were some outstanding individual players on this championship team, such as freshman pitcher Jessica Rhoads, who struck out 53 batters in the final four games (in 28 innings), the remarkable success was the result of excellent team play. As Weaver says, "We won this [championship] because we were a team. Relationships off the field will take you a long way. Sure, you've got to have the talent, but I think this team won because they were a true team in every sense of the word." A team effort, surely, yet the remarkable contribution of pitcher Jess

**2009 NCAA Division III national championship
women's softball team celebrate their success.**

Rhoads, who lost her father to cancer in February 2009, just before the opening of the softball season, strongly supported this amazing spring season.

The success of the softball team was actually the third national athletic championship for Messiah during the 2008–2009 academic year, with *both* men's and women's soccer teams winning NCAA Division III championships, itself a remarkable achievement. What was more amazing was the fact that this was the *second* sweep by the two teams, with the first occurring in 2005. But first a bit of earlier athletic history. In 1997 David Brandt, son of the former dean, was named head soccer coach after serving for several years under his own mentor, Layton Shoemaker, who had built a strong program. Then in Brandt's fourth season as head coach, in 2000, the men's soccer team took a major leap forward when they made the final four in the national playoffs. In the first game of the championship series they fell behind by two goals in the first half of play, but returned in the second half to defeat Linfield College (OR). Then in the championship game they faced Rowan College (NJ), a team ranked second in the nation. Unlike the semi-final game where the Messiah Falcons faced a 2–0 deficit, Messiah scored twice—and then controlled the game. The years of preparation, the strong work ethic, the effective recruitment—all had paid off.

Although there had been many fine athletic teams in a number of sports, the national prominence of a championship in 2000 seemed to bring a new level of pride and determination to Messiah athletes. Indeed that same year the women's basketball team, with coach Mike Miller, had an outstanding season with a remarkable 23–4 win-loss record, concluding the season with their first final-four appearance and a runner-up finish. Despite the loss, the season had been extremely encouraging.

The men's soccer team continued their tradition of excellent play with another national championship in 2002. Meantime, the women's soccer team under the leadership of head coach Scott Frey was becoming a nationally recognized force as well. In 2002 the women had a spectacular season (23–1), losing only their final game, thus becoming, for their first time, the national runner-up team. Frey was honored as Mid-Atlantic Region coach of the year.

And women's field hockey, which, under head coach Jan Trapp, has had many excellent teams, again in 2002 — for the second consecutive year — was the national runner up. Because of their outstanding achievements, the three fall sports teams were featured on a CBS special, "CBS Sports Presents Championships of the NCAA," leaving little doubt that Messiah College was achieving a national reputation for excellence in athletics. One additional note on this remarkable year: in March 2002, the head wrestling coach, Neil Turner, was inducted into the National Wrestling Coaches Hall of Fame after 39 years of outstanding success. After 11 years of coaching at Messiah at the time of his induction, he had compiled a record of 122–64–1 in dual meets.

The winning tradition continued with a third national title for men's soccer in 2004, followed by the stunning achievement of national titles for *both* men's and women's soccer in 2005, as noted earlier. Both the women's and men's soccer team had undefeated seasons, which culminated in the national titles, the first time in NCAA soccer history that a college at any level had accomplished this feat. On the men's soccer team Kai Kasiguran was named the NCAA championship player of the tournament and Commonwealth Conference player of the year, and coach David Brandt was honored as Commonwealth coach of the year. And on the women's soccer team Kacie Klynstra was named NCAA championship player of the tournament, and coach Scott Frey was voted NCAA Division III and Mid-Atlantic region coach of the year.

During this amazing fall the women's field hockey team, which was also having an outstanding season, seemed poised to win a national title as well, though they fell one game short of their goal and ended as runners up. Among other superb athletes, Aftan Fisher, a four-time All-American, was named NCAA Division III field hockey player of the year (2005), an individual honor which Danae Chambers had been awarded the previous year.

Reflecting on their outstanding season, several of the coaches (as cited in *The Bridge*) focused on what it takes to move to this level of achievement. "We hope to have success," said Brandt, "but our focus is on excellence, which is more under our control than success. . . . You have to know the standard for excellence and then live it with discipline and consistency." In Scott Frey's words, "It takes vision by the leadership, belief in the process by everyone involved, and a lot of hard work." And Jan Trapp, the head field hockey coach, said, "There has to be encouragement, leadership, and willingness to work together."

The saga of outstanding athletic successes continued in 2009, the centennial year. The field hockey team had another amazing year, perhaps their most outstanding yet with a 22–0 record entering the NCAA Division III National Championship game. The season ended with a heart-breaking 1–0 loss to Salisbury University (MD), a team which they had defeated earlier in the fall. Among other honors, junior Julie Barton was named Division III field hockey player of the year, along with being named for the second straight year as a first-team All-American. Kourtney Ehly, Ashley Mowery, and Katie Love were also honored with All-American status. And during the season Jan Trapp won her 500th game, becoming at the time only the third collegiate field hockey coach with this distinction.

Meantime both the men's and women's soccer teams were engaged in yet another remarkable fall season — with the centennial year bringing the school its *third* double national championship. The men were under new head coach Brad McCarty, who, after eight years as an assistant coach, now led the team to a remarkable 24–1 record and a season that culminated in a national championship victory over Calvin College (MI) with a 2–0 win. After his first season as head coach, McCarty was named NCAA Division III Men's Soccer National Coach of the Year, and junior Geoff Pezon earned First-Team All American status, as well as being named the Common-wealth Conference Player of the Year. Of his team McCarty says, "They bought into having a new coach; they bought into new leadership; . . . and I wanted to maintain the pride of the program."

Continuing head coach Scott Frey guided the women's soccer team to another stellar finish with a 25–0–1 season record, cul-minating with a 1–0 victory over Washington University (MO) in the NCAA Division III National Championship game. Frey was honored following their amazing season by being selected as the Women's Soccer National Coach of the Year for 2009, this being his second award, the first national honor following the 2005 season. And

Erin Hench was selected by the National Soccer Coaches Association of America as the 2009 National Player of the Year for Division III, as was her teammate Amanda Naeher in 2008. Of Hench's honor, Coach Frey says, "The ultimate compliment I can give her? She makes everyone around her better." Describing the team's success, senior Amy Horst says, "Other places, people have team goals, but they also have personal goals. That doesn't exist here. As you go through the program, you begin to enjoy other people's successes more than your own. Coach always talks about it [Messiah] being a place to play the game you love, with the girls you love, for the God you love."

According to the athletic director, Jerry Chaplin, there are twin goals, simply expressed: "Pursuing athletic excellence . . . Developing Christian character." And, he adds, "I've told our athletes when I've met them at the beginning of the seasons . . . [that] if we don't meet both of those goals then we haven't done a good job." Clearly, the goal of achieving athletic excellence is being accomplished and recognized. In fact, on January 26, 2010, the United States Congress passed House Resolution 1030 honoring Messiah College for the twin soccer championships in the 2009 season and for the history of success in the past decade. To summarize, men's soccer teams have won national championships in 2009, 2008, 2006, 2005, 2004, 2002, and 2000; women's soccer teams have won it all in 2009, 2008, and 2005. The women's softball team won the national championship in 2009. In addition, women's basketball and women's soccer teams have each been national runners up twice, with the 2008 women's basketball team compiling an amazing 30–3 record, the best in school history, and Coach Mike Miller amassing 400 career wins. And the field hockey team has had 13 final four appearances, with seven teams being national runners up, while winning 16 conference titles during Coach Jan Trapp's tenure.

In addition to these outstanding team successes, Messiah has also had three NCAA Division III national individual championships: Mike Helm (wrestling, 2000), Chris Boyles (decathlon, outdoor track and field, 2002), and Amy Reed (heptathlon, outdoor track and field, 2008). In cross country and both indoor and outdoor track and field, head coach Dale Fogelsanger has had an outstanding record of success. Noting these teams, coaches, and individual performers, one needs to add that there have been many other excellent teams, coaches, and individual athletes in the 22 inter-collegiate sports programs.

Moving to this level of athletic performance has made and will continue to make a difference in the identity of Messiah College. As Dr. Douglas Miller, professor of health and exercise science, says, "Athletics is one of the symbols of who we are at Messiah. There are many symbols, but athletics is one because we have been excellent in that area to the point that we are challenging any other Division III school. . . . It's a national type of excellence, and that has brought a different kind of athlete to Messiah, an athlete that is driven, that is turning down scholarships to Division I schools." The identity of the college is quite obviously affected by the national prominence of athletic standings. Jerry Chaplin, the athletic director, says, "We're now . . . on a national stage. People know us for a lot of things, but a lot of . . . [what] we are known for is athletic success." This out-standing success affects the marketing strategy of the college as well, because in a culture where sports are so prominent, potential students (and their parents) may be attracted to a college with a demonstrated record of athletic excellence. The continuing challenge will be to maintain an appropriate balance: to recognize and affirm the hard work and success of coaches and teams in ways that will contribute to the holistic identity of the college as an academic institution committed to bringing all of life under the Lordship of the Messiah, whose name we bear.

A related part of the cocurriculum is the "rec-sports" program, an important venue for athletic development on a very different level. The goal of rec-sports is "to provide students, employees, and alumni with the opportunity to participate in a variety of competitive recreational sports in a safe environment." Under the overall direction of Heather Greer, with the assistance of a core staff of 12 students, rec-sports in 2008–2009 included soccer, basketball, volleyball, flag football, floor hockey, racquetball, softball, and ultimate Frisbee. Almost 900 persons — one-third of the student body — participated in the program, and on many late afternoons and evenings one can see teams playing or practicing on designated fields.

Another level of cocurricular athletics is club sports, which operate at a level closer to varsity sports than to the rec-sports program. To quote from the college's description, "Club sport organizations . . . are student organizations whose members meet regularly to pursue an interest in sport or physical activity that includes outside competition. . . . [These] activities are viewed as sponsored by the college as opposed to being conducted by the college. This distinction has implications for both tax deductibility of potential donations to student organizations and for the College's financial reporting." Club sports may use the college name, word mark, and letterhead. Furthermore, there is administrative support for programming and event planning. On the other hand, the college does not provide athletic trainers for club sports.

In 2008–2009 there were five recognized club sports at Messiah: men's and women's soccer, men's volleyball, ultimate Frisbee, and ice hockey. Most of these had active schedules of competition, with some — particularly the men's volleyball team — having outstanding seasons. Men's volleyball has developed a history of success with MAC championships in each of the last three years and in 2009 winning the Division II National Championship Series for club sports. Clearly, club sports have become another venue for inter-collegiate athletic competition.

These three components of cocurricular athletics — varsity sports, rec-sports, and club sports — function at significantly differing levels, of course, and meet a variety of needs and expectations. In the centennial year it's hard to imagine that intercollegiate sports was not permitted less than a half-century ago at Messiah. In 2009, as we have seen, the college is a national Division III powerhouse in several sports. The on-going challenge will be to keep an appropriate balance between intercollegiate sports and the larger identity of the college.

With the success of the intercollegiate athletic program has come the expectation that major athletic contests will be broadcast on the campus FM radio station WVMM (90.7). From earlier modest beginnings in 1969 as a student-initiated AM station transmitting low-power signals through on-campus utility lines, the radio station received new equipment and an FM license in 1989. The station has been housed in various locations: initially in the library, then in

The Larsen Student Union, which houses many student offices and
the campus radio station, was dedicated on September 24, 2004.

Miller residence hall, later in what is now the Engle Health Center,
then the Musser house (now razed), and finally in the past few years
in its current home in the Larsen Student Union. Students have had
major responsibility (and authority) in the operation of the radio
station, but in 1997 Ed Arke, who was an experienced announcer
with a public radio station, was hired as manager of the college radio
station, as well as being a lecturer in communications.

Working closely with students, Arke gradually brought increasing
sophistication to the station, though he says the biggest challenge
has been to develop a clear identity and focus. The station has been
something of a "hybrid" with funding coming from both academic
and student life budgets, as well as functioning in both curricular and
cocurricular areas. A large number of students, with many different
tastes and interest, serve as DJs for the station. Programming has been
an on-going challenge and has gradually evolved from an earlier
almost-exclusive focus on Contemporary Christian Music (CCM) to
a more inclusive one. The station has also become linked to a few
courses in the Broadcasting major. With the current financial
challenges the radio station was reviewed for its budgetary effectiveness, and as a result of the review process it became more fully

aligned with the academic program, in 2009 again becoming a part of the Department of Communications. Nonetheless, the broadcasting of high-profile athletic contests probably generates the largest listening audiences, though the radio station seemingly has not become an integral part of the college's appeal to a larger off-campus public.

Like radio, theatre, which some years ago was part of the communications area, has both curricular and cocurricular components. Also like radio, theatre performance is public; quite unlike radio, though, is the visual impact of live actors on a stage performing before an assembled audience and connecting with several senses at once. Because of its power and potential impact, theatre was regarded with considerable suspicion by the founding denomination of Messiah. More recently, audiences have become more receptive to a greater variety of theatrical practices.

Theatre has grown and matured in other ways in the last 30 years. In the 1970s and 1980s, for example, theatre faculty members taught several communication courses, as well as teaching selected introductory theatre courses, while at the same time directing major productions. Adding to the difficulty was the curricular need for upper-level students to study for three or four semesters at the Philadelphia campus. Although students often received an excellent education, the Grantham campus missed having the benefit of more experienced students performing at Messiah. Currently, students are required to study for one semester at Philadelphia — or another urban educational setting — thus allowing upper-level students to participate more fully at the Grantham campus.

One recent development which has attracted considerable attention is Theatre for Social Change, a particular interest of Dr. Valerie Smith, co-chair of the department. Although she received in her own words, "a traditional Ph.D. in theatre history," she has found her work in more experimental theatre for social change "much more rewarding." Influenced by the South American Augusto Boal and his theatre of the oppressed, Smith seeks to focus on the need for peace within ourselves (inner transformation) and reconciliation with others (justice and peace).

In recent years, among other plays, Smith has directed *Nickel and Dimed* and *Dead Man Walking*, the former dealing with the inability of the working poor to make a decent living on marginal wages, and the latter play powerfully confronting some of the ambiguities and complexities surrounding capital punishment. For directing that play she received the 2008 Justice Award from the Legislative Initiative Against the Death Penalty. This type of theatre has an edge, a purpose which goes deeper than the evening of light-hearted diversion which some theatre-goers would prefer. Here audiences are often unsettled, challenged — perhaps even offended — but they have been engaged. Theatre for Social Change will likely not appeal to large audiences, but issues of justice and reconciliation link well to the mission of Messiah College.

One campus space of large public appeal — of a very different type — is the Oakes Museum, a natural history museum that is particularly popular with local school districts. Indeed, the museum has logged over 10,000 visitors in each of the last three years, with 94 school groups among those guests. The Oakes Museum is named for generous benefactors Galen and Beulah Oakes, who were both

A youthful visitor has a close encounter with the imposing giraffe.

Located outside the Oakes Museum stands the impressive
elephant skeleton, Tukufu, a Swahili word meaning
"majestic, grand, distinguished."

graduates of Messiah, and who have long been strong supporters of
the college, particularly through Mr. Oakes' extensive (44 years)
service on the Board of Trustees, including a lengthy tenure as vice-
chair, followed by over seven years as chair.

The vision of the Oakes Museum is to promote "the understanding, appreciation, and stewardship of the resources and
creatures of the natural world through a variety of educational
programs." The visitor to the museum is immediately struck with the
visual impact of seeing the enormous skeleton of an African elephant,
prominently featured in the atrium of the Jordan Science Center.
Inside the gallery itself there is something for everybody with a large
display of North American bears, mountain sheep, and deer. The
museum has an extensive collection of over 17,000 bird eggs, 200
nests, and 300 birds. Also featured is the Chesapeake Bay watershed,

including the ecological impact of the Susquehanna River on the Chesapeake. Perhaps most striking is the enormous African diorama created by Jerry Connolly and John Schreffler, which features animals gathered around a large watering hole. The museum's collection of 200 African mammals includes 75 full mounts, the largest collection of its kind in Pennsylvania. Although the visual impact of the dioramas and the mounted animals is impressive, the educational value is greatly enhanced by the tours which the director, Ken Mark, and his education coordinator, Helena Cicero, organize and lead, along with other staff.

A teacher from a local school district writes, "I just wanted to let you know how pleased everyone was with every part of the visit to the Oakes Museum. There is never a time when everyone here [at our school] thinks that something is wonderful, so you accomplished the impossible! The parent chaperones were also raving. What great community relations!" And from a mother, "My children had a fantastic time at your museum. If it would have been only the stuffed

Students working in the Grantham Community Garden, located on campus.

animals, I don't think it would have been such a hit. The young ladies that answered questions . . . are what made our trip such a success."

In addition to the educational tours of the museum itself, the guides may also include other campus sites to promote "understanding, appreciation, and stewardship of natural resources." One such site is the solar panel pavilion located next to the Frey building, the Collaboratory project described earlier. Next to the pavilion is a quarter-acre garden, known as the Grantham Community Garden. Begun by the vision of English majors Francis Eanes and Daniel Webster, along with the help of many others, the garden is intended to be a model of community-supported agriculture. Shares are sold in the garden, and then weekly throughout the growing season, shareholders get a portion of the available produce. The garden, which has now had a couple of successful seasons, is a visible embodiment of sustainability. As Eanes says, "The intent . . . is to get people to ask the question, 'Where does my food come from?'" So children on a field trip with their school or college students on their way to class are visibly reminded that food doesn't grow in shrink-wrapped plastic containers; vegetables grow in ordinary soil around us, as they are cultivated and cared for by many hands.

As this survey has indicated, life outside the classroom of Messiah College is rich and varied. Holistic education certainly must have a strong focus on intellectual development; at the same time, the spiritual, physical, emotional, and social dimensions of life are intimately intertwined in the development of healthy persons who are committed to serving God through serving others. Such persons — both the young and their mentors — continue to have good habits of mind and body reinforced; to have negative habits of mind and heart challenged and changed; and in all things to be committed to grow in "intellect, character, and Christian faith."

Chapter 11

Transitions

The Changing Face of the College

This historical essay has focused primarily on the years following 1972, the year when Messiah College entered into a covenant relationship with the Brethren in Christ denomination and was no longer owned by the church. But there are still many people living in 2009 whose relationship to Messiah long preceded 1972, and who have seen and experienced enormous changes at the college. Perhaps the oldest living alumnus is Dr. Kenneth B. Hoover, who came to Messiah Bible College in 1930, when it was a junior college. Graduating in 1932, he stayed for an additional year of study before completing his degree with a final year at a baccalaureate college in Iowa. After some seminary work, a stint of teaching at Jabbok Bible School in Oklahoma, and then completing a Master of Science degree in biology, Hoover returned to Messiah in 1942 as an administrator and teacher.

As he recalls in his memoirs, "So far as I know, I was the only one in the Brethren in Christ Church at that time with a graduate degree in any of the biological sciences." Happy to have a full-time position, Hoover reports that his total salary for his first full year was $900. Even in 1956, fourteen years later, when the Hoovers built a house on campus, his salary was less than $3,000. For many of these years Hoover—and his colleagues—had multiple assignments in addition to a heavy teaching schedule, including supervising study hours for students, speaking in chapel, and, of course, serving on committees. Along with many others during these strenuous years, Hoover served with grace and cheerfulness despite teaching loads that today would seem quite unreasonable. "These were very good years." Hoover says. "We served with a sense of mission and were very happy in carrying out our responsibilities. . . . If it were not for the fact that we carried heavy loads and enjoyed our ministry very much, the college may not have survived during these small [enrollments] and difficult times." In addition to carrying heavy teaching loads and administrative assignments, Hoover (and other colleagues) needed to find time and space to complete their graduate degrees, as well as regularly find summer employment to help support their families. During the course of those years, a number of changes had come. Messiah Bible College had become Messiah College, but the significant transition of moving from a small, intimate denominational college (with an academy) to becoming a recognized Christian liberal arts college was an identity shift which was an on-going process.

Fast forward, then, some twenty years to the 1970s, the decade when Dr. Hoover would retire from full-time teaching, and the decade when this brief history primarily begins. The college still had a strong denominational identity, at least as the college was experienced by some of the students from other church traditions. Writing in May 1972 one graduating senior offered her views: "As an outsider [to the denomination] with a different religious tradition, you can never really belong to the Messiah College version of the Brethren in Christ community, but the members will be kind to you and let you observe the warmth they feel for other members of their community" (*Ivy Rustles*, Sept. 4, 1972). Her wry comments suggest that she felt some sense of isolation because of her background. The student body was, however, gradually increasing in size, and in the fall of 1972 for the first time reached 800 (FTE), with only a fourth of the students coming from the founding denomination. In second place, with just over 17 percent, were the United Methodists; the rest came from a variety of other Christian churches. By far the largest number of students (80 percent) were from Pennsylvania with most of the others coming from other states on the eastern seaboard. There were only 21 international students, and four of those came from neighboring Canada. The number of "minority" students is not listed.

If one were an Anonymous Visitor at Messiah in the fall of 1972, one would find a rather quiet campus. The political storms swirling on major college campuses during Richard Nixon's presidency have mostly by-passed rural Grantham, though some on campus are passionately interested in issues related to the protracted war in Southeast Asia, as well as in the political struggles of the president and the current presidential election.

Winding his way onto campus, our Anonymous Visitor (Mr. A.), sees an inviting covered bridge spanning the sparkling creek that flows beside the street at the main entrance. He enters the covered bridge with its massive curved beams and (apparently) newly constructed roof. But all he finds on the other side are tennis courts; obviously this is not the entrance to the main campus. He returns over the bridge and drives up the hill, passing a building with tall white pillars, and then he sees an older building, which must be the main administration building. Since it's still early, he parks his car and walks over to another older building nearby which some young people — probably students — are entering.

Mr. A. introduces himself to a friendly looking young man, "Joseph Frey," and tells him that he is doing a survey of some small private colleges. A rather sociable fellow, Joseph invites Mr. A. to join him for breakfast. We're still having our meals here in the Alumni Building basement, Joseph says, because that large new building over there isn't yet ready for use. It will be called the Eisenhower Campus Center; it should be pretty nice when it's finished. We'll have our cafeteria there, as well as the bookstore and a large gymnasium. There's even going to be a bowling alley, I understand.

They pick up their trays and get the simple breakfast of scrambled eggs, toast, and cereal. So what's life like here at Messiah College, Mr. A. asks. What courses are you taking? Well, Joseph responds, the main one that all freshmen are taking is a six-credit course called Shapers of Man. It's supposed to introduce us to college life with a lot of writing assignments, some psychology lectures, and a lot of other subjects — oh, yes, there's quite a bit about Christianity in the course. We meet in a large classroom with maybe 150 other students and the faculty teaching team, who take turns lecturing. We meet three times a week for lecture, and then we have smaller classes with one professor. Actually, I understand that this is the first of five semesters of Gen. Ed. The instructors call it "integrated studies," I think. It's supposed to all link together when we've taken all five courses. I know that it's an awful lot of work for students!

The construction of the Stoner covered bridge, which was moved
from its original location to campus in 1972.

The covered bridge connects the athletic fields to the main campus.
Note the original curved beams.

You mentioned Christianity a little bit ago, Mr. A. says, and I know that your college is named Messiah. So are you a member of a certain denomination, and what are your religious requirements? Yes, Joseph says with a nod, I'm part of the Brethren in Christ Church, which founded the school, but there are lots of students here from other Christian backgrounds. We have required chapel three times a week, and our dorm floor has a weekly Bible study. There are quite a few Gospel Teams, and I've volunteered to teach at the Elizabethtown Crippled Children's Hospital in a neighboring town one evening a week. Besides that, I have signed up to help register voters for the upcoming election. I can't vote yet, but I think that George McGovern deserves a chance because he says he will get us out of Vietnam.

Sounds like a busy schedule, Mr. A. says, but what do you do for fun? Joseph smiles, I love soccer, and men's soccer is a pretty big thing here. It looks like we should have a good team, so when we have Saturday home games, you'll find me there any afternoon I'm free. The women have field hockey; they are getting better and have won a few games this fall. I understand that there is a new assistant hockey coach, Jan Trapp, and the girls are excited about that.

Joseph shifts in his chair: I'm sorry to rush off, but I have a Shapers of Man lecture coming up, so I must run. Feel free to look around campus, though. And if you come back later, we could meet in the new campus center, which should be a lot nicer than this basement cafeteria. With thanks for Joseph's help, Mr. A. says he will explore the campus. You might want to see the Kline Hall of Science, Joseph suggests, it's where we have most of our classes. It's only a few years old and has modern science labs and new equipment. Thanks, Mr. A. responds, I'll take a look.

But after his brief tour Mr. A. doesn't have occasion to return to campus until ten years later in 1982, and then he finds a campus with almost 1,500 students—almost double the numbers from his previous visit. Soon after arriving on campus, Mr. A. meets a friendly admissions counselor, who responds to his questions about the student body. Yes, the ratio of women to men is still about three to two—it's nice for the men! Even though most students (almost 65 percent) are from Pennsylvania, that is almost 15 percent fewer than a decade ago; but the percentage of international students has actually dropped to less than 2 percent. We have some "minority" students, though not as many as we would like to recruit. Currently, the admissions counselor tells Mr. A., there are 22 African American students, 12 Asian students, and 7 Hispanic students, a total of just under 3 percent of the student body. Denominations, you ask? Well, Baptists, with almost 19 percent of the student body, have replaced the Brethren in Christ and the United Methodists (each now with about 10 percent) as the largest identified body, though Baptists come from many different church groups.

The campus has changed, Mr. A. observes, and asks whether he can visit. Of course, the friendly admissions counselor agrees and calls to a student who seems to be hurrying to class. He introduces "Sally Ryder" to Mr. A., a returning friend of the college. Sally is on her way to class in a rather new building, the Climenhaga Fine Arts Center, where she is attending her required freshman Gen. Ed. class, now named Skills and Perceptions. So is this still part of the Integrated Studies course, Mr. A. asks. Well, yes, Sally says, but we students usually call it "Thrills and Deceptions." Nobody gets an "A" for the course — at least that's what the sophomores all tell us. Here we are; this is Miller Auditorium, which is also our theatre and our concert hall. Mr. A. is surprised at the size of this "classroom" — there must be over 400 seats — and the lecturer looks distant and rather small from where he sits near the back of the auditorium. Messiah certainly has grown since his earlier visit. It no longer seems to have the small-town feel of the last decade.

After the lecture, followed by a small-group class discussion in a much smaller classroom, Sally asks Mr. A. if he would like to see Lottie Nelson. Sure, he says, thinking she must be a faculty member. After a short walk, however, he realizes that Lottie is not a person on campus — but a buzzing dining hall, filled with students enjoying lunch. After a short wait, they move to the serving lines. Good food, excellent choices, Mr. A. observes. It's not too bad, Sally allows, not too bad for college food, though it's not like home cooking.

They join a table where some students are animatedly discussing politics. As far as he can determine, most are ardent supporters of President Ronald Reagan, though one student argues that

President Carter could have won the election — had it not been for the American hostage crisis in Iran. But Reagan stands up to our enemies, another student says. He won't let Iran or the Soviet Union — or anyone else — bully us around. Nobody seems ready to challenge her views, and the conversation shifts to more local concerns.

I hear we might be getting some more computers for a computer lab, one student says. I'll believe it when I see it, another responds. I don't think the college is going to invest big bucks in computers. Nobody argues the point, and lunch being finished, Mr. A. thanks the students for their hospitality and excuses himself from the table.

Had Mr. A. returned to campus two years later in 1984, he would have found that the college had in fact made a significant commitment to the use of microcomputers when they purchased 15 Apple computers for student and faculty use, plus equipping additional computer labs. In the next few years Messiah would continue to augment and expand computer services with a variety of "Apples," "Rainbows," and "Zeniths." Far more than most people on campus could have imagined in the early 1980s, the "computer revolution" was coming to Messiah College. By the summer of 1988 the college would begin to implement a decision to provide computers to faculty who requested them. Then, according to Dr. Wayne Cassel, who provided much administrative leadership (along with Dr. Rick Dent), by the fall of 1989 "all freshmen were required to use word processing in Skills and Perceptions." There would be no turning back.

Three years later it's 1992: time for our campus visitor, Mr. A., who is now 60, to make his regular tenth-year visit to Messiah College. Having discovered the college's "Fact Book" on his earlier visit, he requests a copy and pores over the charts before returning to campus. Because of his previous visits he is not surprised to learn that the college has continued to grow and currently lists 2,225 (FTE) students, well over 700 more students than in his last visit. Some things haven't changed though: the ratio of women to men in the student body is still three to two. However, he is surprised to learn that just over half of the full-time students are Pennsylvania residents, a drop of 15 percent from his visit ten years ago; and there are now 59 international students, a significant increase from 24 in 1982.

The percentage of "minority" students has doubled to just over 6 percent, with a total of 134 students: 52 Asians, 44 African Americans, 33 Hispanics, and 5 Native Americans. How has the denominational affiliation and identity changed, he wonders, and finds that Baptists are still the largest group with 442 students, just over 20 percent—a significant increase in numbers and a slight increase in percentage from ten years earlier—while the Brethren in Christ and the United Methodists have each declined in actual numbers as well in percentages from 10 percent to 6 percent. Meantime, in these ten years the number of Mennonites has almost doubled to 145 students and 6.6 percent.

Not needing a campus guide this time, Mr. A. decides to see whether Miller Auditorium in the Climenhaga Fine Arts Center is still being used as a lecture hall. Students are milling around outside the double doors, and he quietly slips into the back of the auditorium. Not much seems to have changed, he thinks: as the lecturer gets underway, some students are still whispering to their neighbors, while others are taking notes from the outline projected on the screen; a few, he notices, though, are using laptop computers for their note-taking. Pausing until the students have left the hall at the end of the lecture, Mr. A. waits to speak with the lecturer for the day. Mr. A. asks about the students and about the course and learns that a major revision of the General Education curriculum has been completed. In a few years, the lecturer says, we won't be having this series of Integrated Studies courses. These team-taught courses are being phased out to be replaced with discipline-based distribution requirements. Surprised, Mr. A. says, I thought that the interdisciplinary courses were a key component of the required curriculum during these twenty years I've visited the college. Well, yes, the professor acknowledges, but we no longer had strong administrative support for the program, and faculty also lost enthusiasm for these interdisciplinary team-taught courses. Most of us think we can do a better job by teaching to our strength in "distribution" requirements, which focus on our own academic discipline areas.

Puzzled at this seemingly major change in educational philosophy, Mr. A. starts to ask another question, but the professor excuses herself, noting that she has another class to teach in a few minutes.

Leaving the lecture hall, Mr. A. decides to do a walking tour of the campus to observe how the campus buildings have changed as the college has continued to grow. Next to the library at the top of the hill, he sees a major new building with its startling blue front providing a postmodern appearance. He discovers the new building is Frey Hall, which houses the Mathematics, Engineering, and Business Departments. An imposing building, he thinks, but he notices that the earlier open space between buildings has now been mostly closed in. Since he still has some time before lunch, he decides to continue on to the periphery of campus where he observes four residence halls that he had not seen on his last visit. Amazing signs of growth: Messiah College seems to be an institution on the move.

Recalling his previous good experiences with the excellent food service at Messiah, he returns to the Eisenhower Campus Center for lunch. There he meets the friendly "checker" at the door as he has in the past — but as he enters the food service area, he sees that much has changed: there is now an attractive food court, complete with a wonderful salad bar, choice of several entrees, various cold cuts for sandwiches, a wide choice of drinks, and best of all, a dessert bar with multiple options. Goodness, he thinks, how cafeterias have changed since he was in college 40 years ago.

The students, though, seem not so different from his memory of those he met ten years earlier. Looking for a space at a table in the noisy, crowded dining hall, Mr. A. asks whether he can join several students. After a brief lull in the conversation, he asks what is on students' minds these days. There's not a lot of enthusiasm for the recently elected President Bill Clinton, he discovers, though a few persons at the table are happy to have a young president for a change. What about campus life, he asks, anything new? Well, says one, there are reports that the old Gen. Ed. program is going out and a new one is coming in. What do you think about that potential change, Mr. A. asks. New students coming in will have it easier, several chime in. Another one remarks that it's about time for something different. This Gen. Ed. program has been here forever. And a third says that probably the grading will be easier when there are classes with individual professors. The conversation dies down, a couple of students excuse themselves to go to class, and Mr. A. leaves the dining

Since the mid-1990s, graduation ceremonies are typically held outdoors.

hall as well, reflecting that Messiah College appears to be a thriving institution.

Had Mr. A. returned the following year—in 1993–94—he would have found major transitions: the academic dean not receiving a new contract, a long-term president retiring after 30 years, trustees scrambling to give direction to the college, and faculty and staff wondering what would happen next. The seemingly placid surface of life at Messiah would have suddenly become a much more turbulent river with surprising eddies and potentially dangerous rocks just below the surface.

During these ten years major changes would come to the college: inaugurating a new president, the first who was not from the founding denomination; administrative restructuring to move from a college with one dean and academic vice-president to an institution with five schools, each with its own dean; a renewed focus on institutional identity with a new mission and identity statement. But in 2002 Mr. A. decides to do a "virtual" visit to the college, rather than make another trip to the campus. As he has come to expect, he discovers that the college has continued to grow with 2,851 (FTE) students—over 600 more than a decade earlier—

but that the rate of growth has slowed considerably. Students now come from 38 states, though by far the largest number of students, about 50 percent, still come from Pennsylvania, with over 35 percent more coming from eastern seaboard states. The number of international students (now from 34 countries) has increased to 69 (from 58 a decade earlier) though the percentage of the total has declined. Mr. A. finds that the number of students from "under-represented racial/ethnic cultural populations" has increased to 193 students, about 6.7 percent (from 6 percent ten years ago).

Checking student denominational affiliations, Mr. A. finds that Baptists continue to be the largest single group with 16.7 percent of the total, though the percentage has dropped from the earlier 20 percent. The next largest group of students are those listed as "nondenominational" with almost 15 percent, nearly doubling those from the previous decade. Presbyterians, Mr. A. finds, are now attending Messiah in larger numbers: almost 9 percent from about 5 percent ten years ago — a significant increase; and Methodists are again attending in larger numbers — almost 10 percent of the total after a dip to 6 percent. But the percentage of Brethren in Christ and Mennonites *together* has dropped from a total of over 12 percent to about 9 percent. Although the categories of denominational affiliations have been changed from the earlier ones, Mr. A. notes a wide diversity of listings, including "Independent/Fundamental" and Lutheran, Pentecostal and Catholic, "Free Church/Brethren" and "CMA/Missionary." He wonders how all these live and work together and wishes he had asked students when he was on campus earlier.

We leave Mr. A. now, but had he visited Messiah College two years later, in 2004, he would have found two more large new buildings: Boyer Hall, the home for humanities, education, and social sciences, and Larsen Student Union, the center for many student activities and services. Not only might he have been surprised at the size of these recent additions, but he would have seen a level of sophistication in design and construction which would suggest that excellent quality was a major consideration. These two significant additions to campus facilities were made possible because of a highly successful $50 million campaign named "To Serve and to Lead," which also included additional funding for student scholarships.

The Phipps family — Brooke, Kelly, and Kim,
the current president of Messiah College.

This major fund-raising effort — by far the largest in the history of Messiah College — was expertly led by D. Kelly Phipps, who was then serving as director of development and who also chaired the "To Serve and to Lead" campaign. Thirty years in the life of the school had brought major changes in expectations, for students, for faculty and staff, and for constituency.

New buildings in 2004 were not the only major changes at Messiah, of course. At least as significant were changes in major administrative posts. Dr. Kim S. Phipps had been eagerly recruited by Messiah College and became academic dean in 1998, following the retirement of Dorothy Gish, who had served during a challenging time of transition. Then in 1999 in her second year as academic dean, Phipps was also named interim provost at the resignation of Donald Kraybill, who had been the first provost at the college. In an earlier chapter we followed the very difficult illness of President Rodney Sawatsky, whose brain tumor was diagnosed in March 2003, followed by subsequent surgeries and aggressive chemotherapy and radiation. Facing his severe health challenges, Sawatsky needed to curtail his activities, finally taking a medical leave from his duties in the fall of 2003, during which time Phipps, as provost, along with the help of other administrators, carried considerable extra responsibility. During this uncertain time — with Sawatsky facing enormous changes — Phipps desired both to be responsive to his personal needs, as well as to attend to the leadership needs of the college. Recalling those months, Phipps says, "I went over to see him . . . probably four days out of five . . . and [would] just update him on what was going on, because I didn't want him to feel isolated . . . and some of the best conversations I had with him about his vision for Messiah and about the theology of hope and grace happened in those moments." On a personal note, she adds, "Although it was a very strenuous time in terms of time commitment and all of that, I received a lot of personal mentoring that I'm grateful for."

Following the difficult decline in the president's health and his subsequent early retirement, the Board of Trustees asked Dr. Phipps to serve as interim president beginning in July 2004, and Dr. Randall Basinger was later named the interim provost. At the same time, the Trustees set in motion the process of forming a search committee and beginning a national search for president. Although the process was confidential, it was widely expected that Kim Phipps would be a candidate for the position. In fact, there were two finalists for the post, and on December 14, 2004, the Board of Trustees announced the appointment of Dr. Kim S. Phipps as the eighth president of Messiah College, an announcement that met with overwhelming support and general acclamation from educators, staff, and students. The college had successfully navigated some uncertain waters. There seemed to be a collective sigh of relief that another major transition had been negotiated, even while mourning the sadness of Rodney J. Sawatsky's death a few weeks earlier.

The transition to a new presidency was, however, not formalized until the following fall with the official inauguration on October 14, 2005, as part of the annual Homecoming activities. Among the special activities were an evening lecture by best-selling author and inspiring lecturer, Anna Quinlan, and a chapel address by Nathan D. Baxter, former dean of the National Cathedral in Washington, D.C. President Phipps had chosen as her inaugural theme "Created and Called for Community," which was also the title of the new "core" course, which would soon become a requirement for all first-year students. Already as provost, Phipps had strongly supported the idea of having a core course, one which would both be a common experience for all students and which would articulate and explore some of the most basic commitments of Messiah College. Thus it was most appropriate that she chose this theme for the inauguration week generally, as well as for her address specifically.

In her inaugural address President Phipps said, "At Messiah College, we understand that we have been called to live as a community characterized by deep Christian conviction accompanied by an attitude toward others that is gracious and kind. We must nurture a campus ethos rooted in humility and respectful dialogue . . ." Supporting her theme that we are "created and called for community," she argued, "We are created and called to use our gifts and abilities in the service of others. We are created and called to share our hopes and dreams with each other. We are created and called to comfort and console each other . . . to confront and challenge each other." Developing her support for the importance of genuine community, she cited the example of Jesus, as articulated by the Apostle Paul in his letter to the Philippians: "Let this same mind be in you that was in Christ Jesus, who though he was in the form of God, did not regard equality with God as something to be exploited, but emptied himself, taking the form of a slave, being born in human likeness. And being found in human form, he humbled himself and became obedient to the point of death — even death on a cross."

Two themes, which Phipps highlighted, virtues essential for Christian community, are humility and hospitality. Humility, she said, "enables us to truly learn from each other . . . to be willing to change our ideas as a result of learning from each other. . . . Humility is an essential ingredient to creating a community where every individual flourishes and succeeds." In his public response to her address, Paul Nisly noted that humility might seem to be a surprising virtue to be highlighted in an academic community, not a value commonly associated with the mission of a college, but one which nonetheless very appropriately acknowledges our dependence on God and on others.

Hospitality, the second virtue, could have been anticipated by those who knew Kim Phipps and had both heard her focus on this theme in her speeches, as well as embody it in her practice. In fact, if "excellence" was one of the late president's key themes, "hospitality" was essential to the new president. As she said, "Physical hospitality requires us to allocate time and space to care for the needs of others. Intellectual hospitality necessitates a spirit of openness to others and the sharing of our knowledge and learning. . . . Spiritual hospitality suggests that we demonstrate respect for and appreciation of the beliefs of others, even while clinging to our convictions." She acknowledged that Messiah College had not yet achieved these high goals, "but we pursue this journey together — as a community." And as she had said earlier in her address, community "is about being human together in ways that acknowledge and accept all of our uniquenesses and our differences of personality, ethnicity, class, race, gender, and faith. Community is for all of us, because community is about being human in all the forms humanity takes."

These are lofty goals, but as Phipps well knew, "community" is never a static condition which can simply be maintained. Always there are challenges which tend to fragment community, particularly challenges which can develop within a larger campus that is no longer knit by deep commonalities of backgrounds and that at the same time faces the difficulty of having more limited resources. A few years before Phipps became president, for example, the college initiated a major internal review of various on-campus services, including campus events (which was the first to be reviewed), followed later by dining services and facilities services. Major goals included improving efficiencies and implementing cost savings. According to Dennis Weller, currently conference and events coordinator, the internal review included careful record-keeping and cataloguing of the time spent on various projects, including, for example, the time that it took to set up and tear down for twice-weekly chapels in Brubaker Auditorium. These records provided hard data on the time needed to prepare for various events, thus making better scheduling possible. Further, Weller says, "We found we could do things more efficiently with our personnel." Very soon, however, employees understood that the review process had a possible goal of determining whether some — or all — of these campus services could be outsourced to off-campus agencies, thus saving money for the college. If services were out-sourced, obviously those people doing that work on campus would lose their jobs.

In addition to this important, practical issue affecting the lives of current employees, some noted the potential effect on students who had developed longer-term relationships with staff, especially those students who had college work-study positions. Kathrynne G. Shafer, vice-president for operations, says, "There's a real commitment from the staff . . . and a real understanding that they're part of the edu-cational process. They're not just here to come and clean and fix the buildings, but they interact with the students, either as supervisors that give students work experience . . . or they provide an environ-ment where they can learn . . . we've indentified our mission and really understand our mission as a college. The employees . . . say we're not here just because of a job but because we are passionate about the students, and we want to provide an environment where they can learn and live." One can then ask, how would more tem-porary outsourced personnel, who would have far less knowledge of or loyalty to the college, relate meaningfully to student workers? After careful evaluation of the internal review, the relevant admin-istrators decided that it would be both more efficient and more beneficial to the college to continue with the current system.

But the concept of "community" had been strained. Some employees felt that their services had not been properly appreciated and valued. Dennis Weller, who is an alumnus of the college and who has served here in various roles for over 27 years, says that the handling of the internal review has had a long-term negative impact on morale. The review, in his words, "created turbulence which lasts until today [2009]." With keen insight he adds, "What was missed at the end of the process was celebration; there was relief, but we missed the opportunity to celebrate." In his judgment an appropriate time of acknowledgement and appreciation could have helped bring more closure and a better long-term feeling about the review process. Clearly, building "community" is never simple, the outcomes of actions rarely fully anticipated. In part, the challenge of a place like Messiah College is precisely that "community" is such an important value. At XYZ Business one may expect to be a cog in the corporate gears, but not at Messiah, where the expectations are much higher.

Another transition — a significant one — has been the growth of the college, which our fictitious Mr. A. observed over the years. What Mr. A., as a periodic visitor, probably didn't recognize or understand is how size affected community. Dr. Gerald Hess, professor of biology and interim dean of the School of Health and Natural Sciences, who is an alumnus of Messiah and now has been a faculty member or administrator for almost 40 years, celebrates the college's growth and the increased opportunities which growth has brought. At the same time he acknowledges, "I think we lost the intimacy . . . that we had when I was a student here [from 1961–65]." Those who were on the faculty in the early 1970s remember social evenings at the college when some faculty would bring ice cream freezers, others would bring toppings and other desserts, and the entire faculty would bring their families for an ice cream social; or when the faculty and staff would gather for an all-employees Christmas party. Barry Goodling, vice-president for advancement, recalls, "I remember we used to have summer picnics . . . down by the creek. And we'd all bring something, and there was that sense of knowing each other and knowing everyone that was a part of Messiah." Nostalgia is a potential temptation for the historian, of course, and selective memory might cause one to minimize the negative effect of limited salaries and heavy responsibilities.

Growth in numbers also brought change in structures, particularly the shift from a single college model to a five-school structure. As President Phipps has said, "The restructuring itself of going to the school model . . . [was] a significant event, and we're still learning . . . the strengths and weaknesses of that system." Later she acknowledged, "I'm still sorting out in my own mind the sense of isolation that has happened because of the schools model." In addition to that change was the move to a Community of Educators Senate, a representative group which largely replaced the earlier Faculty Meeting and the later Community of Educators meeting. Clearly, there was a considerable gain in efficiency, but there was a loss of face-to-face relationships. Hearing colleagues articulate their viewpoints, debate their differences, come to some mutual understanding, and finally make decisions in a large-group meeting—this almost-weekly gathering took much time and energy. So the change of structures to a far smaller Community of Educators Senate was reasonable, but there may have been a concomitant loss of community that discussion and debate via an e-mail network cannot adequately replace.

Clearly, increasing size has brought challenges and adjustments. On the other hand, fewer students in the last several years has brought a different set of challenges which the college continues to monitor and accommodate. To be specific, in 2003 Messiah had 2,914 (FTE) students, its largest student body ever: the college seemingly was well-positioned to reach its (then) goal of 3,050 students. Five years later, however, in 2008, there were 2,763 (FTE) students and, in 2009, 2,730 (FTE), even though the Office of Admissions had redoubled their recruiting efforts. After several decades of almost continuous growth, as we have observed, adjusting to these new realities has not been simple. Most long-term employees of the college have lived in a climate of continual expected growth; moving to a steady-state—or even reduced size—student body has been for many unprecedented. Naturally, with fewer students the budgeting process has become increasingly difficult, with the situation being exacerbated by the national economic downturn of 2008–2009.

The transition to these new economic realities at Messiah College has necessitated adjustments in expectations on various levels, including the hiring of additional or replacement personnel and limiting increased levels of remuneration for current personnel. Closely related to these new economic realities is the major question: How can the college best maintain quality educational programs in the face of fewer resources? Which adjustments are appropriate and reasonable, and which changes will negatively affect the education of students? Further, what new directions need to be explored in order to lead rather than to be in a defensive posture? Already in May 2007 Mrs. Eunice Steinbrecher, chair of the Board of Trustees, said, "Higher education—and the way higher education is delivered—is obviously changing. . . . It's a new day, and if we don't address the way we are delivering education . . . I'm afraid we are going to be left back in the woods somewhere."

One of the ways in which the college is attempting to address change is to offer a number of online summer school courses. In 2009 a total of 248 students chose online courses, a sizable increase from the 197 students in 2008. Completing courses online is, of course, a significantly different experience than the multiple inter-actions — student with students and students with faculty — which one experiences in the classroom and will not replace an effective Messiah College classroom experience. But in the current educational environment Messiah no doubt needs to explore multiple options, including online courses.

Another new direction has been the movement toward offering a limited number of graduate programs. In June 2009 Messiah College was approved by the Pennsylvania Department of Education (PDE) to begin offering a Master of Arts program in counseling, which features three specialized tracks: mental health counseling, marriage and family counseling, and school counseling, with Dr. John Addleman serving as counseling graduate program director. Two additional graduate programs, one in music conducting, the other in art education, have been approved by the college and are in various stages in the formal PDE review process. Quite obviously, this entry into graduate school offerings is a significant transition for Messiah College. As with any major transition there are great hopes for the success of the new programs, as well as some concerns about the costs and risks of new initiatives. Only in retrospect can one say with assurance whether new directions in educational programs were wise and timely or not.

Clearly, Messiah College in 2009, the centennial year, is almost unbelievably changed from the small institution she was when the young Kenneth B. Hoover came to the junior college in 1930 at the beginning of the Great Depression. Even in these last forty years — as we have seen — there have been major transitions: two new presidents, both from traditions other than from the founding denomination, in contrast to the expectations and practice of the first 85 years of Messiah's history; a number of new deans and vice presi-dents; major additions of administrators, educators, and staff; significant structural changes in organization with the shift to the five-school model. During these years of enormous growth, the student body was recruited from a wider geographical area, though most Messiah students continued to come from the eastern seaboard states.

In recent years the college has faced the adjustment of steady-state — or even somewhat declining — enrollments. Coinciding with the significant adjustment of having reduced revenue and increased expenses has been the national and international financial crisis. As President Phipps said in her 2009 State of the College address, "I must tell you that 'tweaking' and making minor adjustments to our program offerings and financial model are *insufficient* for meeting our challenges." In short, as Kurt Anderson, whom Phipps cited, has written, "It's the end of the world as we know it. But it's not the end of the world." Thus some changes in administrative structures and reductions in personnel are being implemented. But taking the long view reminds us that Messiah College survived the Great Depression and two major world wars. A much stronger institution than it had been earlier, Messiah College will not only survive: by God's grace it will thrive. To quote Dr. Hoover in a very different context, "Things change — and God is in it all."

Chapter 12

Personal Views

Looking Back, Looking Forward

In this brief historical overview of the last 35 or 40 years at Messiah College, we have seen many evidences of shared faith, bold vision, and enduring promise. We have also seen times when the vision has been somewhat clouded and the promise delayed. While all of those reflections have — quite obviously — been filtered through the mind and words of the writer, the "voice" has primarily had an objective tone. In this concluding chapter, however, I will speak more personally from the vantage point of one who has had over 35 years of teaching and administrative experience and as one who is committed to Messiah College and cares deeply about her future. At the same time we will hear from a number of other "voices" for their perspectives on a variety of key issues. There are numerous things to celebrate — and we will here reiterate only a few; there are challenges which we face — and we will discuss some of them; finally, there are many who have blessed us with their commitment to Messiah College — and we will listen to a few representative voices.

Throughout the 2009-2010 academic year there will be many celebrations, times of thanksgiving for the growth and health of the college, times of honoring the many people who have contributed immeasurably to help Messiah College become the thriving institution of the present. We have noted the growth in the last half-century from an academy and junior college with a few hundred students to a complex, multifaceted institution with nearly 3,000 students, along with the equally dramatic growth in the numbers of staff and educators to serve this greatly enlarged student body. Concomitant with the significantly increased number of students has been the growth of campus facilities: classrooms and laboratories, faculty and administrative offices, traditional residence halls and apartment-style buildings, athletic fields and gymnasiums—the changes have been little short of phenomenal in this half-century.

During these years Messiah has grown from being a small school without academic accreditation to receiving accreditation by the Middle States Association of Colleges and Secondary Schools, as well as by many specific disciplinary accrediting agencies; at the same time academic offerings have increased from a small handful of majors to over 55 majors. The addition of the Philadelphia campus to the "home" campus at Grantham made available a major urban center at Temple University with all the vast resources of the large city; and the recent development of the Harrisburg Institute provides an excellent urban connection within a dozen miles of the Grantham campus. On the global scene the relationship with Daystar Communications (later Daystar University) in Nairobi, Kenya, dramatically enlarged the international focus. Currently, there are approximately 40 off-campus international and national sites available to Messiah students with a wide range of educational possibilities. In the cocurricular area the college moved from having no intercollegiate athletic program 50 years ago to 22 NCAA Division III athletic teams in 2009 and from primarily regional competitions to a number of national championships.

In other public performance areas, music has long been important—indeed central—to the religious and aesthetic tradition of Messiah College; that tradition continues to mature and flourish. In the summer of 2009 President Phipps announced that the Susquehanna Chorale, a 36-voice chamber choir, is now an ensemble in residence at the college and "will collaborate with the college on creating mutual, increased opportunities for visibility with both organizations." Besides the many contributions of the music program to the college and community, the visual arts and theatre have in these years moved from a marginal existence on campus to a greatly enhanced and significant presence. The quality of the art shows, for example, including the annual spring senior student shows, has become increasingly sophisticated. And the theatre program has matured and grown, particularly since upper-class theatre majors are now on the Grantham campus for most of their academic careers.

One celebrates also the greater presence of the humanities at Messiah, particularly because of their wonderful home in Boyer Hall. The addition of the Boyer Center, with the remarkable gift of the Ernest L. Boyer materials and the leadership of Dr. Richard Hughes, distinguished professor of religion and senior fellow at the Boyer Center, has brought a new visibility and presence to the cause of effective teaching and holistic education. The annual naming and recognition of student Boyer Scholars effectively promotes many of the ideals which Dr. Boyer emphasized in his distinguished career. And the Center for Public Humanities, which the former dean of the Humanities School, Dr. Joseph Huffman, conceived and championed, has brought new vitality to the humanities through the Hoverter Course, the annual week-long Humanities Symposium, and a number of lectureships.

Another major area of outreach beyond the campus has been the work of the Collaboratory under the leadership of Dr. David Vader. Although the Collaboratory was initially conceived by faculty in the Engineering Department, it has its home in the School of Mathematics, Engineering, and Business and now includes many students and some faculty members from various disciplines across several schools. The work, both in the United States and in a number of international sites, embodies the service emphasis which we hope that Messiah College graduates will accept as part of their calling as citizens of the Kingdom of God and members of a global community.

Similarly, the Agape Center with its various programs — ranging from the initial "Into the Streets" experience required for first-year students to various week-long service opportunities during the school year to longer-term summer service options — all these bring concrete applications to the ideals of service and reconciliation which Messiah's mission statement articulates. The multiple learnings of these opportunities are well framed by Chad Frey, the director of the Agape Center, who says, "Good service is reciprocal in many ways ... [because] the guest-host relationship in service is inverted. When you serve, you may think that you're going to a country, say Tanzania or Zimbabwe, to do service to this community. But [you] come away having experienced radical hospitality and realize that you were the one being served. And service does that as a context for education: it inverts typical roles." These learnings are indeed important to a full-orbed view of education — and cause for our celebration and thanksgiving.

On a rather different level, I am grateful for those who had the vision to plan for and then engage in developing a community garden on the Grantham campus. Forming tillable, productive soil from tough Grantham clay takes persistence. Learning through patient hard work that growth from seed to harvest requires weeks — and sometimes months — teaches that nutritious food is a gift to be cherished, not a right to be taken for granted. And being engaged with the actual physical production of food helps to link concretely the pleasure of eating with its source in ordinary soil.

There are many other causes for celebration at Messiah College, such as the support services which are regularly so good that they are assumed, rather than noted. One thinks of the outstanding food and dining services area, which day after day, meal after meal, provides an amazing variety of good food, as well as serving capably in multiple venues besides the main facility in Lottie Nelson Dining Hall. And the campus buildings are routinely so clean and well maintained that one needs to visit other campuses to be reminded that those personnel working in conference and facility services ought to be honored, not taken for granted. Or, if one pauses in the midst of a hectic schedule, one can relax in the serenity of the well-kept grounds, surrounded by the luxuriant beauty of the many trees, bushes, flowers, and other plantings, so well designed by Elizabeth Sobrevilla, herbaceous plant care specialist at Messiah. On a campus stroll on a bright blue October day, one could well say with the nineteenth-century poet Gerard Manley Hopkins, "The world is charged with the grandeur of God" — indeed cause for celebration.

At the same time, as we reflect on the many reasons to celebrate at Messiah College, we also recognize that we face challenges in a number of areas. At times we both celebrate and acknowledge challenges. An example: we celebrate our urban connections with Harrisburg and Philadelphia, but we continue to face the challenge of maintaining strong ties and encouraging students to live, study, and work in these urban centers. We celebrate Daystar University, but for many years now we have had limited direct involvement — in part because of our government's travel advisories. In 2009-2010, after a long hiatus, Messiah College is again being represented at Daystar by Dr. Lamarr Widmer, associate professor of mathematics, who, with his wife Margaret, is teaching and serving there during his sabbatical refresher leave. One hopes that this return (for Messiah) to Daystar will be the beginning of a renewal of the important relationship the college has had with this dynamic African university.

A major challenge which Messiah College faces — one common to many educational institutions — is finances. As Dr. Lois J. Voigt, vice-president for finance, says, "Finances is the engine; it's not the goal. Finances is how you accomplish what you want to accomplish, but it's not the goal of what you're doing. So it's just a support function." But obviously, as Voigt knows as well as anyone, having adequate finances is essential for a strong institution. So the issues, she says, are "enrollment and expenses, and juggling these . . . [in order to] still have the quality education that you need to attract students without having to charge so much that you can't attract them! Finding that balance of maintaining the quality, attracting the students, and finding the finances for the students, I think is the challenge of the next few years." Voigt's comments seem particularly prescient because she offered them in 2007, well before the major national and international financial crises in 2008, which have affected many educational institutions, in addition to many other agencies and institutions. Although Messiah would have faced financial challenges, as Voigt noted, these have been exacerbated by the difficulties in the larger economic climate. It requires no financial wizard to recognize that the general economic downturn creates a greater challenge for both parents and their children to arrange finances for education, thus in turn making it more difficult for the college to recruit the number of students needed for an efficient operation. In addition to enrollment challenges, the college also faces a decline in its endowment with the battered stock market, thus providing less additional revenue to support the budget.

Currently, Messiah College is raising funds for two major projects: $20 million for endowing student financial aid and a much larger amount for a performance/worship center, both worthy projects. For student recruitment the efforts to increase the endowment available for financial aid deserve high priority. Even with recent more conservative increases in tuition rates, the potential debt load for graduates becomes a daunting issue for prospective students and their parents. Thus making available more financial aid for students must be a high priority.

One component in this financially challenging environment, of course, is controlling—and even reducing—expenditures. Part of that cost reduction may need to be staff reductions. As President Phipps noted in her June 15, 2009, "Campus Update," "Several positions were eliminated including staff, administrative, and full- and part-time faculty employee groups." Such reductions are never easy, as Phipps notes: "Decisions that involve the reduction of personnel are extremely difficult, and I realize that these changes have created concern and anxiety. The College is doing all that we can to assist employees affected by these decisions, including out-placement services and other resources." Nonetheless, despite whatever services are offered, the dislocations experienced by affected personnel—especially for those who have served Messiah College for many years—are painful. And the concern and anxiety filter into the larger campus community as well. One can, however, safely say that Messiah is a strong institution that will weather this difficult economic turbulence, though the adjustments from the "growth mentality" of earlier decades will not be easy.

Although developing budgeting priorities is rarely an easy or straightforward process, stressful economic times intensify the chal-lenge. To recruit students one needs—in many cases—to provide substantial financial aid. How does one decide priorities among student groups? As we have seen, under President Sawatsky a decision was made to offer more academic merit-based scholarships, thus channeling some funding away from (financial) need-based aid. At the same time, one of Messiah's institutional priorities has been increasing the numbers of students (and faculty) from "under-represented racial/ethnic cultural populations." From 2002 to 2008 the size of this student group has been fairly steady at about 7 percent of the total student body, with another (approximately) 2.5 percent international students. Messiah is blessed to be able to offer three full-tuition Martin Multicultural Scholarships through the generosity of Lloyd and Lois Martin. These scholarships attract a number of "under-represented racial/ethnic" students to the campus, and for those we are grateful. At the same time, much remains to be done. Dr. Lawrence A. Burnley, who has been associate dean for multicultural programs and special assistant to the provost for diversity affairs, says, "I think diversity is important at Messiah College, [but] I don't think it's an institutional priority yet. . . . Institutional priorities show up in budgets, so it's clear where . . . priorities are."

Not only is significant funding needed for student recruitment, but support is needed for adequate programming and staffing. To bring students and not provide the necessary academic and other needed support will not contribute to the long-term success of these efforts. Dr. Neryamn Nieves, assistant professor of Spanish at Franklin and Marshall College, says, "I think back on . . . what made me successful at Messiah; I remember being in a summer program [START] really prepared me for college. . . . I needed something to transition me from the skills I had, but also to adjust to being at the college away from home [by] creating a group of people around me that were my support." The twin outcomes of developing better study skills and habits and finding a support group in the more intimate environment of this two-week intensive experience led to her successful completion of a *double* major in college, followed by successfully completing the long, arduous journey through graduate school. Besides that, Nieves became a loyal alumna of Messiah, including returning for an early two-year stint as an admissions counselor, followed, after graduate school, by nine years as a faculty member.

Not all stories end so well, of course, but Nieves' experience supports the idea that investing in adequate support services is time and money well spent. Nieves cites the experience of another reputable university that has accepted students to whom Messiah had denied admission on the basis of inadequate academic preparation, but whom she has seen succeed at that institution. There are some students, she says, who "aren't even given a chance to succeed [at Messiah] that may be [successful] if we had . . . some kind of starting program that would help them be able to succeed." Coming from one who both cares deeply for Messiah and who herself has experienced the benefit of a good beginning, her words deserve serious consideration. The college needs to continue to wrestle with how it can best recruit top academically qualified students while helping somewhat less prepared students to succeed.

Beyond needed finances and specific programs—both essential areas—are attitudinal changes. Ms. Debra Cruel, who was a Board of Trustees member for eight years and who had a key role in the Multicultural Diversity Subcommittee of the Committee on Education, offers a profound insight: "The remaining barriers [to increasing under-represented groups] are not what people think. I don't think it is financial; that can be overcome. It is knowing in your heart that the Kingdom of God is every tongue and kindred and tribe and nation, and feeling absolutely incomplete until you experience that. . . . When you feel that you are missing something without your brothers and sisters from other cultures, that creates a welcoming community. That breaks down every barrier because you, all of us, are desired in the same way." Developing this welcoming culture, this enlarged concept of the Kingdom, is both a gift of divine grace and the result of the on-going work of education. As Debra Cruel says so well, persons should "go where they are celebrated, and not where they are tolerated. So there has to be a culture of celebration . . . created from the leadership, that every time a new student steps foot on the campus, the culture is [that] we celebrate our gifts, our cultures, our distinctions, our differences, our similarities." Her definition of a welcoming celebration sounds very much like President Phipps' favorite word, "hospitality."

Part of that hospitality can be the honoring of people who have been "pioneers" (to use Ms. Cruel's word), persons like Dr. Wilma Ann Bailey, former associate professor of Old Testament at Messiah. In Cruel's words, "There is tremendous recognition of someone who may have given a million dollars [to the college]," but we don't have pictures and plaques honoring the "pioneers," such as Dr. Bailey. In that context one ought also to mention Dr. Robert Suggs, professor of psychology and, later, half-time director of personnel at Messiah, who came to Messiah in 1980 and served with distinction for a number of years. Many years later Dr. Joseph Jones came as the first dean of the School of Education and Social Sciences, where he served for six years, initiating—among other things—the Harrisburg Institute. All three of these African American "pioneers," not surprisingly, were heavily recruited by other schools. Bailey took a position as professor of Old Testament at a seminary; Suggs became an academic dean and later a provost; Jones was named as provost at another college.

Noting that each of these three—and one could name others—*had* been at Messiah reminds one that recruiting faculty is only part of the issue: *retaining* faculty in "under-represented racial/ethnic populations" continues to be a challenge. The 2008 Messiah Fact Book lists an average of 14 or 15 non-Caucasians in the "full-time instructional faculty" of 170 to 173 in each of the last five years from 2004 to 2008. Again in 2009 a few non-Caucasian teaching faculty members were recruited for faculty/administrative posts elsewhere to the considerable loss of Messiah College. Amanda A. Coffey, director of human resources, has an interesting perspective, "We can't change the location of Grantham, and Grantham is not in a diverse community." Recognizing that this area may not be one in which to "put down roots," she says, we "design a program by which faculty from diverse backgrounds and heritages and racial and ethnic make-up come to prepare themselves. . . . Maybe one of the things we think about is how do we make ourselves the most attractive middle step in someone's academic career." Coffey's insight is thoughtful, yet one hopes that increasingly this can be a home where people of "every kindred and tribe" can be fully welcomed, where the Kingdom can grow and flourish, and where people can put down deep roots.

As with any situation involving a rich diversity of people, there will be no single answer to such complex issues. One long-term direction will be for faculty and administrators and mentors to encourage strong students from many backgrounds to attend graduate schools, finish their degrees, and return to Messiah to teach. If students have had a positive, nurturing, challenging educational experience at Messiah, as well as having the ability to complete graduate degrees, more of these "under-represented" groups may be inclined to return to their alma mater. No approach by itself is enough; but we should be committed to try some long-range approaches.

Included in our efforts needs to be developing long-term relationships with churches, particularly in Harrisburg, York, and Lancaster, as well as in Philadelphia, where we have an urban campus. Neryamn Nieves notes the importance of having students participate in churches: "The churches, especially the smaller ones, always appreciate those types of connections, somebody coming in and just encouraging the young people. . . ." Often there are family networks in churches, and those students who have been accepted at Messiah and who have had good experiences are unofficial recruiters for the college. "In the Hispanic community," Nieves says, "it is a family affair as to where the young person is going to go to school. . . . And so you've got to make Messiah appear to be a place that is going to care for their young person."

Some, of course, do find Messiah a welcoming place. Andrew Samuel, a 1984 graduate of the college and later a member of the Board of Trustees, reflects on his experiences as a student. Mr. Samuel, currently founder and president of a bank, was born in India, moved to Zambia when he was six, and enrolled at Messiah when he was 17. He speaks with appreciation of the scholarship aid which made possible his coming to the college and says that he always felt welcomed. "Either," he says, "I was real naïve . . . or there truly was a desire [at Messiah] to embrace folks like me who were coming in . . . and I never really felt different or an outsider . . ." Encouraging, hopeful words.

For some, the challenges lie not with differences in racial or cultural backgrounds from the dominant culture, but with specific individual challenges. In the past, students coming to the college with a variety of disabilities often found the adjustments difficult and the accommodations rather limited. According to Dr. Keith Drahn, currently director of disability services, too many students "apparently were coming in the front door and going out the back door after about two years. It was rare that an individual who would identify themselves as having a disability was actually graduating." In 1996 Messiah administrators perceived that the college needed a person with specific background education and experience to lead and coordinate disability services. Drahn initially began his service with a combination teaching and administrative role, which in 2007 became entirely administrative, a change which he welcomed as a necessary development because of the enlarged need.

Drahn says, "We have turned the corner in terms of disability finally being accepted as part of the diversity discussion." He credits the coming of Dr. Larry Burnley with his "passion for equality and full participation and acceptance and appreciation for diversity among people of color, along with disability, for that to happen." In the years since 1996 Drahn has seen the number of students with disabilities increase from 35 students registered his first year, to 50 the second, and to 75 the third; now typically between 100 and 125 students are registered annually. At the same time, Drahn says, "The demand and the severity of the disabilities that are represented among our students have changed." Recently, for example, some have needed major assistance simply to move from their wheelchair into bed at night and up again in the morning.

The types and severities of disabilities vary greatly, and Drahn has also initiated the use of electronic text format—with the capable assistance of the Information Technology services area—for some students. He has found that e-texts have been very helpful for students who have major difficulty in concentrating. These students, he says, "would read maybe ten or fifteen minutes, and then they had to get up and do something; or they couldn't stay focused well enough, and so they would end up reading and rereading something four or five times." For many of these students, *hearing* the text provided the focus they needed. In a few years, he adds, graduation rates went up from 12 or 15 students to 30 or 35 students and "about half of those were graduating with honors."

Whatever the particular need of students, Drahn is keen to help them find "how their own disability can inform their own experience and inform God's call upon their lives. . . . [It] is reassuring to me in knowing that I am doing God's will, not just in helping these students find accommodations in the classrooms, but sometimes helping them integrate the way God has made them, and he makes no mistakes." In the process of assisting these students with particular needs, Drahn is also assisting the larger Messiah College community—staff, students, and teaching faculty—to enlarge their concept of hospitality, to embrace the amazing diversity of individual humans.

How, we might ask, should our Anabaptist, Pietist, and Wesleyan theological perspectives shape our understandings of human diversity in all its manifestations? How are we preparing our students for lives of reconciliation, as our mission statement proclaims?

The question of diversity at Messiah is one part of the larger on-going discussion of identity, which has been a significant theme in this historical essay. Diversity, of course, is much larger than the two important areas which we have just addressed. How do we value and emphasize our theological moorings, and at the same time provide a hospitable place for Catholics and Evangelicals, charismatics and those in liturgical traditions, Eastern Orthodox and fundamentalists, Reformed and Mennonite and Brethren in Christ?

At a place like Messiah College, identity is never a fixed position; always it is fluid, dynamic, evolving. Identity, in short, is a continuing challenge for Messiah. An essential component of our identity needs to be a welcoming place, as we have argued. At the same time we need to maintain clarity of focus. The fact that in 1999 an earlier president could seriously propose to the Board of Trustees that Messiah should consider choosing a new name may — among other things — suggest some uncertainty about our corporate identity.

Former academic dean of the college, Dr. Daniel R. Chamberlain, says, "I guess the fear any of us have who have been in leadership positions is that a college may lose its way in thinking that it is finding its way. . . . [Some colleges try to be] all things to all people; and they have lost any sense of centeredness." A current dean, Dr. Ray Norman, from the School of Mathematics, Engineering, and Business, says, "I think our identity in this [religious] area is still being worked out. At this point in history, in Messiah's history, who are we?"

Developing the college's identity and mission statements has been part of our response, as has the recently required first-year course, Created and Called for Community. The Provost's Seminar, a weekly meeting which is required of all new faculty in their first semester, is another aspect of the college's giving attention to issues of common identity. Then during the course of their academic careers, faculty members are required to write, revise, and expand an essay "which reflects on their vocation as Christian scholars and on the connections that exist between Christian faith and their academic disciplines." Nonetheless, Dr. Richard Stevick, professor emeritus of psychology, raises concern about faculty faith commitments: "I just worry about the accountability issue," he says, though he agrees that there can be no simple or formulaic guidelines. Expressing concern, though of a rather different nature, Richard Hughes, senior fellow of the Boyer Center, says, "I don't see the slippery slope here as the slippery slope from a seriously Christian school to a secular school. . . . I see the slippery slope as one in which we lose sight of . . . [our] roots, forget what Anabaptist means, forget what John Wesley was all about, forget what the Pietist vision really was, and just become one more generic, evangelical institution." Having clearly distinctive Christian commitments, while at the same time maintaining a posture of openness, will be a continuing challenge for Messiah College. The conversation needs to be sufficiently focused to be meaningful: never should the college assume or take for granted an inherited Christian identity.

Some years ago, the late president Rodney Sawatsky coined the phrase, "Rigorously Academic; Unapologetically Christian," a tag line which had been used earlier in other venues but which was first printed on the cover of the 1998–2000 Messiah College Catalog. As President Sawatsky certainly knew, having memorable descriptors is important to any institution, but he knew as well that more difficult is giving meaning to the phrase. Probably there is more agreement on the first part (which is a largely shared goal in academe), than there is for the second (which is unique to a particular kind of academic institution). That essential task of continuing self-definition is surely appropriate at a time of centennial celebration, but it will be a work in progress, not a static place of assumed identity. The 2008–2009 Messiah College Catalog continues to reference the college motto, "Christ Preeminent," a worthy reminder of our ultimate loyalty as well as our calling and responsibility. But each generation of educators will need to ponder how that commitment will order institutional and personal priorities.

One recent significant effort which President Phipps and Provost Basinger have initiated is, as President Phipps has said, "to involve every employee group, as well as student leaders, in conversations around the college's mission and identity, where we have restated our core commitments . . . and then talked about areas where we may have a breadth of perspectives." In 2009, Basinger, who was formerly a professor of philosophy, has made presentations to faculty and staff groups, to the Provost's Seminar, to student leaders, and in orientation sessions with new employees. Among other things he discusses differing types of Christian schools, along with the varying expectations which those institutions hold. According to Basinger, those institutions which may be described as "orthodox" in their affirmations of Christian faith have three levels of belief: (1) There are some beliefs which all educators and administrators are required to affirm; (2) there are some beliefs which the college affirms and which are privileged by the institution, but only some ("a critical mass") are required to affirm; (3) there are beliefs on which the institution is neutral. But what, Basinger asks, are the beliefs and commitments which all educators need to affirm? What, on the other hand, are the "beliefs which an institution affirms while allowing educators/ administrators to disagree (i.e., beliefs on which an institution and educators/administrators can agree to disagree)?" For Messiah College, the affirmation, "Jesus is the son of God," might be an example of the former. On the other hand, "Participation in war is inconsistent with the teachings of Jesus," may be an example of the latter. These questions — and others — along with the ensuing conversations are essential to a continuing engagement with the issue of our identity as a particular Christian college.

Other areas — though of lesser magnitude than these specifically religious ones — will continue to be important challenges. We value excellent athletic teams and celebrate their outstanding achievements, which have become increasingly important to the identity of Messiah College. How do we keep an appropriate balance with other educa-tional goals of the college? In a climate of tight financial budgets, how do we decide about the appropriate allocation of funds? What do those decisions indicate about our identity?

Other important decisions involve the development of graduate school programs, a significant shift from a century-long tradition of focusing solely on undergraduate education (with the earlier inclusion of an academy for secondary education). How will these graduate programs relate to the undergraduate program? How will financial resources be allocated? How will the identity of the college be enhanced or challenged by the inclusion of these programs? How will graduate programs affect the college's Christian identity?

The tremendous growth of the 1980s and to a lesser degree throughout the 1990s led to the decision to restructure the college academically into five schools. How do we continue to foster commitment to the whole, at the same time that many find significant identity in the individual schools? How do we balance essential commitment to the good of the entire institution with the needed focus on one's own discipline? Further, how do we as educators maintain some sense of cohesion in the Community of Educators, when most major decisions are discussed, debated, and decided in the COE Senate? And to cast the net further yet, how can all the support and service staff and administrators become more fully included as integral parts of the whole that is Messiah College? How can all persons feel valued, so that "community" can become more than a buzz word?

Finding and identifying challenges lead probably to more questions than resolutions—and the knowledgeable reader no doubt will add his or her own to the list. But asking the questions, focusing the issues, and working toward consensus will be important to assure the on-going vitality of the institution into the next century.

Fortunately, there have been many people who have been deeply committed to Messiah College throughout her history. In his history of the college, Dr. E. Morris Sider notes, for example, the sacrifices of Enos Hess, who taught without salary for several years, as well as later returning major portions of his salary, all the while living an extremely frugal lifestyle. In the course of interviewing many persons in preparation for this current historical essay, I have spoken with at least three persons who accepted salaries that were one-half or less of what they had been earning before coming to serve at Messiah. Several others experienced dramatic reductions in their incomes.

One thinks also of the commitment of one family, the Hostetter family, who through three generations of sons served as president for 61 of Messiah's first 85 years. One specific outstanding example of commitment and hospitality was the invitation of C. N. Hostetter, Jr.

The Harvey Sakimura family, brought to campus in 1944
by college president C. N. Hostetter, Jr.

to the Sakimura family to come to Messiah College in 1944 during
World War II. The family had lost their flower shop and greenhouse
business, as well as their home, in 1942, when they were forcibly
moved to an internment camp during the anti-Japanese war fever.
When the family later was allowed to move to Michigan, they
attended a summer Brethren in Christ vacation Bible school, where
the three children excelled in Bible quizzing. Their achievements
and the needs of the family were communicated to President
Hostetter, who invited the family to move to Grantham and live on
campus. He offered Harvey, the father, a job as groundskeeper and
made arrangements for the children to attend the Messiah academy.
Despite several threatening letters and phone calls which Hostetter
received, he persisted in supporting the Sakimura family, surely an
outstanding example of the spirit of reconciliation and peacemaking.
Clarence, one of the sons, writing in 1997, says, "Despite all the
emotional tensions that swirled around us due to our Japanese
ancestry, the family felt safe and secure."

To name personal heroes may not be appropriate in an historical essay, but perhaps in this concluding chapter the writer may be forgiven. Coming to Messiah in 1972, I had been asked to serve as chair of the Division of Language, Literature, and Fine Arts, a position which I did not seek nor particularly desire. But three distinguished faculty were serving as chairmen (in addition to Dr. Daniel Chamberlain, who capably served in a dual role as academic dean and division chair). Dr. Carlton O. Wittlinger, professor of history and former dean of the college, chaired the Division of Social Sciences, and knew through experience and vast research probably more about the Brethren in Christ denomination than any other person at that time; Dr. Kenneth B. Hoover, professor of biology, chaired the Division of Natural Sciences, and loved, understood, and explained the created world better than anyone I had known; and Dr. Martin H. Schrag, professor of history of Christianity, chaired the Division of Religion and Philosophy, and grasped, taught, and practiced the central commitments of Anabaptism more meaning-fully than I had ever experienced. These all were giants at Messiah College and in the denomination. Yet each of them willingly, humbly served as mentors to this untried, inexperienced recent graduate student, who knew neither administrative work, Messiah College, nor the Brethren in Christ denomination. By their lives and words they demonstrated how one could be both loyal and, occasionally, critical. Their commitment to The Messiah — and to the college which bears his name — was exemplary.

To name a few exemplars of commitment is dangerous, of course, because there have been hundreds — probably thousands — of committed persons who have served in public, visible roles as well as in quiet, often unnoticed, roles at Messiah. One such person whom many persons at the college would not know is William S. Woods, Jr. who served as chair of the Finance Committee of the Trustees for a number of years. Dr. Glen Raser, past director of institutional finance, notes the importance of Mr. Woods in giving guidance to the developing of the endowment funds from the Fry Coal Company trust, funds which eventually became a major part of the total college endowment. As Raser says, there were "millions of dollars that needed to be taken care of; so at that point in time Bill

Woods was just the perfect person to join the [finance] committee." A committed Christian (and father of a Messiah alumna), Woods demonstrated his faith through his guidance in the financial area.

Another person with deep commitment to the college was much better known to many. Indeed, hers was the pleasant voice which most callers to the campus first heard when they contacted Messiah. Nancy Busch, who was for two decades the switchboard receptionist, touched thousands of people, many of whom she never saw. Her warmth and hospitality, whether on the phone or in person, and her willingness to help others, whether timid student or senior administrator, embodied an ethic of service which we hope to foster at Messiah.

Messiah College has been blessed with the long-term commitment of many people, whether staff, administrators, educators, or trustees. One almost legendary person is Dr. Harold ("Doc") Engle, who, with his late wife Mary Elizabeth, was a 1937 graduate of the junior college. Despite his busy medical practice, Doc Engle served as chair of the Board of Trustees for over 20 years under three different presidents. Reflecting over the many years of his committed leadership, Doc Engle says, "I was thrilled to see the Philadelphia campus open. I was part of that, and being from Temple [University] I appreciated that connection and felt it was a good move. . . . I was [also] a part of the Daystar [University] connection, which I thought was a good idea and still do."

Another trustee with extraordinary longevity and commitment is Galen Oakes, who served for 44 years on the Board, including five years as assistant chair and over seven years as chair. Although Oakes lived in Ohio and always needed to travel for hours to Board meetings, he says that for 40 years he never missed a meeting. One time in the fall of 1973 he had gone on a hunting trip in a remote area of Ontario, where the train dropped him off beyond the road "in the middle of nowhere." Oakes had made arrangements with the train conductor to be picked up on a certain day and time. On that day he signaled the train with a white flag, "The train slowed up, and I was getting ready to go on the train — and then it took off again — didn't completely stop. So I was 13.6 miles away from Hornepayne at that point. And I had my dress shoes [on] . . . and [carried] a suitcase. And

I walked those 13.6 miles on the railroad [tracks] that day . . . and I remember that was a painful day, but I did get to the college [Trustee] Board meeting on time." Oakes travelled some other difficult miles for the Board — though less physically painful — as he helped negotiate the transition between presidencies in 1994, as noted earlier.

Naming people from various areas of service to Messiah College, one begins to feel like the writer to the Hebrews (in the New Testament), who referred to his catalog of the faithful as a "great cloud of witnesses." Surely many will not be named here, but one should yet mention the chair of the Board of Trustees in this year of the centennial, Mrs. Eunice Steinbrecher, who has given significant leadership and support through ten years, and particularly during the latest presidential transition with the extended illness of Rodney Sawatsky. Speaking of that difficult time, Barry Goodling, vice-president for advancement, says, "I think a key during that time . . . [was that] Eunice Steinbrecher exhibited exceptional leadership." Mrs. Steinbrecher made many additional trips from Ohio, particularly to support and encourage the chief administrators, many of whom were carrying more than their usual responsibilities.

Through the past century Messiah College has been blessed with the commitment of many trustees, administrators, staff, and educators. One always hopes that their modeling of deep commitment to God through service to others will be internalized by students, who in turn will lead lives of "service, leadership, and reconciliation in church and society." Relatively few may be called to serve as trustees or administrators, though some surely will. But many will serve responsible roles in "church and society," whether they will be listed in college catalogs or not.

In the course of interviewing persons in preparation for the writing of this historical essay, I spoke with a number of graduates working in various capacities; several have returned to Messiah, their alma mater, where they serve as administrators, educators, and secretaries in a host of different roles. Off campus, among others, I interviewed a bank president (Andrew Samuel, '84 accounting), a pastor (Anthony Alexander, '75 behavioral science), a judge (Melinda Fisher Nowak, '76 English), and a professor (Neryamn Rivera Nieves, '87 Spanish and English). Speaking with these graduates, I was enormously encouraged to see how these persons who had been shaped and challenged by Messiah were now, in turn, positively influencing others. Dr. Neryamn Nieves offers her perspective: "I am from a very traditional Hispanic church, and going to Messiah just opened a whole other world for me of different ways of thinking . . . [for example] thinking about the Christian faith. . . . It goes both ways . . . I learned a lot, and I know that Hispanics can bring a lot, African Americans can bring a lot, or Asians [can] . . . all different groups. Try to get them there!"

Finally, a short summary of the work of one recent graduate, Ryan M. Keith ('02 politics), who is the founder and president of an organization called Forgotten Voices International. The mission of Forgotten Voices "is to demonstrate the love of Jesus Christ by equipping local churches in southern Africa to meet the physical and spiritual needs of AIDS orphans in their communities." Forgotten Voices is working in Zimbabwe and Zambia, with twelve projects and currently a network of 160 churches; and through those churches 4,800 orphans are being helped. In the United States some ten churches are part of a supporting network, and Ryan Keith has a volunteer team of seven who provide major assistance. All seven are Messiah College graduates (from 2000 to 2007) "that volunteer on average 10 to 15 hours per week in very specific roles," Keith says, "whether it be church relations or communications or development or administration processing checks . . . or prayer ministry." The leadership team meets in alternate weeks for several hours of planning and prayer. Because Keith is currently a student at Harvard University in the Kennedy School, where he is a candidate for a master's degree in public policy, Matthew Hoover is presently serving as executive director of Forgotten Voices, while also working full time in the commercial real estate business.

A few years earlier Keith had been accepted at Harvard Divinity School and, as he says, had "rented an apartment, picked out classes, [and] signed up for an internship in Boston." But then his church (West Shore Evangelical Free Church in Mechanicsburg, PA) asked him — along with eleven others — to go to Zimbabwe on a two-week mission trip to see what their church might do to help AIDS orphans. So Keith gave up his lifelong dream of going to Harvard, changed his plans, and went on the trip—which gave him a new focus on his life's direction. In subsequent years (since 2004) Keith has been working to organize and assist national churches to meet some of their almost overwhelming needs. In the process, Keith says, "I've learned so much about God's faithfulness; I've learned so much about the way God cares for the orphans and widows."

In 2008 after working hard to found and establish the ministry of Forgotten Voices, Keith believed that he needed further education to learn how best to lead and expand the ministry. And providentially Harvard accepted him and offered a Pforzheimer Fellowship, which pays his tuition. Besides that, the Kennedy School has approved his work with Forgotten Voices as his internship, so he can travel to southern Africa three times a year, usually for three-week stints. The needs are stunning; resources and personnel are always limited. Yet Keith, his leadership team, the supporting churches, and all the cooperating staff and churches in Africa are making a difference in the lives of 4,800 orphans. Obviously, Ryan Keith's story is not typical, yet one hopes that those principles that he learned at Messiah will change the lives of many other students. What he learned, Keith says, "is an integration between the Word of God and my own spiritual development and how that fleshes out tangibly into the way I minister to people around me." He has needed not so much the specific skills that he learned at Messiah "but principles of trusting in God, being able to think critically about very complicated things, and make a plan on what I thought was best, given the information that I had." Surely in this story—and in the stories of many Messiah College graduates—there is cause for thanksgiving and celebration.

In the personal musings of this final chapter we have reflected on reasons for celebration; we have considered some areas of concern; and we have honored the commitments of several persons, who are only illustrative of the commitments of a large host of the faithful. Whatever our particular calling—whether accountant or lawyer, pastor or teacher, mechanic or college president, farmer or social worker, leader or follower—may the educational ministry of Messiah College lead to the continuing growth of the Kingdom of God. Soli Deo Gloria!

List of Persons Interviewed

Anthony C. Alexander
Edward T. Arke
James H. Barnes, III
Randall G. Basinger
Debra L. Berke
H. David Brandt
Merle/Ila Brubaker
Lawrence A. Burnley
  (twice)
D. Wayne Cassel
Daniel R. Chamberlain
Jerry A. Chaplin
Amanda A. Coffey
Debra R. Cruel
Keith W. Drahn
John W. Eby
Harold H. Engle
Melinda Fisher-Nowak
John Fite
Emerson C. Frey
Chad W. Frey
Eldon E. Fry
Mark G. Garis
Dorothy G. Gish
Barry G. Goodling
Shirley A. Groff
Gina R. Hale
Robert E. Hamilton
Kristin M. Hansen-
  Kieffer

Harold Heie
Gerald D. Hess
David A. Hietala
Mary Ann Hollinger
Erma L. Hoover
Kenneth B. Hoover
  (twice)
D. Ray Hostetter
Carol A. Hostetter
Joseph P. Huffman
  (twice)
Richard T. Hughes
Robert B. Ives
Douglas Jacobsen
Joseph Jones
Hierald E. Kane-Osorto
Donald B. Kraybill
Jonathan D. Lauer
Philip J. Lawlis
Martha M. Long
Ronald E. Long
Kenneth M. Martin
Douglas K. Miller
Donald L. Minter
Jeffrey A. Moshier
Neryamn Rivera Nieves
W. Ray Norman
Galen M. Oakes
David L. Parkyn
Timothy J. Peterson

D. Kelly Phipps
Kim S. Phipps
Glen A. Pierce
Glen A. Raser
Richard E. Roberson
Clyde A. Ross
Andrew S. Samuel
Dorothy A. Schrag
Kathrynne G. Shafer
Layton Shoemaker
E. Morris Sider
Ronald J. Sider
Ronald R. Sider
Valerie R. Smith
Deborah R. Snyder
Eunice F. Steinbrecher
Richard A. Stevick
William G. Strausbaugh
Deborah E. Tepley
David T. Vader
Lois J. Voigt
Cynthia A. Wells
Donald L. Wingert
Douglas M. Wood
John R. Yeatts
Marvin D. Zercher

Almost all the tapes and transcriptions are available in the Messiah College Archives.

Index

(Please note that this listing is selective.)

Hostetter, D. Ray, 4–8, 11–12, 17–18,
20, 32, 35, 41, 43, 63–64, 67, 69–73,
78–79, 81–87, 90–94, 97, 99–106,
109, 112, 115–16, 122, 176, 227
Hostetter, C. Nelson, 82
Hostetter, S. Lane, 5, 82–83
House Resolution 1030, 184
Hoverter Course in the Humanities,
161, 172, 215
Hoverter Foundation, 161–62
Huffman, Joseph, xiii, xv, 161–62, 172,
215
Hughes, Richard, xvi, 169–70, 215, 225
Human Rights Awareness (HRA), 147
Hunter, Matt, 146

Institutional Identity Committee,
112–116
Integrated Studies, 54–61, 195, 198, 200
Interdisciplinary Studies, 54–61
International Business Institute (IBI),
158
Internship Center, 158–59
Issachar's Loft, 168–69
Ives, Robert, 116
Ivy Rustles (student newspaper),
23–27, 30–31,34, 38, 194

Jackson State University, 26
Jacobsen, Douglas (Jake), 112–13, 115,
136, 170, 176
Johnson, Florence, 151
Johnson, Dale, 151
Jones, Erin, xvi
Jones, Joseph, 159, 220–21
Jordan Science Center, 132, 190
Jordan, Richard, 85–86

Kaisiguran, Kai, 182
Kane-Osorto, Hierald, ix, 30
Kasparek, Rebecca (Ebersole), xvi
Keefer, Luke L., Jr., 174
Keith, Ryan, 163, 232–33

Kent State University, 23, 26
Kenya, 70, 72, 74–77, 214
Kilbourne, Jean, 173
King, Martin Luther, Jr., 145, 177
Klynstra, Kacie, 182
Knadig, Thomas, 25
Kraybill, Donald B., 117–19, 123,
128–30, 204
Kreamer, Carolyn, 120
Krikorian, Meshach Paul (M. P.), 28
Kroeker, Charlotte, 125

Landis, Howard, 24
Larsen Student Union, 138, 187
Lawlis, Philip, 48
Lederach, John Paul, 101–02
Lewis, Melissa, xvi
Library book walk, 89–90
Lilly Foundation, 175
Lippert, Wendy, 157
Logue, Niles, 101
Long Range Planning Committee,
52–53
Long, Martha, 75
Long, Ron E., 45–46, 72, 111
Longenecker, Joseph, xvi, 151
Longenecker, Julie, 156
Love, Katie, 183

MacVaugh, Kimberly, 175
Mageria, James, 70, 72, 73
Mahadaga, 151, 154
Malcolm X, 177
Mark, Beth (Hostetler), xvi, 25–27
Mark, Ken, 191
Martin Multicultural Scholarship,
218–19
Martin, Kenneth, 92
Martin, Lloyd and Lois, 219
Marty, Martin, 177
McCain, John, 177
McCarty, Brad, 183